IN THE STEPS OF GEORGE BORROW

BY THE SAME AUTHOR

George Borrow, by Henry Wyndham Phillips

IN THE STEPS OF
GEORGE BORROW

by
EILEEN BIGLAND

With 28 Illustrations

RICH AND COWAN

London   New York   Melbourne   Sydney   Cape Town

First Published 1951

Made and Printed in Great Britain by
GREYCAINES
(Taylor Garnett Evans & Co. Ltd.)
Watford, Herts.

TO

IAN BIGLAND

ACKNOWLEDGMENTS

My most grateful thanks are due to Sir John Murray, K.C.V.O., D.S.O., Sir Orme Sargent, K.C.B., K.C.M.G., Mr. R. Green-Armytage, the City Librarian, Norwich, the Executors of the late Mr. Herbert Jenkins, and the British and Foreign Bible Society.

E. B.

CONTENTS

ILLUSTRATIONS

"MY FATHER WAS A CORNISH MAN"

(*Lavengro*, Chap. 1)

I

THE market-place of Liskeard dreamed in the noonday heat. The shops were closed for the lunch hour. Blinded windows and shut doors reproached the sun. The only sign of life was a vigorous child who propelled himself across the square on one roller-skate. Standing in the doorway of *Webb's Hotel* my mind went back nearly a hundred years to a very different scene. . . .

It was Christmas Eve, 1853, and round the log fire in *Webb's* coffee-room sat four worried men. They were Mr. Henry Borrow of Looe Down, Mr. Robert Taylor of Penquite, Mr. James Jago, the Town Clerk of Liskeard, and Mr. Bernard Anstis, an ex-Mayor of the town. Since noon they had been waiting to welcome an illustrious and much-travelled kinsman but the Plymouth coach, delayed by a heavy fall of snow, had arrived over an hour late and none of its shivering passengers bore the remotest resemblance to the man they had come to greet. Now it was past three o'clock and still no sign of him. Whatever could have happened?

Occasionally one of the men strode to the door, flung it open, and peered out into a snow blizzard so thick that visibility was reduced to a few yards; then, with a shake of the head, he rejoined his companions.

In an effort to raise the company's spirits Mr. Henry Borrow drew a dog-eared cutting from the *Plymouth Mail* of 20 September out of his pocket and read it aloud:

"GALLANT CONDUCT OF MR. G. BORROW

Intrepidity.—Yarmouth jetty presented an extraordinary and thrilling spectacle on Thursday, the 8th inst., about one o'clock. The sea raged frantically, and a ship's boat, endeavouring to land for water, was upset, and the men were engulfed in a wave some thirty feet high, and struggled with it in vain. The moment was an awful one, when George Borrow, the well-known author of *Lavengro* and the *Bible in Spain*, dashed into the surf and saved one life, and through his instrumentality the others were saved. We ourselves have known this brave and gifted man for years, and, daring as was this deed, we have known him more than once to risk his life for others. We are happy to add that he has sustained no material injury."[1]

It was this thrilling account of bravery which had aroused the interest of Henry Borrow, his brothers William, Thomas, and Nicholas, and his sister Elizabeth. The hero of Yarmouth must assuredly be their first cousin, a son of their Uncle Thomas who had left the Duchy in 1783 to join the Army. A long time ago, of course, and Thomas had not seen fit to send his family any news of his doings, but Cornishmen were clannish folk and Henry immediately held a conclave at the old homestead of Trethinnick where it was decided that his son-in-law, Robert Taylor—the best pen-man among them—should write to George congratulating him and inviting him to visit the home of his fathers.

A most satisfactory answer to this letter had been received about the middle of October:

"Yarmouth, 14 Octr., 1853.

"MY DEAR SIR,—I beg leave to acknowledge the receipt of your letter of the 10th inst., in which you inform me of the kind desire of my Cornish relatives to see me at Trethinnick. Please to inform them that I shall be proud and happy to avail myself of their kindness and to make the acquaintance of 'one and all' of them. My engagements will prevent my visiting them at present, but I will appear amongst them on the first opportunity. I am delighted to learn that there are still some living at Trethinnick who remember my honoured father, who had as true a Cornish heart as ever beat. . . ."

[1] The Press report was copied from the Bury *Post* of 17 September, 1853.

This very proper acknowledgment of kinship had pleased the Cornish Borrows and they were delighted when their famous cousin wrote again on 15 December that he would like to spend Christmas with them.

And now, despite the most explicit instructions as to his journey, George Borrow had failed to arrive! The four gentlemen grouped around the fire shuffled their booted feet on the stone floor and glanced anxiously at each other. For weeks past their womenfolk had been sweeping and scouring, baking and cooking. Family parties embracing every forty-second cousin, every connection by marriage, had been arranged. The whole countryside, from Jamaica Inn to Menheniot, from Crowsnest to Lamellion, was agog to meet this hero who not only risked his life to save his fellow men from stormy seas but actually *wrote books*. It would be too humiliating, decided the deputation of welcome, if they had to trail home ignominiously and announce their cousin had not come.

The hands of the clock pointed to four-thirty and Mr. Henry Borrow had just said in a sepulchral voice that it was no good waiting any longer when the door burst open and the most astonishing figure appeared on the threshold. It was immensely tall, wrapped about in a long black coat and crowned by a wide-brimmed black hat. From one hand dangled a much-worn carpet-bag, while the other hand grasped a "green, manifold and bulging"[1] umbrella by its middle. For a full minute the figure stayed silhouetted against the whirling snow; then in one gesture—or so it seemed to the awestruck quartette by the fire—the bag and umbrella were dropped, the cloak unfurled, the hat doffed, and a remarkably handsome man stepped forward, his arms outstretched.

" 'Look out, look out, Svend Vonved!' " he sang in deep, bell-like tones.

Henry stumbled to his feet. "You be . . . ?" he stammered, "you be . . . ?"

The stranger bowed. "My name is George Borrow."

It took the Cornishmen several minutes to recover their wits. In all their speculations as to what their kinsman would be like they had never envisaged such foreign mannerisms,

[1] Theodore Watts-Dunton's description.

such outlandish garb. But he proved so friendly, so eager to know all details about his relatives, that by the time the maid-servant bustled in with a huge pot of tea they were quite won over, and during the meal their liking for this new-found cousin became tinged with admiration. In intervals of praising the ham, the pasties, the cold chicken and the clotted cream, George told them how he had arrived in Plymouth at midnight, slept for a few hours at the Royal Hotel, and emerged only to find that every seat on the Liskeard coach was booked. Nothing daunted he inquired the way and set out blithely on the twenty-mile walk.

The Cornishmen nodded wisely to each other. Here was a man worthy of the Borrow clan—twenty miles over rough and unknown roads and he arrived showing no sign of tiredness! What a wealth of knowledge he had too! There wasn't a country he had not visited, a language he could not speak; yet he was full of questions about the Duchy. Would they take him to see Celtic barrows? Where was the Trevethy stone? Were they ever troubled by the *piskies*? Their hearts warmed as they thought of the fine Christmas they were going to have with this wonderful relation.

After the meal the party broke up. Robert Taylor, with whom George was to stay at Penquite, had brought an extra horse, and the ease with which the new-comer swung himself into the saddle set the final seal on his popularity. Heads bent against the snow-laden wind he and Robert galloped off on their four-mile ride, while the other three hastened home to tell their families the exciting news.

The market-place stirred from its lethargy. Blinds were rolled up, doors unlocked, purposeful ladies with shopping-bags and ration books peered into windows. No longer could I stand in the doorway of *Webb's Hotel* dreaming of happenings ninety-eight years back in time. I, too, must be up and about the business which had brought me to Cornwall and take the road leading to St. Cleer.

A gruelling road it proved, striking northward out of Liskeard over what the Cornish folk call a "Down". When

Borrow had climbed this bluff he had gazed down on a rugged, windswept landscape patched with snowdrifts: now, under the benison of a strangely un-English sun the moorlands, shimmering silver and purple in the heat haze, rolled gently to Plymouth in the south and the Bristol Channel in the north. Ahead of me the hundred-foot spire of St. Cleer Parish Church rose from the valley, a landmark too lovely to belong to the grey, tin-mining little town that sprawled around it; but it was in the Parish Register of St. Cleer that I found what I sought, the pedigree of the Borrows of Trethinnick.

Here was the first name on a yellowed page: *John Burrow or Burrough, farmer, m. Mary Lyne, May 29, 1690.* Further on were the names of his four children, John, Richard, Henry, and Joan, and in their case the name was spelt Borrow. Very nearly the family petered out in this generation, for only Henry and his wife, Elizabeth Sibly, had a child, a son named after his grandfather. This John followed his father's example and also married a Sibly, who gave him no fewer than eight children, including two sets of twins. The youngest, Thomas, was born in December 1758, shortly after the death of his father.

Good, sturdy yeoman stock, these Borrows, men who lived close to the land, attended church with great regularity, and were noted for their intelligence and common sense. They were not, perhaps, so exalted in station as their descendant painted them in *Lavengro*:

"My father was a Cornish man, the youngest, as I have heard him say, of seven brothers. He sprang from a family of gentlemen, or, as some people would call them, *gentillâtres*, for they were not very wealthy; they had a coat of arms, however, and lived on their own property at a place called Tredinnock (Trethinnick), which being interpreted means *the house on the hill*, which house and the neighbouring acres had been from time immemorial in their possession. I mention these particulars that the reader may see at once that I am not altogether of low and plebeian origin; the present age is highly aristocratic, and I am convinced that the public will read my pages with more zest from being

told that I am a *gentillâtre* by birth with Cornish blood in
my veins. . . ."

Borrow never could resist drawing a long bow. In this
case he was probably right in doing so, for the Victorian reading
public were undoubtedly attracted by anything "highly
aristocratic". Besides, when he wrote *Lavengro* he was a man
in his forties looking back nostalgically to a youth rose-tinted
by time. But as I left St. Cleer and turned towards Trethinnick
I reflected that his forebears were none the worse for their lack
of gentility.

On the left-hand side of the road leading from Liskeard to
Redgate and Jamaica Inn I found Trethinnick, a cluster of
old buildings tucked in a fold of the hills. Against the golden
stubble of a sloping field the farmhouse stood out dark and
squat. The little gardens of its two cottages were ablaze with
dahlias; but some of the out-buildings showed signs of decay
and there was no trace of the blacksmith's forge which had
once been the family's pride.

Here the Borrows had lived for generations; tilling their
soil, growing their *Gillyflower* and *Tom Knight* apples, shoeing
their neighbours' horses, greeting birth and marriage with
decorous pleasure, death with decorous mourning. They believed
in the God of the Established Church and the King of England,
were he Stewart or Hanoverian: they believed equally in
Holy Wells and *piskies*. Their thoughts were bounded by the
Duchy border, and although their native hospitality never
faltered they were wont to welcome any visitor from beyond
the River Tamar with slight reserve lest he prove "over
gorgious".

II

Thomas Borrow, the father of George, was the first member
of the family to break away from farming and Cornwall.
Perhaps some ancient Iberian strain within him clamoured

Menheniot, Cornwall

George Borrow's birthplace, Dumpling Green, nr. Norwich

for expression; perhaps the mere fact of his posthumous birth induced in his infant mind the feeling that he was different from his elder brothers and sisters. Whatever the cause young Thomas was a mischievous child continually in hot water, and the never-failing protection of his mother, who found in her lusty Benjamin recompense for her struggles to cope single-handed with the farm, the forge, and eight hungry mouths, did not endear him to his kith and kin.

Henry, the eldest brother, bore an especial grudge against Thomas. Ten years old when his father died, Henry had been forced to abandon childhood and became the buffer between his mother and the world. He filled the role admirably. By the time he was twenty he was virtual master of Trethinnick, a preternaturally aged youth always on the alert for a bit of sharp dealing on the part of older farmers, always antagonistic to anything which threatened the crops or stock on his fifty acres. To Henry, Thomas was that unforgivable creature, an enemy within the gates. Thomas allowed the cattle to stray; Thomas forgot to feed the chickens; Thomas airily refused payment when strangers brought their horses to be shod; Thomas was never there when he was wanted; worst of all Thomas evaded his brother's wrath by hiding behind his mother's skirts.

The growing Thomas realized neither his mother's championship nor his brother's dislike. He lived for the day—and the day was good. From earliest childhood he had scampered bare-foot over the moors, and by the time he was twelve had developed an exceptional physique. By nature gregarious, he made friends with all manner of people, from aristocratic landowners to horse-copers and gypsies. Everybody liked the lad with the tanned face, eager blue eyes and bright brown hair; the more disreputable among his acquaintances encouraged him to play truant from the Parish school, telling him that since he showed signs of becoming a "proper man with his hands" practice in the art of fighting would do him more good than mere book learning.

So Thomas, unbeknown to his family, spent many stolen hours trying to emulate the prowess of Mendoza, Belcher and other famous bruisers of the day. Presently he extended his interests to certain sports frowned upon by the law—cock-fights held in the courtyards of lonely inns and badger-baiting, a horrid pastime in which the poor badgers were nailed together by their tails and driven into the midst of a pack of hounds. Thomas was revolted by the cruelty but ashamed to say so—it would never do to be thought a coward.

The death of his mother in the spring of 1773 came as a tremendous shock to the boy. Dazed with grief he wandered about the homestead until Henry called him into the musty, little-used parlour and delivered a long speech about responsibility. Since the Lord had seen fit to call their dear mother to her rest—his tone inferred that the summons had been precipitated by her youngest son's behaviour—it was his, Henry's, bounden duty to rule as patriarch over the family. Out of honour to her memory and that of their dear father—here it was implied that if Mr. Borrow had lived Thomas would have proved a more amenable child—his first duty was to ensure the continued prosperity of Trethinnick. Thomas must realize, therefore, that schooldays were ended and that in future he must devote all his energies to farm-work.

As Henry droned on, sorrow gave way to rebellion in Thomas's heart. How dare Henry, with his domineering ways, his disapproval of all pleasure however innocent, his little pettifogging meannesses, usurp their mother's place? For the first time the boy understood just how blank and colourless life was going to be without her. Heedless of his brother's exclamation he turned and fled from the house.

High up on the moors Thomas wrestled fiercely with himself, Should he go home, floor Henry with a blow, pack his few clothes and voyage forth to seek his fortune? Ah, but how did you seek fortune when you were only fifteen, without a penny to your name, with hands that might be "proper" at fighting but were unskilled at anything else? Should he stay on the farm, pretending to fall in with Henry's plans? No, not the farm, the *forge*! That was it—he would work in the forge, learn the blacksmith's craft. Then, bitter as the parting must be, he would say good-bye to Trethinnick.

But as spring passed into summer Thomas found it more and more difficult to do as he wished. Each time he scurried through his early morning tasks and slipped into the smithy with an offer of help so Henry appeared, dour and menacing against the sunlight streaming in through the open doorway, to remind him of duties undone. Duty . . . duty . . . duty . . . the word pursued Thomas the day long. As the youngest he was given all the dullest, dirtiest jobs and it was no use grumbling to his other brothers and sisters, for they were completely under Henry's thumb.

By the winter, when Henry brought a bride to Trethinnick, Thomas had grown into a sullen youth who spoke but seldom and avoided his family except at meal-times, when he gobbled his food to the detriment of his digestion. His sole comment on his new sister-in-law was the scornful remark that Henry thought a great deal more of her father's rich lands at Looe Down than he did of the douce Temperance Trenniman herself. There was certain truth in this statement, for the shrewd Henry had picked his wife with care, but the fact that Thomas was aware of the reason behind his choice did nothing to sweeten his mood.

For the next five years there was open antagonism between the eldest and youngest brother. Henry piled work on to Thomas: Thomas retaliated by disappearing from the fields every time Henry's back was turned. Rumour had it that the boy had renewed his friendship with the wilder young men of the neighbourhood and by 1778 Henry decided that the troublesome Thomas must be put out of his, and temptation's, way. To this end he journeyed to Liskeard and interviewed a very grand gentleman indeed, a Mr. Edmund Hambly, a leading maltster and the Headborough, or Constable of the Hundred of West. He then called a family conclave at which it was solemnly announced that Thomas had been bound as apprentice to Mr. Hambly for five years.

To Henry's chagrin Thomas showed elation at the news. The sparkle came back into his blue eyes as he clattered up and down the slate-floored kitchen collecting his goods and chattels. Liskeard spelt freedom, for since his mother's death he had lost his deep attachment to Trethinnick, regarding it merely as the one place where he could not escape Henry's all-seeing eye.

The grandeur of that remote being, Mr. Hambly, did not worry Thomas. He settled down happily in his lodgings, worked with a will during the day, and spent his evenings drilling with the newly formed Yeomanry Militia—an occupation which thrilled him to the marrow and was to prove of immense help to him later on. This full and exciting life was exactly what he needed and he quickly became a favourite with everybody, while his employer's excellent reports of his progress were received with surprise at Trethinnick.

During his apprenticeship Thomas seldom visited his family, although the farm was within easy walking distance. There was always far too much to do in his spare time—extra technical instruction in the use of arms, practice fights with his fellow militiamen, excursions to the many fairs for which the Duchy was famous. It was one of these outings, alas, which led to his downfall.

On a fine July evening Thomas walked over to Menheniot Fair with one or two friends. He was feeling particularly pleased with himself for not only had he just become a qualified maltster but the next week would bring the annual Yeomanry Militia exercises, a fortnight of open-air life which he greatly enjoyed. But when he and his companions reached the fairground they found a terrific battle being waged between the young men of Menheniot and those of Liskeard. How the affair had started nobody knew, but Menheniot fancied that some insulting remark had been passed by one of the visitors, and tempers quickened by the heat and copious draughts of ale had blazed. Stalls were knocked down and gaudy wares trampled underfoot in the scrimmage, whereupon the fair vendors, the circus folk, even the freaks, had thrown in their weight on the side of the villagers.

The Liskeard boys were in bad shape when one of them caught sight of Thomas and besought his aid. Nothing loath—who could resist fighting for his own town?—he stripped off his coat and plunged into the fray. Shouting encouragement and using his fists for all he was worth he led his side to within an ace of victory. Suddenly a constable with uplifted baton appeared in his path. This was too much for Thomas, who considered that policemen should keep to their proper place.

With one well-directed blow he sent the man sprawling and when a second constable came forward he dealt with him the same way.

Even in 1783, however, one could not insult the law with impunity. From the crowd stepped Mr. Hambly, very much in his official capacity, to warn Thomas that if he did not desist from his savage brawling immediately he would be placed under arrest. Thomas, whose success had gone to his head, dodged lightly round his outraged employer inviting him to come and get him. Mr. Hambly made a dart forward and received a fist full on his nose. He tried again and an upper cut so dazed him that he performed several somersaults before he even realized he had been hit. Two of his henchmen picked him up, dusted him down and hurried him from the scene while the crowd roared themselves hoarse in praise of Thomas.

For the moment Thomas was a hero. Escorted by his battered but exhilarated friends he marched back to Liskeard; but the morning brought retribution. The penalty for assaulting a policeman was severe; the penalty for assaulting the Head-borough, the Constable of the Hundred of West, varied, according to report, from ten years to a life sentence. It was a chastened Thomas who took the hill road to Trethinnick and when he got there it was to find Henry standing like an avenging angel at the gate. He had always known, he averred, that his youngest brother would bring shame upon their honoured name. He deserved no help and he would get none. If he didn't take himself off that instant the police would be sent for.

Thomas turned on his heel and made for the moors. For five long months there was no news of him. Then a curious story filtered through to Trethinnick. A gaunt and ragged young man had presented himself before Captain William Morshead[1] of the Coldstream Guards at Bodmin and said he wished to enlist as a private soldier. Upon taking his particulars Morshead, himself a Cornishman, discovered who he was and did everything in his power to persuade him to stick to the trade he had already learned. The young man was

[1] Afterwards General Morshead

adamant. He was going to join the King's army and nothing was going to stop him.

The sisters at Trethinnick wept, Temperance tried to soften her husband's heart, the brothers argued that whatever young Thomas had done they could not allow him to leave the Duchy without a word from home. Henry's answer was to reach for the Family Bible and draw a thick line through Thomas's name. He was not to know—the mere idea would have given him apoplexy—that seventy years later his eldest son was to head a deputation of welcome to Thomas's illustrious child.

III

I left Trethinnick dreaming in the August sunshine and that night boarded a train at Bodmin Road. The light was fading as we crossed Saltash Bridge and as I gazed down at the pale waters of the Tamar so I fished two bits of paper from my pocket. The first read:

"Coldstream Guards—'C' Company.

"Name	. . .	Borrow Thomas.
"When enlisted	.	29th December, 1783.
"Where born	.	St. Clear, Cornwall.
"Years old	. .	23 (he was really 25).
"Size	. .	5 ft. 7¾ inches.
"Hair	. .	Light brown.
"Complexion	.	Fresh.
"Trade	. .	Maltster.
"By whom enlisted	.	Capt. Lt. Morshead.
"Where	. .	In Cornwall.
"Former service	.	5 years—0 months.
"What corps	.	Cornish Militia (Yeomanry added in pencil.)"

The second read:

"*Service of Capt. Thomas Borrow*—1783–1824.

"*Coldstream Guards:*
"Private in Co. C.   apptd.   .   Dec. 29, 1783.
"Corporal in Co. C.   ,,   .   Sep. 17, 1784.
"Serjeant in Co. H.   ,,   .   Oct. 18, 1789.

"*West Norfolk Militia:*

"Serjeant Major,   apptd.   .   Feb. 25, 1792.
"Quarter Master,   ,,   .   May 27, 1795.
"Adjutant W.N.M.   ,,   .   Feb. 27, 1798.

"Served 45 yrs. 2 m. (including his five years
            with the Yeomanry Militia.)
"'Retd. on full pay, July 23, 1819."

A good soldier, Thomas Borrow, but reading his military record I remembered how he must have journeyed, outcast and miserable, from Cornwall to London in the bitter January of 1784.

There were no trains then; no sleepers from Plymouth, North Road, to Paddington, London. The army of the day travelled rougher than most and every step of the road from Bodmin Thomas realized more clearly the gulf separating Private Borrow of the Coldstreamers from the light-hearted lad who had joined battle against Menheniot. He could forget neither the circumstances leading to his enlistment nor the memory of Henry's harshness; and as he left the Duchy so he left his youth in a misty, half-faery realm echoing with lovely, familiar names—Penquite, Trewarrick, Lamellion, Jamaica Inn, Trethinnick . . . always Trethinnick. . . .

He buried those names deep. During the ten years of his service in the Guards—spent mostly in London—he seldom referred to them. Only one thing remained of his early life; his interest in pugilism. Here the truant hours of childhood bore fruit. Sergeant Borrow was a "proper man with his hands". Strolling through Hyde Park somewhere around 1790 he paused to listen to the challenges thrown out by the famous warrior Big Ben Brain[1] and could not resist an argument with that fearsome man.

In Big Ben's opinion there was only one answer to an argument, but in the ensuing contest he found to his surprise that his opponent possessed more skill than most professional fighters. George Borrow gave a glowing account of the event in the first chapter of *Lavengro*:

> "... I opine that even Wellington or Napoleon would have been heartily glad to cry for quarter ere the lapse of five minutes, and even the Blacksmith Tartar (Tamerlane) would, perhaps, have shrunk from the opponent with whom, after having had a dispute with him, my father engaged in single combat for one hour, at the end of which the champions shook hands and retired, each having experienced quite enough of the other's prowess."

George's talent for exaggeration showed itself in this passage, but from other sources we know that the fight was regarded by experts as being more closely matched than the meeting staged a few months later between Big Ben and Johnson, which resulted in Ben becoming "champion of England". There seems little doubt either, although the date given is wrong, about George's statement that Brain, "worn out by the blows which he had received in his many combats, expired in the arms of my father, who read the Bible to him in his latter moments. . . ."

Far more significant, however, is a much later passage from *Lavengro*. George, then twenty years old, asks his dying father for details about Big Ben:

> " 'You are a strange lad,' said my father; 'and though of late I have begun to entertain a more favourable opinion than heretofore, there is still much about you that I do not understand. Why do you bring up that name? Don't you know that it is one of my temptations? You wish to know

[1] Sometimes alluded to as Big Ben Bryan.

something about him? Well, I will oblige you this once,
and then farewell to such vanities—something about him.
I will tell you—his—skin when he flung off his clothes—
and he had a particular knack in doing so—his skin, when
he bared his mighty chest and back for combat; and when
he fought he stood, so—if I remember right—his skin, I
say, was brown and dusky as that of a toad. Oh, me! I
wish my elder son was here!'"

That paragraph reveals the whole tragic relationship
between the father who was determined to forget youthful
indiscretions and the son who wanted passionately to recall
them. In George, Thomas saw the reflection of the wild boy
who dodged brother Henry and sent the Headborough of
Liskeard head over heels at Menheniot Fair; and because he
knew the bitter result of such rebellion he did everything in
his power to quench his son's exuberance.

The encounter with Big Ben marked the last occasion on
which Thomas gave way to his fighting instincts. As he strode
back to the barracks he was appalled to think that he, a
trusted Sergeant in the Guards, should have so lost control
of himself. His feeling of shame was intensified by the congratulations heaped upon him by his officers as well as his
fellow sergeants, and the awed glances of the privates in his
company. When H.R.H. The Duke of York was graciously
pleased to suggest that Sergeant Borrow be transferred to the
West Norfolk Regiment of Militia as Sergeant-Major in charge
of recruiting, Thomas leapt at the chance. The keen, sweet
winds of East Anglia would sweep away all memory of a mad
and ill-spent youth.

Many men have suffered strange conversions: none stranger
perhaps than that experienced by Thomas Borrow at the
hands of Big Ben Brain. From his arrival at the Norfolk depot
in the spring of 1792 to his death thirty years later he frowned
upon all manner of violent sports, telling first his soldiers
and then his children that they were sinful.

It was at the little town of East Dereham that Thomas
met his future wife. One evening he went to see a play performed by a travelling company and was immensely struck

by a young actress with an "oval face, olive complexion and Grecian forehead". Her name was Ann Perfrement and greatly to his relief Thomas found out that she was not a regular member of the company but a talented amateur merely engaged to fill a minor role for a few weeks. Her father, a solid farmer of Huguenot descent, disapproved of his lively daughter's interest in the stage and welcomed the sturdy Sergeant-Major as her suitor. A year later Ann and Thomas were married; and if the twenty-one-year-old bride missed the footlights she found plenty of excitement in the roving life her husband's duties obliged them to lead.

The situation in France added urgency to Thomas's efforts in recruiting. During the remaining years of the century he and Ann moved from East Dereham to Colchester, from Sheerness to Dover and back again to Essex. In February 1798 Thomas received just reward for his labours, a commission from George the Third, which made him Adjutant with the rank of Captain. The roll of parchment, addressed to *"Our Trusty and Wellbeloved Thomas Borrow, Gent"*, was his most prized possession.

The new century brought an added happiness to the pair, the birth of their elder son, John Thomas Borrow. Two years later the Militia was disbanded after the Peace of Amiens, but almost immediately the threat of Napoleon made it necessary for a new regiment to be recruited. Thomas was kept continually on the move and in the summer of 1803, as the war clouds piled up over Europe, he took Ann home to her father's farm, there to await the birth of her second child.

On the 5th of July, while Thomas marched through East Dereham to the beat of the drum, George Henry Borrow came into the world.

CHAPTER ONE

"OCEANS OF ENCHANTMENT"

(*Lavengro*, Chap. III)

(1803–1816)

I

A SNATCH of conversation between Theodore Watts-Dunton and George Borrow rang through my head as I took the Yaxham road out of East Dereham.

"What is the real nature of autobiography?" asked Watts-Dunton.

Borrow answered him obliquely, with two more questions: "Is it a mere record of the incidents of a man's life? Or is it a picture of the man himself—his character, his soul?"

Already, at the very start of my journeys in Borrow's footsteps, I was aware that I must always discard his first definition of autobiography and keep the second in the forefront of my mind. Practically all the information about Borrow's wanderings lay in his own works, and while he himself was the central figure in every major book he wrote from *The Gypsies of Spain* to *Romano Lavo-Lil* it was often a figure more than life size. He was a man with a strong creative faculty and a sense of theatre. To him the impression made on the reader's mind was far more important than the strict truth of the narrative. He had a puckish habit of embroidering certain incidents which appealed to him. He was a natural exaggerator and sometimes things read became inextricably mixed with things experienced.

To his devoted biographer, the erudite and meticulously minded Dr. Knapp[1], Borrow's way of altering dates and place-names, of blandly ignoring some years in his life and cramming others with references to astonishing and probably

[1] Dr. William I, Knapp, Ph.D., LL.D., *Life, Writings and Correspondence of George Borrow*, 2 vols. (John Murray, 1899).

apocryphal adventures, of adding fiction to fact, was a continual
worry. And not only to Dr. Knapp, who remained a fervent
admirer of his hero even while he ploughed through countless
manuscripts and records in search of corroboration. Many
lesser men grew so irritated by Borrow's deviations that they
spent the rest of their lives in destructive criticism of his
writings.

In the very first sentence of *Lavengro*, Borrow wrote:
"On an evening of July, in the year 18——, at East D——, a
beautiful little town in a certain district of East Anglia, I
first saw the light."

Tramping along the Yaxham road on my way to Borrow's
birthplace I felt a little sorry for the gentlemen who had spent
so much time and trouble in accusing Borrow of what they
termed "distortions of truth". Did it really matter that he
had said he had been born at East Dereham when he had been
born some two miles away at Dumpling Green? Perhaps he
hadn't liked the name, or perhaps his affection for the town
where he spent much of his childhood was uppermost in his
heart. In either case it seemed a tragedy to miss the magic
of Borrow's prose for such a trumpery cause.

At a cross-roads I found the *Jolly Farmers* inn, where
Thomas Borrow, his father-in-law and other cronies sipped their
pints of ale of an evening. On this spring morning the sole
customer was an ancient man who complained bitterly of the
present price of beer. I took the hint and, since he looked so
very old, asked if he had ever heard of a family called Perfrement who once lived at Dumpling Green. He glared, said
he didn't approve of women in saloon bars, and turned his
back. As I rose to go he lifted his head and roared at me:
"*Parf*ment be what you mean, *Parf*ment!"

He was the only link with Borrow provided by Dumpling
Green. The very landscape had altered, the commons cultivated,
the high table-land neatly divided by rows of hedges. But as
I walked on eastwards I came to a pool—known as a pit in
this part of Norfolk. On the opposite side of the road was a
farmhouse. Here in all likelihood Samuel Perfrement and his
wife had brought up their eight children; here George Borrow
had been born; here by the pool his mother, then a little

girl of ten, had shivered with fright as she watched her older sister rinsing a new linen chemise in the water.

Long afterwards, when George told his mother of the Danish mythological figures, Frey and Freya, she recalled this tale of the supernatural:

The sister, whose betrothed had died, was so anxious to know her matrimonial future that she invoked the aid of those gods who said that if a girl washed her linen at night in running water and then "watched" it dry before the fire she would, on the stroke of midnight, have revealed to her the face of her future husband. So the "giddy and rather unsettled" sister chose an evening when her father had gone to East Dereham market and, with the trembling Ann, awaited the verdict of Frey and Freya. The garment was hung before the fire, the door left ajar. The clock boomed one . . . two . . . On the third stroke the farm gate shut with a "tremendous noise". In answer to that ominous sound the sister ran to the door, closed and bolted it, and fell to the floor in a fit of convulsions.

"Poor thing," said Ann, "she never throve, married poorly, flung herself away."

Poor thing indeed, I thought, as I skimmed a stone across the pool: yet the Perfrement obeisance to mythology and the Borrow belief in Holy Wells and pixies played equal parts in the formation of George's character. It was thanks to this dual inheritance that he shouted against the wind of time: it was owing to the warring forces between native Celt and adopted Anglo-Saxon that his romanticism flowered, many-petalled and triumphant, on a back-cloth deliberately painted in half-tones.

Stone-skimming brought an invasion of small, round-eyed children. "What youm look for?" they asked. "Be you 'Merican?" "Whaffor you throw stones . . .?" A singing chorus of "Whaffor?"

In their opinion I, too, was a poor thing. Middle-aged women who spent their mornings throwing stones into pools and had no proper feeling about the distribution of largesse were to be discouraged. They marched off and left me to my contemplation of a muddied pond.

There was a tug at my skirt. Looking down I saw a boy of about seven, spindle-limbed and weasel-faced. "I'll show you way to East Dereham," he said.

"I know the way. I've just come from there."

He wagged his head. "Youm don't know short cut."

Off he set and I followed. Why? He had the bright dark eyes of a child who trotted regularly from Dumpling Green to East Dereham long, long years ago. "Thorough bush and thorough briar" we scrambled; and while my body protested at crawls under hedges my mind was busy with that other child's memories of East Dereham:

"I love to think on thee, pretty quiet D——, thou pattern of an English country town, with thy clean but narrow streets branching out from thy modest market-place, with thine old-fashioned houses, with here and there a roof of venerable thatch . . ."

My guide parted from me in the High Street, clutching the coin with which I had retrieved my reputation. I wandered on to the church, and although my real objective was Cowper's tomb I went first to the bubbling spring that had appeared—a veritable Holy Well—when the body of Withburga, daughter of King Annas of the East-Angles, was removed. That the worthies of East Dereham had regarded the lady's exhumation as an act of vandalism was made plain by the lettering cut into the stone above the spring.

"The Abbot and Monks of Ely
ſtole this precious Relique
and tranſlated it to Ely Cathedral
where it was interred near her three Royal Siſters,
A.D. 974."

The sad story of Withburga had been a favourite of George Borrow's and as I entered the church porch I paused before the memorial to another, very different, personality who coloured young George's Sundays. This was James Philo, the cordwainer, High Church Clerk of East Dereham for fifty years and owner of the most stupendous voice in Norfolk. To George, sitting beside his mother in a black leather-lined pew, the rolling cadences of the liturgy as read by the Rector and Philo brought a fearful yet fascinating belief in the phrase, "Thou God seest me!"

"*Rector.* 'Thou didst divide the sea, through Thy power: Thou brakest the heads of the dragons in the waters.'

"*Philo.* 'Thou smotest the heads of Leviathan in pieces: and gavest him to be meat for the people in the wilderness.'

"*Rector.* 'Thou broughtest out fountains and waters out of the hard rocks: Thou driedst up mighty waters.'

"*Philo.* 'The day is Thine, and the night is Thine: Thou hast prepared the light and the sun.' "

But when the congregation had filed out into the sunshine and Mrs. Borrow was greeting various friends, George, his infant mind seething with awful visions, would creep back to the side chapel of St. Edmund, the martyr-king, and stand beside the grave of his hero, William Cowper, who had died three years before his birth. "England's sweetest and most pious bard" gave balm to the hypersensitive little boy who was one day to write a perfect tribute to the poet.

"Yes, pretty Dereham, I could always love thee, were it but for the sake of him who sleeps beneath the marble slab in yonder quiet chancel. It was within thee that the long-oppressed bosom heaved its last sigh, and the crushed and gentle spirit escaped from a world in which it had known naught but sorrow. Sorrow? do I say? How faint a word to express the misery of that bruised reed; misery so dark that a blind worm like myself is occasionally tempted to exclaim, Better had the world never been created than that one so kind, so harmless, and so mild, should have undergone such intolerable woe! But it is over now, for, as there is an end of joy, so has affliction its termination. . . . Peace to the unhappy one, he is gone to his rest; the death-like face is no longer occasionally seen timidly and mournfully looking for a moment through the window-pane upon thy market-place . . . ; the hind in thy neighbourhood no longer at evening-fall views, and starts as he views, the dark lathy figure moving beneath the hazels and alders of shadowy lanes, or by the side of murmuring trout streams; and no longer at early dawn does the sexton of the old church reverently doff his hat, as, supported by some kind friend, the death-stricken creature totters along the church path to that mouldering edifice with the low roof, inclosing a spring of sanatory waters, built and devoted to some saint . . ."

For Cowper, no less than the small George Borrow, knew affiliation with the lady "ſtolen by the Abbot and Monks of Ely". Cowper, like the frightened child who worshipped his memory, sought sanctuary from the stern Jehovah conjured up by Philo's voice.

Cowper, Withburga and Philo, a curious trio to whom another figure must be added if the picture of East Dereham is to be complete. In Borrow's childhood the town was ruled by a benevolent despot, the widow of Sir John Fenn, editor of the *Paston Letters*. Every morning this old lady walked slowly through the market-place, leaning on a gold-topped cane, while behind her marched a footman carrying a basket filled with gifts of food for the sick and aged of the parish. Occasionally the little procession halted for her ladyship to inquire why this or that girl had failed to attend the Sunday school she had not only started but had kept supplied with the instructive books she wrote under the names of "Mrs. Teachwell" and "Mrs. Lovechild". To a child already conscious of the need for expression Lady Fenn, purveyor of food for ailing bodies and healthy minds, appeared as an omnipotent being somehow connected with Philo's all-seeing Jehovah.

II

George Borrow might have been a less sensitive little boy had he entered the world before, instead of after, his brother. John, three years old when George was born, was so beautiful

The Borrow House in Willow Lane, Norwich

Robert Hawkes, Mayor of Norwich, 1822, by Benjamin R. Haydon

even as a tiny baby that a woman once tried to snatch him from his mother's arms, while on all his outings people admired his "rosy, angelic face, blue eyes and light chestnut hair". As he grew his beauty became yet more dazzling and was unusually matched with a mind so alert that he "mastered his letters in a few hours, and in a day or two could decipher the names of people on the doors of houses and over the shop windows".

It was inevitable that Captain and Mrs. Borrow, absorbed in this wonder-child, knew disappointment when they looked upon the infant George. His body was puny; his skin swarthy. He cried a lot and was slow in walking and talking. During the first few years of his life—which were spent in constant movement from camp to camp—he showed a tendency to creep away into some corner, where he sat with his long head slumped forward on to his chest, staring into vacancy and muttering gibberish to himself. Such behaviour did not pass unnoticed; and while the ladies of the regiment tapped their foreheads significantly the parents began to fear that their younger son was what the country folk called a "natural".

George was in his third or fourth year when, as he squatted by the doorway drawing with his fingers in the dust, a Jew pedlar shuffled up and hailed him. George turned his head away so the Jew knocked on the door and, having cried his wares, asked the maidservant: "Who is that child sitting in the sun?" The girl snapped that he was the son of her mistress and "a bit weak in the head". To her astonishment the Jew launched out upon a terrific peroration:

" 'Pon my conscience, my dear, I believe that you must be troubled there yourself to tell me any such thing. It is not my habit to speak to children, inasmuch that I hate them, because they often follow me and fling stones after me; but I no sooner looked at that child than I was forced to speak to it. His not answering me shows his sense, for it has never been the custom of the wise to fling away their words in indifferent talk and conversation. The child is a sweet child, and has all the look of one of our people's children. . . . Were it not for what you tell me, I should say it was a prophet's child. Fool, indeed! he can write already, or I'll forfeit the box which I

C

carry on my back, and for which I should be loth to take two hundred pounds!"

The Jew then whirled about and bent to scan the lines George was busily tracing in the dust; but no sooner had he looked than he straightened and doffed his greasy hat. "Holy letters, young master," he chanted, "holy letters!"

This episode, retailed by the frightened maidservant, was seized upon by Mrs. Borrow as direct evidence that the boy whom everybody regarded as peculiar was in reality possessed of miraculous, if incomprehensible, powers. Captain Borrow took the opposite view. Since his "conversion" after the fight with Big Ben he had become a man of stern convictions. "Love your country and beat the French, and then never mind what happens!" was a phrase always on his lips. He had small patience with a son who looked like a wizened monkey, burst into tears when spoken to, and preferred sitting by himself to playing with other children. He had even less patience with pedlars, and the visit of this particular one disturbed him profoundly. The man's words confirmed his suspicions that George was a very odd little boy indeed who required the strictest possible upbringing.

It would be wrong to suggest that Captain Borrow was in any way unkind to his younger son. On the contrary he was, according to his lights, a most devoted father; but he was also a man who had deliberately shut a door in his mind upon all memories of his own youth, and each time he looked at George the door opened. It seems doubtful whether he actually realized this—he was a man of action and not given to self-analysis—but there is ample evidence that George knew from a very early age the cause behind his father's disapproval of him.

The incident of the pedlar led Captain Borrow to issue a multitude of instructions. George must be shaken out of his unhealthy habit of brooding; he must be disciplined and a vigilant eye kept on his comings and goings lest he strike up any more undesirable acquaintanceships.

Happily for George the Napoleonic Wars kept his father tremendously busy and his mother, chronically involved in packing or unpacking the family's belongings as they moved from married quarters to lodgings and lodgings to married quarters, was too harassed to carry out her husband's dictates. Besides, her instinct was to protect the little goose she firmly believed to be a swan and within a very few months she had further proof of his strange gifts.

The Borrows were living most uncomfortably under canvas at Pett Camp in Sussex and Mrs. Borrow, anxious to escape the close confines of their tent, spent as much time as possible out of doors with the children. On a warm evening the boys were playing between the high hedges of a sandy lane while their mother sat with her sewing a little way off. Suddenly she heard a panic-stricken cry from John: "Oh, Mother, Mother, the viper! My brother has a viper in his hand!"

As she sprang to her feet Mrs. Borrow saw that in truth George was clutching a snake by its middle; but even in her distress she noticed that neither George nor snake seemed the least perturbed until John darted forward to his brother's aid. Only then did the snake hiss, and when George dropped it the reptile sent John into a paroxysm of fear by rearing its head on its coiled body and hissing yet more furiously.

Poor Mrs. Borrow—to whom all snakes were poisonous creatures—scolded George roundly. To her surprise he did not, as was his wont, dissolve into tears, but told her, in his halting speech, that he loved the snake and regretted its departure. It was, he said, *friendly* towards him.

Possibly it was the word "friendly" that reawakened in Ann Borrow's mind memory of the Jew pedlar who had declaimed so passionately that her boy was a "prophet's child". More likely the half-remembered knowledge of that agonizing moment when she saw the infant George fearlessly clasping the snake caused her to send him tearfully to bed and then sit outside the tent brooding on this new manifestation of her gosling's power.

Was the snake really the viper of George Borrow's imaginings? It appears so in the second chapter of *Lavengro* but—and here the follower of George Borrow falls into the pit dug by several of his biographers—was Borrow telling the truth?

No, he was gilding a lily better left ungilded. "The beautiful and glorious object . . . like a line of golden light" may have been an adder, may just as well have been a common or garden grass snake. But we have, willy-nilly, to grow used to George's gildings and to understand how little they matter in the mosaic which forms the pavement trodden by the man who was the Ulysses of the Nineteenth Century.

A Jew pedlar; a snake; a surfeit of berries; a Danish skull . . . from these fragments we build the mosaic piece by piece.

The berries may have been those of deadly nightshade. George ate of them voraciously somewhere near Canterbury while his nursemaid was languishing in the arms of a dragoon. The poor redcoat was riven from his love-dreams by the necessity of George, "who suffered from strong convulsions for several hours" and only awakened to consciousness when he saw his parents and the regimental surgeon standing beside his bed in the barracks.

"Up to this period," he says, "I had been rather a delicate child; whereas, almost after the occurrence to which I allude, I became both hale and vigorous. . . ."

It was when Captain Borrow was stationed at Hythe that George saw the skull which was to make such an impression on his mind that all through his life he studied Norse languages and legends. His mother took the boys to see an ancient church, and while she talked with the sexton John and George slipped out to explore the churchyard. Here they found a small building half-full of objects they thought to be large grey stones. Boy-like, they seized upon the biggest and were struggling to drag it into the light of day when the booming voice of the sexton arrested them:

"Skulls, madam, skulls of the old Danes! Long ago they came pirating into these parts; and then there chanced a mighty shipwreck, for God was angry with them, and He sunk them; and their skulls, as they came ashore, were placed here as a memorial. There were many more when I was young, but now they are fast disappearing. Some of them must have belonged to strange fellows, madam. Only see that one; why, the two young gentry can scarcely lift it!"

This ghoulish recital caused John to drop his share of the burden, but George squatted down beside the mammoth skull, running his hands wonderingly over its surface. "Strange fellows" indeed, these Danes must have been—huge, war-like men moved by the spirit of adventure to launch their ships on stormy seas. From that moment the Norsemen were his heroes.

III

George Borrow was six years old when his family returned to East Dereham, a move which delighted Mrs. Borrow since it meant nearness to her relations and friends and, wonder of wonders! a house of her own. John was sent to school, where he won golden reports, and Captain Borrow found that at last he had some leisure to spend with his wife and children. Only George felt vaguely unhappy. He loved East Dereham. It was associated in his mind with long exciting holidays at his grandfather's farm, but to live in?—that was a different matter. He missed the hurly-burly of camp and barrack; the flash of sunlight on the bayonets of marching men; the men-of-war sailing out of harbour with buntings streaming from the top-gallant masts. Most of all he missed freedom.

Whether the mysterious berries had anything to do with it is a debatable point; but it is certain that after his recovery from the convulsions which had so upset his nursemaid and her dragoon his physique had immensely improved. Wiry, possessed of inexhaustible energy, the roving life had suited the child admirably. Now, cooped up in a little house in a small town, he knew something akin to panic. His outings consisted of decorous walks during which he inevitably met Lady Fenn, and church attendances coloured by the terrifying pronouncements of Philo: his home life was one long ding-dong battle with parental authority.

Captain Borrow's pleasure in John's scholastic ability was marred by his disappointment over George's backwardness.

Six years old and unable to write—ridiculous! Yes, yes, he could read in a halting fashion, but the boy needed spurring on—and did Mrs. Borrow remember that regrettable episode of the Jew pedlar? Tsch, Tsch! High time such a state of affairs was remedied.

So the gallant Captain threw himself into the task of educating—and disciplining—his younger son. He ranted, cajoled, threatened: to no purpose. "The lad's a dunce!" he raged to his wife and she, her gentle heart torn between two loves, was forced to agree that the boy seemed to have absolutely no interest in lessons. Moreover, he had reverted to those habits which had so distressed her two or three years earlier. He wouldn't play with other children, he refused to answer when spoken to, and he spent far too much time moping in corners.

Child psychology was still unheard of, and nobody realized that George was a very unhappy little boy. He was acutely conscious of his brother's brilliance, his father's antagonism, his mother's pitying glances, and his own shortcomings. What he wanted to do was to *think*, but as this was the last occupation to be encouraged in the Borrow household he was eternally chivvied from study of Lady Fenn's *The Child's Grammar*, *The Mother's Grammar*, and *Cobwebs to Catch Flies* to the church pew where he writhed in fear of Jehovah.

It was his brother's godmother who, all unwittingly, provided him with a "magic casement". She called one day with a *History of England* for John and, not wishing to hurt Mrs. Borrow's feelings, whispered she had included in the parcel a book for George. When his mother had gone out with this lady the boy crept to the table where the books lay loosely wrapped. Why he did so he knew not, for he disliked all books at this period, but, as he wrote forty years afterwards in *Lavengro*:

"A strange sensation came over me, such as I had never experienced before—a singular blending of curiosity, awe and pleasure, the remembrance of which, even at this distance of time, produces a remarkable effect upon my nervous system . . ."

The book was revealed, bound in dingy leather. George opened it idly and gave a gasp of sheer pleasure. Before him, limned in vivid colours, was the picture of

"a heavy sea and rocky shore, with mountains in the background, above which the moon was peering. Not far from the shore, upon the water, was a boat with two figures in it, one of which stood at the bow, pointing with what I knew to be a gun at a dreadful shape in the water; fire was flashing from the muzzle of the gun, and the monster appeared to be transfixed. I almost thought I heard its cry. I remained motionless, gazing upon the picture, scarcely daring to draw my breath, lest the new and wondrous world should vanish of which I had obtained a glimpse.

" 'Who are those people, and what could have brought them into that strange situation?' I asked myself."

Such was George Borrow's introduction to *Robinson Crusoe*, the book which transformed him from a dull, morose child into one eager to learn anything which could enable him to follow the adventures of the shipwrecked mariner and his man Friday. For the next few months his parents, unaware of the cause behind this sudden change, congratulated each other upon George's quickness in assimilating the profound truths contained in *Cobwebs to Catch Flies*. Frowns gave place to smiles, but it is doubtful if George even noticed, so absorbed was he in the reading of *Robinson Crusoe*. Hour after hour he spent poring over this treasure, at first spelling out the words laboriously, later skimming the pages at speed only to turn back to the beginning so that he might savour to the full the meaning of every line.

"Hail to thee, spirit of De Foe! What does not my own poor self owe to thee? England has better bards than either Greece or Rome, yet I could spare them easier far than De Foe, 'unabashed De Foe', as the hunchbacked rhymer styled him."

IV

In his *George Borrow and His Circle*[1] Clement King Shorter stressed the fact that Borrow was always an imaginative writer and added that "Dr. Knapp's worst banality was to suggest that he 'invented nothing'." A true criticism, but perhaps because the present writer is a woman her chief grudge against that careful and loving biographer is his lofty dismissal of Borrow's early years. Beyond recording his birth—the exact place of which worried him considerably—he gives no details of his experiences before the year 1810, merely saying superbly:

"We pass over the well-known accidents and exploits of our bantling at Pett Camp, Hythe, and Canterbury, because the interesting period (to mothers) of the differentiation of a tot into something intelligent does not stimulate our enthusiasm. In short—it is a time when the animal is most admirable to its friends within the four walls of the nursery."

If ever the adage, "The child is father to the man", rang true, it was in the case of George Borrow, and if we discard his early childhood we have not the faintest hope of understanding the motives which prompted his writings or his way of living. It is by no means enough to point, as did Dr. Knapp, to the first three chapters of *Lavengro* and say: "Well, here is your infant animal, study it if you will." We have to go every step of the way from a little child's fumblings for expression to a dour old man's hypochondria if we are to gain—as we surely must, for otherwise why write about him?—a portrait of a figure unique in English literature. . . .

But we are in East Dereham, Norfolk; the year is 1810; the fife is shrilling and the drum is beating; the regiment is again on the march—this time to Norman Cross in Huntingdonshire.

The Borrow family reached this junction on the Great North Road in early summer, but the only genial thing about

[1] Published, Hodder & Stoughton, 1913.

the place was its climate, for the wooden barracks were in a swampy field and immediately opposite them, obliterating the view, towered the huge prisons—also of wood—which the Government had built to house their French prisoners. These grim buildings were surrounded by palisades and closely guarded, and since there were no windows the wretched inmates were obliged to poke their heads through gaps in the steeply slanting roofs if they wished to glimpse the outside world.

There wasn't a soldier in the British army who relished a posting to Norman Cross; there wasn't a soldier's wife who failed to grumble at the poorness of the married quarters, the nearness to the prisons, and the general atmosphere of gloom. The low-lying fen country was unhealthy enough in ordinary times: now, so people averred, it provided a breeding-ground for all the germs spread by the prisoners in whom confinement and bad food had induced every imaginable disease.

Only young George, his mind steeped in Defoe, found Norman Cross a thrilling and romantic place. He pitied the prisoners—especially when their guards carried out the famous "straw-plait hunts"[1] at the point of the bayonet in search of contraband articles—but he felt selfishly grateful to them since they kept his father so busy that the discipline of East Dereham went by the board, while his mother spent her days scouring and scrubbing their meagre quarters lest some plague attack her family.

Each morning after he had done his small share of the household tasks, George slipped out of the barracks to wander around the countryside. Hour after hour he would crouch in the reeds by Whittlesea Mere, watching the birds, listening to the croaking frogs, thinking how wonderful it was to be alive and free. Tired of staying still he would rise at last and scamper across the tussocky grass until he reached Yaxley with its dark tangled woods, its wilderness that had once been parkland, its deserted, tumbledown house. Yaxley was paradise to George. He crawled through the prickly undergrowth stalking imaginary robbers; he followed every twist

---

[1] The prisoners plaited straw for hats and bonnets so exquisitely that this occupation was forbidden as being bad for English trade.

of its weedy garden paths; he studied the habits of its rooks, pigeons, rabbits, stoats, weasels and moles; he lay on his stomach under its great trees, devouring some book of adventure.

It was on his way to Yaxley that he often met the tall old man with a leather bag on his shoulder, who had a queer habit of poking among the furze and bramble bushes with his stick, muttering to himself as he did so. This behaviour so intrigued George that one morning he crept close enough to hear the old man say, as he stared at a mark on the dusty road: "He must have been a large one, or he would not have left such a trail, I wonder if he is near; he seems to have moved this way." He then began raking in some bushes and presently emerged holding a snake in his hand.

"What do you think of that, my boy?" he cried, spying George, "what do you think of catching such a thing as that with the naked hand?"

George remembered the "beautiful and glorious" viper which had caused all the commotion at Pett Camp. "Why," he said, "that I could do as much myself."

"You do, do you?" shouted the old man angrily as he squeezed some foam from the snake's jaws and thrust it into his leather bag. "Lord! how the young people in these days are given to conceit; it did not used to be so in my time when I was a child, childer knew how to behave themselves; but the childer of these days are full of conceit, full of froth, like the mouth of this viper."

This outburst alarmed the seven-year-old boy and he ran off towards Yaxley; but all day as he wandered round his favourite haunts he thought about the encounter. Perhaps his answer had been rude? If so, it was his duty to apologize— besides, it was now clear that the old man collected vipers, a delicious occupation of which George dearly wished to know more. So he left Yaxley earlier than usual, keeping a sharp look-out for the tall figure in skin cap, breeches and gaiters. Soon he saw him tramping along the road ahead and hurried to catch up with him.

"Good evening to you, sir," he panted, sweeping off his cap.

The old man peered at him. "How's this? You aren't, sure, the child I met in the morning?"

"What makes you doubt it?" asked George.

"Why, you were then all froth and conceit, and now you take off your cap to me."

"I beg pardon," said George, "if I was frothy and conceited; it ill becomes a child like me to be so."

This humble speech quite melted the old man's heart, and for the next few weeks he allowed George to accompany him on his snake hunts. Yaxley and Whittlesea Mere were forgotten in the excitement of helping to catch the snakes and listening to marvellous stories of how unguents made from their fat effected cures for different ills. But the old man assured George solemnly that his real trade was that of herbalist. Soon, he said, he would have to give up the snake-catching part of his business because he was growing frightened of the reptiles. He put his fear down to an experience seven years earlier "on the other side of England" when he had been awakened from a snooze on the hillside by a huge and monstrous snake he insisted was the very "king of vipers".

George drank in every word of this fascinating tale, nodded his head when the old man swore the viper king had been angry with him for meddling with his people, and was dejected beyond measure when his companion said that it was time he moved from Huntingdonshire. A string of eager questions failed to elicit the old man's exact destination and brought the rebuke that the child asked too many questions. Most probably the herbalist sold his cures at fairs up and down the country; but he seems to have grown genuinely fond of George, for on his departure he gave him his own tame snake from which he had removed the fangs.

This horrid small pet did much to recompense George for his friend's absence. It "had been taught to dance and perform various kinds of tricks", it lived on milk, and it curled up contentedly inside its new master's shirt. George was enchanted with the creature, always carried it with him on his walks abroad and, we may be sure, kept it hidden from his parents.

The Borrows remained at Norman Cross for fifteen months

and at some period during their stay it seems fairly certain that George met the gypsy lad who was to have such an effect on his life. Several eminent men have argued that the meeting did not take place until five years later, when the family had settled in Norwich and George had taken to wandering among the gypsies on Mousehold Heath—yet at that first meeting George still had the snake, and the whole account of his introduction to Ambrose Smith, whom he calls Jasper Petulengro, points to the earlier date.

George came on the gypsy encampment in a clearing in the woods and was attracted by the thin column of smoke rising from their wood fire. As he drew nearer he saw a man and woman, wild swarthy folk, crouching by the fire intent on their tasks. The man was carding plaited straw while the woman was rubbing white powder on some metal objects. When they caught sight of the child they made towards him, the man brandishing a ladle and the woman screaming threats. Didn't he know what happened to strange boys who pried into gypsy doings? Why, they were either drowned in the nearest pond or beaten within an inch of their lives!

They were a fearsome-looking pair. The man had a deep scar on his face and the woman's black hair hung down either side of her face like horses' tails. Most children would have fled without delay, but George, with his insatiable curiosity regarding anything unusual, stood his ground. Indeed, in his own version of the story, he boldly accused the couple of straw-plaiting and the making of counterfeit coins, adding rhetorically:

"I tell you what, my chap, you had better put down that thing of yours; my father lies concealed within my tepid breast, and if to me you offer any harm or wrong, I'll call him forth to help me with his forked tongue."

It seems doubtful whether even the odd little boy who was George Borrow really made such a brave speech. More likely he took the snake from his shirt and held it out silently as a protection against attack. Certainly it was the casual manner in which he handled the reptile that caused the gypsies to drop their threats and back away from him in awe. To their superstitious minds any child who nursed vipers in such nonchalant fashion was clearly a devilkin, a goblin, a supernatural being to be placated by ordinary mortals.

They brought a little stool for him to sit on, fawned and fussed over him, called him "gorgious angel" and "tiny tawny", gave him candied fruits and beseeched him to stay with them and become their "little God Almighty". Even when George —who had difficulty in following their strange talk—told them bluntly that his father was a soldier and that the snake was a tame one with drawn fangs, the gypsies still entreated him to join them, saying they could make "a mort of money" out of him and his viper.

"I shouldn't wonder if you would make a prime hand at telling fortunes," said the man, "and you might still be our God Almighty, or at any rate our clergyman, so you should live in a tilted cart by yourself and say prayers to us night and morning. . . . I shouldn't wonder if you could read."

Proud George immediately whipped his tattered copy of *Robinson Crusoe* from his pocket and read a long passage while the man and woman stared at him in amaze.

"That's the kind of prayers for me and my family, aren't they, wifelkin?" exclaimed the man. "I never heard more delicate prayers in all my life! Why, they beat the rubricals hollow!—and here comes my son Jasper.[1] I say, Jasper, here's a young sap-engro that can read, and is more fly than yourself. Shake hands with him; I wish ye to be two brothers."

The two boys faced each other; the small wiry George still clutching his snake, the bigger gypsy boy, his face already lined and wary, holding a great whalebone whip under one of his long arms. Their glances met and into both pairs of dark eyes came a flicker—was it of recognition?

"There, Jasper!" said the gypsy. "Shake hands with the sap-engro."

Jasper's expression changed to one of surliness. "Can he box? I should think not, he looks so puny and small."

"Hold your peace, fool!" ordered his father. "He can do more than that—I tell you he's fly; he carries a sap about, which would sting a ninny like you to dead."

"What, a sap-engro!" Jasper bent forward, leered at

[1] Ambrose Smith.

George, then patted his head. "A sap-engro," he repeated softly, "lor!"

His parents began a loud discussion about George joining them, and he might well have gone with the gypsies had it not been for the sudden arrival of a burly man on a sweating grey horse. Evidently he brought news of moment, for immediately the gypsies struck their tents, whistled their lean ponies, packed their gear into carts while the new-comer swore at them impatiently.

"Curse ye, for Romans, how slow ye are! Well, it is no business of mine, stay here all day if you like; I have given ye warning, I am off to the big north road. However, before I go, you had better give me all you have of that."

Everyone had forgotten about George. He stood hesitantly in the background as the horseman, whom they called Nat, seized two heavy knitted bags from the gypsy woman, stuck his spurs into the grey's sides and galloped off down the grassy ride. From the depths of the wood came other members of the gypsy tribe to help in the preparations for departure and in a very few minutes the company moved off in their creaking carts without so much as a backward glance at the little boy with the snake.

George blinked away his tears. He had liked them so much, these strange folk with their uncouth speech. He had wanted to travel with them, to live in a "tilted cart" of his own and be their "little God Almighty". Would he ever see them again?

There was a touch on his shoulder and wheeling around he came face to face with Jasper.

"Good-bye, Sap," he whined, thrusting out his hand. "I dare say we shall meet again, remember we are brothers, two gentle brothers." Then he grinned. "What a sap-engro, lor!" he whispered, and turned to run after his people.

George watched until his ragged figure had disappeared; then he looked down at his right hand. "*Brothers*," Jasper had said, "*gentle brothers*." He squatted down beside the smouldering ash of the gypsy fire and drew the little snake from his shirt. "You're a sap," he told it gravely, "and I am a sap-engro!"

V

From the gypsies to *Lilly's Latin Grammar*[1] is a far cry, yet it was thanks to George Borrow's meeting with the Petulengro family that he undertook the stupendous task of learning Lilly's work off by heart. The August of 1811 found the Borrows back at East Dereham, and as Captain Borrow resumed his recruiting so he resumed his interest in George's education. He had no anxiety now about his younger son's delicacy or apathy; rather he complained of his lawless ways and his fondness for tales of adventure and straightaway visited a clergyman of his acquaintance, who agreed to teach the boy.

This gentleman assured the Captain that if George was to grow up an honest citizen it was absolutely necessary for him to master the Latin language: so for the next four months George endured an intensive introduction to that classic tongue. Early in 1812, however, Captain Borrow was ordered to rejoin his regiment at Harwich and was told that for the next year or two they would be continually on the move. Since he could not afford to leave his family in East Dereham they had perforce to go with him, a circumstance deplored by the clergyman, who harangued the Captain in these words:

"You are now removing him (George) from my care; you do wrong, but we will let that pass. Listen to me: there is but one good school-book in the world—the one I use in my seminary—*Lilly's Latin Grammar*, in which your son has already made some progress. . . . If you can by any means, fair or foul, induce him to get by heart *Lilly's Latin Grammar*, you may set your heart at rest with respect to him; I, myself, will be his warrant."

No scholar himself, the Captain was deeply impressed by his friend's remarks. This book he talked of must be wonderful indeed if it could work such alchemy—so when the Borrows left East Dereham a copy of Lilly was included in their baggage and the Captain insisted that each day, wherever they might be, George should study it. Indeed, it is not putting the matter

[1] William Lilly, 1468–1523.

too strongly to say that he became positively fanatical about Lilly. As the regiment marched northwards by slow stages, remaining at this town or that for a few weeks, he chivvied poor George to a succession of schools, his first question to every headmaster being—"Do you use *Lilly's Latin Grammar*?" If the answer was in the negative then he arranged that the master should give George extra coaching in the contents of that marvellous volume; and on the many nights the family were forced to spend in lodgings while actually travelling, he himself sat frowningly while the tired child stumbled his way through declension after declension. By means either "fair or foul" his younger son was going to learn Lilly off by heart.

And in sheer desperation George did so! He was not in the least interested in Lilly—he grew to detest the sight of the dog-eared book; but Lilly was the mountainous barrier separating him from the changing scenery he wanted so desperately to enjoy, from the people he wanted to talk to and the games he wished to play, above all from the search he longed to start up and down these roads of England for the gypsy boy Jasper whose memory he hugged close to his heart. That Lilly should keep him from Jasper was unthinkable; therefore Lilly must be conquered.

Blessed with a remarkably retentive memory George learnt to gabble lines, pages and chapters of Lilly like a parrot. When his family spoke to him he rolled out sonorous Latin phrases; when other boys asked him to play he chanted strings of verbs; when he lay in bed he crooned himself to sleep with passages from Cæsar's Gallic Wars until at last the great day came when he could recite the whole of Lilly right through without hesitation. Without understanding either, of course, but that mattered little beside the parental approval of his accomplishment.

"Truly this is more than I expected," said Captain Borrow. "I did not think that there had been so much in you, either of application or capacity; you have now learnt all that is necessary, if my friend Dr. B . . .'s opinion was sterling, as I have no doubt it was. You are still a child, however, and must yet go to school, in order that you may be kept out of evil company. Perhaps you may still contrive, now you have exhausted the barn, to pick up a grain or two in the barnyard. You are still ignorant of figures, I believe, not that I would mention figures in the same day with *Lilly's Grammar*."

The somewhat qualified approval of this lecture and the pointed hint that the perils of arithmetic still had to be faced worried George not at all. His victory over Lilly appeared to him as a symbol—in retrospect he even developed a nostalgic fondness for that grim grammarian. Arithmetic? Pooh! he would take it in his stride. Meanwhile he was free —gloriously free.

At exactly what period in the regiment's wanderings George "graduated in Lilly" it is hard to determine. From Harwich the Borrows had travelled to Leicester, then to Melton Mowbray and by way of Tamworth and Macclesfield to Stockport; and since they reached that town in June their stops at the earlier places must have been short. At the end of July they began the long march through the bare hilly country of Lancashire and Yorkshire to Huddersfield, where they remained until the end of the year when they moved on to Sheffield. At both the Yorkshire towns the energetic Captain made arrangements for his sons to attend "classical academies", though one cannot think that the boys had much opportunity to learn a great deal at either.

In the spring of 1813 the order came that the regiment would "proceed to Berwick-on-Tweed in two divisions", the ultimate destination being Edinburgh Castle. By this time everybody was heartily sick of journeying, and the prospect of a further two hundred and fifty miles over rough country and among alien people brought lamentations from most of the wives. One cannot blame them. The industrialization of the north of England had scarcely begun; the bleak rugged landscape and its uncouth inhabitants struck terror into the hearts of those accustomed to the flat lands and comfortable countryfolk of East Anglia; the travelling conditions were appalling, since inns were few and poor and food hard to come by. But orders were orders, and on 19 March they took the high road for Barnsley and Leeds. Captain Borrow was on horseback, his wife and children in a fusty, jolting post-chaise.

Perhaps George had achieved his victory over Lilly at

D

Sheffield? At all events, he now displayed a lively interest in his surroundings missing from his account of the journey from Harwich to that city. For the first time he became aware of geography and pestered everybody with questions as to which county they were in. The wildness of their route excited him almost as much as the queer dialects spoken in deep, guttural voices by the lodging and shopkeepers they met. Surely, he thought, as he poked his head eagerly out of the chaise window much to Mrs. Borrow's annoyance, this was just the sort of country where gypsies might be found?

The cavalcade wound wearily on through Leeds, Wetherby, Boroughbridge, Northallerton and Darlington to Durham, where George's allegiance to that "stupendous erection, the aqueduct at Stockport" wavered in favour of the beauty of the Cathedral, and he had "a capital dinner off roast Durham beef, and a capital glass of ale, which I believe was the cause of my being ever after fond of ale". Then on again to Newcastle-upon-Tyne, where they passed an uncomfortable night in crowded barracks, and George had an opportunity of exploring the river as it was Sunday and the British Army did not march on the Sabbath Day.

The next part of their journey was the worst, and a full week passed before they limped into Berwick-on-Tweed, where George found a second river—one he never forgot.

"The river was a noble one; the broadest that I had hitherto seen. Its waters, of a greenish tinge, poured beneath the narrow arches of a long and massive bridge of antique architecture to meet the sea, close at hand, as the boom of the billows breaking distinctly upon a beach declared. There were songs upon the river from the fisher-barks; and occasionally a chorus, plaintive and wild, such as I had never heard before, the words of which I did not understand, but which at the present time, down the long avenue of years, seem in memory's ear to sound like 'Horam, coram, dago'. Several robust fellows were near me, some knee-deep in water, employed in hauling the seine upon the strand. Huge fish were struggling amidst the meshes—princely salmon—their brilliant mail of blue and silver flashing in the morning beam; so goodly and gay a scene, in truth, had never greeted my boyish eye."

Was it the beauty of the scene that made George weep as he lay on the river bank? He said himself he did not think so, but believed his emotion sprang from "something rather connected with the world of spirits and dreams". His scrappy education had not taught him much of history, but in later life he swore that on that far off spring morning he had been affected by the ghosts of the Scots, the English, the Norsemen —all the warriors who had fought and died for possession of the walled city which rose glimmering beyond the bridge.

His tears attracted the attention of a fisherman, who asked him if anyone had hurt him. George, who could only follow his speech with difficulty, asked the name of the river.

"Hout!" said the old man, "I now see what you was greeting at—at your ain ignorance, nae doubt—'tis very great! Well, I will na fash you with reproaches, but even enlighten ye, since you seem a decent man's bairn, and you speir a civil question. Yon river is called the Tweed; and yonder, over the Brig, is Scotland. Did ye never hear of the Tweed, my bonny man?"

"No," said George slowly, as he picked himself up and began to walk towards the bridge. "I never heard of it; but now that I have seen it, I shall not soon forget it!"

VI

On 6 April the regiment halted on the outskirts of Edinburgh. Both officers and men were tired out, but everybody, down to the drummer boys, realized that it would never do to give the savage Scots a bad impression of the West Norfolk Militia. Uniforms were brushed down, horses groomed, brass polished, and colours unfurled. At sunset the brave march into the city began to the thunder of drums and the blaring of trumpets, and as the post-chaise swung round the corner of the High Street in the wake of the baggage-wagons an exultant

George flattened his nose against the window-pane. Here was life! Here was adventure! The uneven cobbles between the tall grey houses were thronged with the townsfolk—barbarians to his childish eyes—who were clad in coarse garments and yelled at each other in outlandish tongues, while they ran to and fro brandishing torches the better to see the strangers within their gates. Up creaked the coach, and up, until of a sudden it reached the level of the esplanade and stopped with a jerk.

George was the first to scramble out. Ahead of him towered the castle, its turrets and ramparts black against the evening sky. A keen salty wind blew in his face as he ran to the northern parapet and peered over. Far below the castle rock lay the Nor Loch; all around it the lights of the city bobbed and twinkled; beyond them showed the sliver of silver that was the Firth of Forth. He ran to the southern parapet—there again was a dark pit studded with lights and in the distance the humped shapes of the Pentland Hills. He drew in a long whistling breath of sheer delight—gracious, he was on the very roof of the world!

George liked everything about this miraculous city of Edinburgh. From the windows of their quarters in the barracks, clamped tightly to the castle on its rock, he never tired of gazing across the Firth to the Fife coast and the Lomonds, the "hielan' hills", as he was told to call them. He spent long hours prowling down the Royal Mile leading to the Palace of Holyrood House; squinting up at the Mercat Cross, the Talbooth Church, or John Knox's house; examining all the narrow closes, once the homes of Scotland's nobility, now poor dwellings that swarmed with humanity and stank of garbage; staring round-eyed in Holyrood House itself at the rusty patch on the floor—reputedly stained afresh each year with sheep's blood—where Mary of Scots' musician Rizzio was killed by the daggers of her nobles.

With his brother John he went farther afield, climbing Arthur's Seat, that hill which lay, like a *lion couchant*, guarding the eastern approach to the city; trotting down the long slope to the Port of Leith, with its tarry smells and its multitudes of ships; catching tiddlers in Craiglockhart Ponds; shivering on the banks of Duddingston Loch where—so it was whispered—

nobody knew how deep the water was; walking sedately to the High School where Walter Scott had been educated and where, so Dr. Adam had declared, "more work was done in an hour than at any other school in Europe".[1]

George even liked the High School to which, upon hearing that the teaching in Greek and Latin was excellent, Captain Borrow had despatched his sons. (One feels that if he could have looked forward in time and learnt of King Edward VII's attendance at that same school he would have regarded it even more favourably than he did.) George's liking for the school was based on the fact that *Lilly's Latin Grammar* was a book abhorred by Aglionby Ross Carson, the Classics master; and on his admiration for the stalwart janitor, William Bowie, whom he invested with all the attributes of the great Norse Viking, Bui Hin Digri.

One of the first things which John and George learnt at the High School had nothing to do with the classics. It was the pugnacity of their classmates. Anything served as an excuse for a fight—or, to use their own word—a bicker. Unfortunately, owing to the deep-rooted dislike of the Scots for the English, the Borrow brothers were usually the target for attack. John quickly became adept at evading any racial insults, but George could never resist answering his tormentors with the result that he was beaten black and blue in the playground for making fun of his Scottish comrades.

Even this did not daunt him. He soon discovered that Edinburgh teemed with rival gangs of youthful fighters, and that the two most notable were known as the Old Town and the New Town, between whom a bitter feud was perpetually waged. One autumn day he was standing on the green brae below the castle (known as the Mound) when he heard cries coming from the swampy ground by the Nor Loch. As there was a thick mist George immediately scrambled down to see the fun, but just as he reached the path across the swamp he was met by the Old Town brigade in full retreat from their enemies. Always a fighter for lost causes George dashed to their aid, but in the act of hurling a stone at the New Town boys he slipped off the path and sank to his shoulders in the

[1] Dr. Alex. Adam, 1741–1809.

quagmire of the Nor Loch. Without ado the Old Town gang formed a protective square around him and continued the fight until darkness fell. They then hauled him out and congratulated him on having a "right dangerous aim".

Thereafter, George's chief sport was fighting, and in the last bicker before the authorities took stern measures to squash the gang warfare he very nearly lost his life. On this occasion the New Town were led by a fully grown man who, so legend had it, wanted to avenge the loss of his younger brother's eye in an earlier battle. Armed with a wheel-spoke and protected by a wickerwork shield, this character advanced on George, struck him to the ground, and was just about to belabour him with the spoke when a wild, red-headed drummer-boy came charging down the brae and took a running jump at the enemy.

This incident was the beginning of an odd friendship between George and the drummer-boy, the notorious David Haggart.[1] A short while afterwards George, who had taken to crag climbing on the castle rock, came across Haggart sitting hunched on a dangerous spur just above Wallace's Tower.

"What are you thinking of, David?" asked George.

"I was thinking of Willie Wallace," answered Haggart.

"And why were ye thinking of him? The English hanged him long since, as I have heard say."

"I was thinking," said Haggart sombrely, "that I should wish to be like him."

George clutched at the slippery rock in sudden fright. "Do ye mean," he whispered fearfully, "that ye would wish to be hanged?"

Haggart nodded. "I wad na flinch from that, Geordie, if I might be a great man first."

This gloomy and, if he had but known it, prophetic utterance intrigued George immensely. Thereafter he and Haggart were boon companions and spent their time scrambling about the castle rock looking for owls' nests and weasels, and learning of each other's very different upbringing. Haggart, surly, rebellious child of an Edinburgh slum, was soon to get

[1] *The Life of David Haggart:* written by himself while under sentence of Death, Edinburgh, 1821.

his discharge from the army and become in turn pick-pocket, highway robber, and murderer. Over Scotland, northern England and Ireland he roved in search of plunder, being twice sentenced to death and escaping by killing his warders before being executed at Edinburgh in 1821 at the age of twenty. While in the condemned cell he dictated his astonishing life to the prison chaplain, confessing to a variety of crimes under no fewer than six aliases, and this blood-thirsty work was published soon after his death.

A blackguard if ever there was one, this David Haggart, yet to George Borrow he remained a hero. In *Lavengro* he went so far as to compare him to Tamerlane, insisting that if he had managed to reach America as he had wished to do, he might have risen to be a great and famous leader of men. This extravagant belief in Haggart's qualities owed nothing to fact and was probably due to Captain Borrow's detestation of one whom he described as the worst drummer-boy he ever knew. Despite *Lilly's Latin Grammar* the Captain still suffered lingering doubts about his younger son's character, and George's association with Haggart distressed him—incongruously enough, what upset him most was the "braid Scots" speech the boy picked up from his singular friend.

The Captain sighed relievedly when, in the early summer of 1814, the regiment embarked at Leith for Yarmouth and Norwich. The long drawn-out war was over at last—or so he and everybody else thought at the time—and he looked forward to a well-earned retirement during which he would be able to devote himself to his family. With Mrs. Borrow and the boys he journeyed south by post-chaise, arriving at Norwich just in time to attend a grand dinner presided over by the Colonel, Lord Orford, in the Maid's Head Inn on 18 July, while after the mustering out of the regiment he took lodgings in the Crown and Angel in St. Stephen's Street and—energetic as ever—bustled off to see the Rev. Edward Valpy, headmaster of the Grammar School.

Mrs. Borrow was delighted to be back again among familiar faces. John, who had lately shown a decided gift for drawing and painting, was in the seventh heaven because it was arranged he should study under that great man, John Crome. Captain

Borrow enjoyed his unaccustomed leisure. Only George, as usual temperamentally at variance with his parents and brother, was miserably unhappy. Once again he found how impossible it was to escape his father's vigilant eye, and on a September day he crawled unwillingly through the Erpingham Gate into the Upper Close of the Cathedral, where the ancient Grammar School was situated.

There he sat, listless, head on his chest, making half-hearted attempts to construe Virgil and Cicero while the master's voice droned through the stuffy class-room. Ah, how he hated Latin, he thought, jabbing a sputtering pen at the exercise book. Latin was dead, Norwich was dead, he himself was dead! He remembered the mist swirling round the castle rock, the strident life of the Canongate, the wail of the pipes, the keen wind that blew from the "heilan' hills" . . . and farther back he remembered the tussocky grass between Whittlesea Mere and Yaxley, the tangled undergrowth in the woods, the smouldering ash from a gypsy fire. . . . He bent closer over his book. With an intensity that caused his whole body to ache he remembered his live, free friends, Jasper Petulengro and David Haggart.

VII

It was Napoleon's escape from Elba that rescued George from his death-in-life at the Grammar School. All through March, 1815, rumours flew round Norwich. The dreaded Boney had landed at Antibes—he was at Cannes—he was marching on Paris—he was reinstated at the Tuileries. Captain Borrow hastily donned his uniform and set about an unofficial muster of his nine hundred men before the order came to embody the militia again. The victory of Waterloo occurred before the muster was complete; but the authorities decided to send the regiment to Ireland, then in a more troubled condition than usual. On 31 August, they sailed in two ships from Harwich, arriving at Cork a week later. With them went a tearful Mrs. Borrow, a joyful George, and a sulky Ensign John Thomas

Borrow—for poor John had been wrested from Crome by his soldierly papa, who thus achieved his ambition to have a son of commissioned rank.

So soon as he looked on Cork harbour George knew in his bones that Ireland was going to better Scotland. His apathy disappeared during the long march northwards to Clonmel, and he strode alertly beside his father, sniffing the sweet tangy scent of bog myrtle, glancing from the blue mountains of Tipperary to the tall, cloak-wrapped men who passed them driving carts drawn by oxen. They were bone-poor, these men, yet they had a proud look; but what particularly interested George was the language they spoke.

"A strange language that," remarked a young officer to Captain Borrow, "I don't understand a word of it; what can it be?"

"Irish," retorted his senior, "and a bad language it is!"

"A queer tongue," said George thoughtfully, "I wonder if I could learn it?"

His father rounded on him. "Learn it! What should you learn it for?—however, I am not afraid of that. It is not like Scotch; no person can learn it, save those who are born to it, and even in Ireland the respectable people do not speak it, only the wilder sort, like those we have passed."

George held his peace, but once they were settled in Clonmel at the house of the Protestant Mrs. Hyne from Londonderry —whose blarneying husband welcomed them by drinking to the health of "King George, God bless him; to the 'glorious and immortal'—to Boyne water—to Captain Borrow's speedy promotion to be Lord Lieutenant, and to the speedy downfall of the Pope and Saint Anthony of Padua"—he wandered round the little town listening to all the conversations he could and trying to make sense out of them.

It was the garrulous Mr. Hyne who persuaded Captain Borrow to send his younger son to an old clergyman who taught "the most elegant Latin". The first morning George went reluctantly, fierce memories of Lilly in his heart—but oh, what a different school to any he had known! It was held in a dilapidated, dirty, stone-floored hall; the master sat at a desk of black oak absorbed in an enormous *Elzevir Flaccus*; the pupils squatted on stones by a roaring wood fire. Occasionally the clergyman would raise his head, mumble out a few instructions as to Latin or Greek tasks, then bend again to his own reading. Nobody paid any attention. The boys held their books on their knees and talked in low voices but they were not construing Latin or Greek; they were telling each other wild stories of adventure.

For a week or two George listened intently to his companions' tales of the wonderful experiences which had befallen them—how one had been sucked into a bog, and another visited by the leprechauns, and a third chased by a dog as big as a bear. All very exciting, but since none of the lads had been farther than Cork their stories held a certain sameness. At last George could contain himself no longer. He told them about his tame snake, and the old man with the leather bag, and the meeting with Jasper. Inspired by their round eyes and open mouths he went on to recount his Edinburgh adventures; the bickers, the crag-climbing, the friendship with David Haggart.

By the end of the morning he was a hero. Never, so his schoolmates averred, had they met such a traveller or one to whom so many astonishing things had happened. They clamoured for more, and George was only too willing to oblige them. For the three or four months he remained at Clonmel he occupied a position similar to that of the story-tellers of ancient times. Naturally his stock of true—or partly true—tales ran out, so he supplemented it by anecdotes taken from the many books of adventure he had read including, of course, *Robinson Crusoe*.

The blarneying Mr. Hyne had not spoken quite frankly when he assured Captain Borrow that George would only make friends with the young Protestant gentry at school. There were among the pupils three "Papist gossoons", sons of local farmers, and one of them was George's ardent admirer. "Faith, Shorsha dear!" he would say, "that snake bates anything about Finna-ma-Coul or Brian Boroo, the thieves two, bad luck to them!"

This boy's name was Murtagh. He was enormously tall with a pronounced stoop, though whether this was because he had outgrown his strength or because he always wore a grey coat far too small for him nobody knew. His eyes stared anxiously out of his freckled face and he made perpetual movements with his hands as if he were shuffling a pack of cards. This, indeed, was exactly what he was doing, for he confided to George that his thieving Uncle Phelim had stolen his precious pack and gone off to Waterford. Since then, so Murtagh said, he had been "frightened" by the silent loneliness of the farm kitchen in the evenings. If only he had the cards then his brother and the farm-hands would play a game with him and thus enable him to conquer his fears; but, alas, he had no money for a fresh pack.

"And now the Christmas holidays is coming, when I shall be at home by day as well as night, and then what am I to do? Since I have been a saggerting (studying), I have been good for nothing at all—neither for work nor Greek—only to play cards! Faith, it's going mad I will be!"

Poor Murtagh's wretchedness gave George a brilliant idea: "I say, Murtagh! I have a pack of cards."

"You don't say so, Shorsha mavourneen! You don't say you have cards fifty-two?"

Then George unfolded his scheme. Murtagh should have the cards provided he taught George Irish.

"And is it a language-master you'd be making of me?" asked Murtagh.

"To be sure!—what better can you do?—it would help you to pass your time at school. You can't learn Greek, so you must teach me Irish."

By Christmas time Murtagh was cured of his fears and George was speaking fluent if execrable Irish. The "Papist gossoon" had done what Lilly had failed to do; he had awakened George's interest in philology.

VIII

The New Year brought a move to Templemore, near the famous Bog of Allen. It was a desolate region wreathed in drifting mists which lifted sometimes to show a ruined, ghostly castle or the sinister Crag of Cashel. There was no school, and George felt doubly lonely since his brother John had been sent to another detachment some ten miles away. Not yet sixteen, yet in charge of twenty men, he had marched bravely out of the barrack-yard to the tune of—

> Marlbrouk has gone to the wars,
> He'll never return no more!

and as George watched he felt sad. Despite his father's irritating habit of holding John up as a paragon of all the virtues he was exceedingly fond of his brother, and he knew full well the inner war that went on between John the artist and John the soldier.

But as the days passed George's spirits rose. He roamed the bog-lands, knocking on lonely cabin doors and talking to the inhabitants in his curious Irish until they invited him in to sit on the "stranger's stone" and told him all their woes and troubles. He made an expedition to a derelict castle once built by the Protector where he found an ancient crone living all by herself, and from her he learnt of the undying hatred the Irish bore against the English.

"Is this your house, mother?" he asked her.

"Yes, my house, my own house; the house of the broken-hearted."

"Any other person's house?"

"My own house, the beggar's house—the accursed house of Cromwell!"

He met queer folk and queerer dogs; he heard the legends about Jerry Grant, the outlaw; he became familiar with the strange superstitions that abounded in Cashel—where, so it was said, the Crag was a piece of rock dropped from Satan's mouth as he flew above the earth; and he learnt to ride on an Irish cob.

"Oh, that ride! that first ride—most truly it was an epoch in my existence; and I still look back to it with feelings of longing and regret. People may talk of first love —it is a very agreeable event, I dare say—but give me the flush, and triumph, and glorious sweat of a first ride, like mine on the mighty cob! My whole frame was shaken, it is true; and during one long week I could hardly move foot or hand; but what of that? By that one trial I had become free, as I may say, of the whole equine species. . . .

"Oh, that cob! that Irish cob!—may the sod lie lightly over the bones of the strongest, speediest, and most gallant of its kind! Oh! the days when, issuing from the barrack-gate of Templemore, we commenced our hurry-skurry just as inclination led—now across the fields—direct over stone walls and running brooks—mere pastime for the cob!—sometimes along the road to Thurles and Holy Cross, even to distant Cahir!—what was distance to the cob?"

In the spring of 1816 it was decided that the regiment should be recalled to Norwich and disbanded. The news was a blow to George, yet not so bitter a one as the removal from Edinburgh had been. Ireland had dispatched the last sign of his early delicacy—he was exceptionally tall and broad for a boy of scarcely thirteen. Ireland had done more—she had given him a passion for languages and a passion for horses, and these were to last his life long. Through them Ireland herself lingered in his mind. Years later he wrote to Mr. John Murray, his publisher[1]: "I wish I were acquainted with Sir Robert Peel, I could give him many a useful hint with respect to Ireland and the Irish." In all his books, too, are scattered references to Ireland and in *Lavengro* he relapsed into rare pomposity when he wrote: ". . . . My education, at the present day, would not be what it is—perfect, had I never had the honour of being *alumnus* in an Irish seminary."

Not by the widest stretch of imagination could the stone-flagged room at Clonmel be termed a "seminary". Borrow's education was sadly imperfect. His knowledge of Ireland was of the flimsiest, and his debt to her had nothing to do with matters academic or political. But Ireland had wrapped him about in a cloak of Celtic mysticism: Ireland had fanned the flicker of romanticism within him until it burned with a steady glow nothing could quench.

[1] Letter of 6 November, 1843.

CHAPTER TWO

"FOR WHAT WAS I BORN?"

(*Lavengro*, Chap. xxv)

(1816–1824)

I

THE return to Norwich marked the end of army wanderings. For the first time in their married life Captain and Mrs. Borrow were able to settle down in a home of their own, and within a very few weeks they had taken a little house in King's Court off Willow Lane.

You may still visit that house—I did so only the other day, walking up St. Giles and taking the turning opposite Rigby's Court. Just before the lane curved into Cow Hill I saw a vaulted arch and above it a notice which showed that Norwich had honoured her roving son, for it read *Borrow's Court*. Beyond the arch was a narrow tunnel which led into a courtyard and there, facing me, was the house itself with a plaque above the doorway.

In Borrow's day it was "shaded by lofty poplars" and covered with ivy, but about 1850 the then owner, a Mr. Goodwin, caused quite a sensation among his friends by removing these adornments. "It is quite changed," wrote Cecilia Lucy Brightwell to Mrs. George Borrow, "all the trees and ivy taken away, and the house cleaned up and new done." Now its stucco front stared blankly at me and when I first entered its door I found little to remind me of the boy who had once lived there. The tiny hall, the decorous front parlour, the kitchen that opened off a small dining-room behind it might have belonged to anybody's house; but as I mounted the creaking stairway I almost imagined that the ghost of John Crome walked ahead of me on one of his periodic visits to John's study so that he might criticize the work of his pupil, and in the bare room that had been George's I stayed awhile, picturing how he had sat crouched at his table, a lock of dark hair falling across his face, bony wrists thrusting out from too short sleeves, as he pored over his French, Italian, Danish, Welsh, Irish—all the languages of romance.

Yes, the house yielded something, but not enough. George Borrow was too much a bird of passage to leave a lasting impression within the four walls which had sheltered him for a space. I made my way out of the city to the wide Newmarket road with its great elms on either side; then I turned and looked back to the sudden narrowing that marked where the city gate used to stand, and pulled my *Lavengro* from my pocket. . . .

"There it (Norwich) spreads from north to south, with its venerable houses, its numerous gardens, its thrice twelve churches, its mighty mound, which, if tradition speaks true, was raised by human hands to serve as the grave heap of an old heathen king, who sits deep within it, with his sword in his hand and his gold and silver treasures about him. There is a grey old castle upon the top of that mighty mound; and yonder, rising three hundred feet above the soil, from among those noble forest trees, behold that old Norman master-work, that cloud-encircled cathedral spire, around which a garrulous army of rooks and choughs continually wheel their flight. Now, who can wonder that the children of that fine old city are proud of her, and offer up prayers for her prosperity? I, myself, who was not born within her walls, offer up prayers for her prosperity, that want may never visit her cottages, vice her palaces, and that the abomination of idolatry may never pollute her temples."

I read on, and scurried through the city to the Lollards' Hole, which lies to the right of the old bridge under a chalky cliff.

"Many a saint of God has breathed his last beneath that white precipice, bearing witness against Popish idolatry, midst flame and pitch; many a grisly procession has advanced along that suburb, across the old bridge, towards the Lollards' Hole: furious priests in front, a calm pale martyr in the midst, a pitying multitude behind. It has had its martyrs, the venerable old town!"

Once more I retraced my steps until I came to the Guildhall where I found a precious relic described by Borrow.

"A sword of curious workmanship, the blade is of keen Toledan steel, the heft of ivory and mother-o'-pearl. 'Tis the sword of Cordova, won in bloodiest fray off St. Vincent's promontory, and presented by Nelson to the old capital of the much loved land of his birth. Yes, the proud Spaniard's sword is to be seen in yonder guildhouse, in the glass case affixed to the wall; many other relics has the good old town, but none prouder than the Spaniard's sword."

Last of all I wandered through the Erpingham Gate into Upper Close and gazed long at the statue of Nelson opposite the class-room where he once conned Latin verbs and where, years later, the boy who thought Nelson's sword the proudest possession of Norwich read grammars of living languages under cover of his desk while pretending to study grammars of dead ones.

II

So soon as the family had moved into King's Court the indefatigible Captain Borrow turned his attention to the future of his two sons. He wrote to the Duke of York, praying that His Royal Highness might, out of his graciousness, grant a regular commission to John, who had been gazetted a lieu-tenant in the militia. The answer was discouraging. The war was over, there was a long waiting-list, many of the candidates had far better claims than young Borrow. The Captain grunted —he had a suspicion that money talked in a peace-time army—and agreed to his wife's suggestion that John should resume his studies with "the little dark man with the brown coat and the top-boots", John Crome.

George's future was another matter. Nobody, least of all the Captain, knew what George was fitted for. There was, he asserted, something very strange about George. To begin with he looked like a gypsy: to end with—well, look how he had behaved in Ireland?

"I know that he kept very strange company," fumed the Captain, "people of evil report, of whom terrible things were said—horse-witches and the like. I questioned him once or twice upon the matter, and even threatened him, but it was of no use; he put on a look as if he did not understand me, a regular Irish look, just such a one as those rascals assume when they wish to appear all innocence and simplicity, and they full of malice and deceit all the time. . . . That ever son of mine should have been intimate with the Papist Irish, and have learnt their language! . . . Irish! why, he might go to the university but for that. . . . How did you learn it? they would ask him; how did you become acquainted with the language of Papists and rebels? The boy would be sent away in disgrace."

Mrs. Borrow immediately took up the cudgels in defence of her younger born. She was sure he had quite forgotten Irish speech and Irish ways and was now turning his thoughts to more serious studies. "Why," she added, "I heard him say the other day that he could read St. John in the original tongue."

Captain Borrow, as was his habit when cornered, took refuge in the Old Testament, muttering darkly of Jacob and Esau and voicing the pious hope that God would protect George. "What," he demanded of his wife, "is that text about the young ravens being fed?"

But Mrs. Borrow was thoroughly roused. "I know a better than that," she answered, "one of David's own words, "I have been young and now am grown old, yet never have I seen the righteous man forsaken, or his seed begging their bread."

This was too much for her husband, who ambled off to apply for a Town Scholarship to the Grammar School for

E

George; yet even as he wrote the letter he knew misgiving. Of course he loved his son; of course it was not the boy's fault that his eyes and skin had an alien appearance—but his ways and manners, his unnatural absorption in outlandish foreign tongues, his fondness for Papists!

George was granted his scholarship and once again came under the jurisdiction of the celebrated Dr. Valpy. This time, however, he was not so affected by the heavy atmosphere of the class-rooms in Upper Close. His sojourn at Clonmel had taught him the art of evading the master's attention by pretending to study the subject under discussion while really studying one nearer to his heart. He had picked up on some bookstall a remarkable volume which purported to teach its readers the rudiments of French, Italian and Low Dutch. Each morning he smuggled it into school under his coat and propped it inside his desk. With his retentive memory it was an easy matter to achieve the required minimum of marks in a quarter of the time allotted to Greek, Latin, or whatever it was, and the reminder of the period was devoted to his hidden treasure.

Within a very short while George had learnt all the book could teach him concerning French and Italian, and, his appetite whetted, begged his mother for proper lessons in these languages. She in turn persuaded Captain Borrow, who was still smarting under her quotation from David, to enlist the services of the Rev. Thomas d'Eterville, an *émigré* from Caen University who eked out a living by teaching at young ladies' seminaries in Norwich.

This gentleman and George took to each other at once. The master was enchanted with his pupil's quickness; the pupil with his master's erudition. Together they skimmed through the works of Spanish, French and Italian writers, and at the conclusion of their study of Dante's *Inferno* old d'Eterville clasped his hands and said with tears in his eyes: *"Vous serez un jour un grand philologue, mon cher!"*

He was wrong. George Borrow never became a great philologist. He did develop what is known as "a gift of tongues", but he was every bit as interested in the men who spoke them as in the languages themselves.

D'Eterville's coaching provided a welcome leaven to the stodgy meal of classics George had perforce to nibble at in the Grammar School, where the staff disapproved of his idleness and the other boys eyed him askance, partly because he was a "free boy" and partly because they thought him an appalling liar. Poor George, the stirring tales which had so impressed his fellow scholars in Clonmel were received with raised eyebrows in Norwich!

He was a proud lad. He resented the snobbish attitude of his class-mates, was frankly dismayed by their accusations that he did not tell the truth—how on earth could one tell a dramatic story without exaggerating a trifle?—and disliked his schoolmasters so much that he made no effort to placate them. They could do and think as they pleased, all these stupid folk; he had a world beyond their ken to wander in.

D'Eterville was not his only guide to that glorious, secret realm of romance and adventure. In the Borrow house there hung an ancient, condemned musket (it bore the inscription, "Tower, 1746") with which he prowled around the countryside shooting blackbirds, bullfinches and linnets. Also in the house was an old fishing-rod, and in the summer he used to wander out to Earlham and fish in the Yare. This river ran through the grounds of Earlham Hall, the home of the Gurneys, the famous Quaker banking family, and one evening, unaware that he was trespassing, George crossed the sloping lawn in front of the house. He sat down on the river bank, trailing his float on the water, thinking less of his fishing than of Dante, and scarcely noticing the amount of fish he detached from the hook and flung on the ground. Suddenly a sonorous voice startled him:

"Canst thou answer to thy conscience for pulling all those fish out of the water, and leaving them to gasp in the sun? Surely that is a very cruel diversion in which thou indulgest, my young friend."

George scrambled to his feet, recognizing Joseph Gurney, then a man of about twenty-eight but already, owing to his father's death, head of his house and guardian to his unmarried sisters. "I am sorry for it, if it be, sir," he stammered, "but I do not think it cruel to fish."

"What are thy reasons for not thinking so?"

"Fishing is mentioned frequently in Scripture," ventured George. "Simon Peter was a fisherman."

"True," said Gurney drily, "and Andrew his brother. But thou forgettest: they did not follow fishing as a diversion, as I fear thou doest. Thou readest the Scriptures?"

George assured him that he did, though not daily as his questioner seemed to think he ought, and added the information that he also read Greek and Dante: whereupon Mr. Gurney invited him to visit Earlham Hall whenever he liked and undertake the study of Hebrew from the works of Zohar and Mishna, Toldoth Jesu and Abarbenel, saying that he himself derived much satisfaction from these writers, and did not like Abarbenel the worse for having been a money-changer since his own family belonged to a glorified branch of that trade and Quakers had often been likened to Jews because of their desire for amassing wealth.

After this conversation with Joseph Gurney, George's fondness for fishing lessened. He never went to Earlham Hall —he fell in with two vastly different companions—but when he was a middle-aged man he dined there and wished afterwards that he had "learned both wisdom and righteousness from those calm, quiet lips", and that he had met Joseph's sister Elizabeth who became, after her marriage to Joseph Fry, the famous prison reformer.

III

George's interest in fishing may have waned, but he still went on shooting expeditions, and it was in all likelihood on one of these that he met John Thurtell, "gentleman" boxer who, like David Haggart, was to meet death on the gallows. The Thurtells lived near Harford Bridge on the Ipswich road, some two miles out of Norwich. The father must have been an estimable man, for despite his son's horrible end he lived down the resultant scandal and became Mayor of Norwich, having been first alderman and then sheriff of that city since 1814. The son, John, had returned from the wars to go into business, but spent most of his time promoting boxing matches. He himself was a noted pugilist and something of a hero to the youth of the neighbourhood.

George was completely fascinated by this curious character. In all probability Thurtell already knew of Captain Borrow's contest with Big Ben Brain, for it had passed into legend; if he did not we may be sure George told him of it. In any event, he flattered the boy by offering to teach him how to box and George, exclaiming that it was only dutiful for the child of his father to put on the gloves, became an apt pupil.

The ludicrous part was, of course, that the Captain would have suffered an apoplectic seizure had he known of the bouts fought in a field near Eaton Church. Fortunately he remained in ignorance—as he did about so many of George's activities.

Thurtell did not confine his sporting interests to boxing. He was a keen judge of horses and it was he who suggested that George should attend the famous Tombland[1] Fair, which took place every Easter on the castle hill. Here prize cattle and sheep were displayed while a little farther up the hill, between the Bell Inn and the York Tavern, was the horse show.

George thrust his way through the crowds, thrilled by the sights, sounds and smells all around him, until he wriggled between the people gathered outside the hospitable door of the Bell and slipped into the Horse Show to watch the parade. . . .

"There were long-tailed steeds, and dock-tailed steeds of every degree and breed; there were droves of wild ponies, and long rows of sober cart-horses; there were donkeys, and even mules. . . . There were—oh, the gallant creatures! I hear their neigh upon the wind; there were—goodliest sight of all—certain enormous quadrupeds only to be seen to perfection in our native isle, led about by dapper grooms, their manes ribanded and their tails curiously clubbed and balled."

[1] Formerly held on "Tomland", a great empty space lower down the hill.

Wild with excitement, George stood on tiptoe to peer over the heads of the throng at the wonderful trotters he had heard and read so much about. Suddenly the shouts of the throng gave way to an expectant hush as an aged man on a lean pony led a dun horse into the ring. At first sight the animal, smaller than the other trotters, appeared rather insignificant; but the crowd surged forward, chanting his name in rapt whispers, *"Marshland Shales! Marshland Shales!"* [1]

For this was the horse to beat all horses, the miracle horse who lived to the age of thirty-three, and whose sale in 1827 called forth this delicious advertisement in the *Norwich Mercury*:

1827.
That well-known trotting Stallion,
MARSHLAND SHALES,
Will be Sold by Auction,
On Tombland Fair-Day,
Unless previously disposed of by Private Contract.

THIS is the Horse which, on 3d August, 1810, trotted 17 miles in 56 minutes, carrying 12 st. 2 lb. and was then sold by auction for £305.
For particulars apply to Mr. Moneyment, vet. surg., Norwich.

George, who had not caught the name, nudged an ancient yokel in a white smock. "What horse is that?"

The old man looked scandalized. "The best in mother England," he said. "He is old like myself, but can still trot his twenty miles an hour. You won't live long, my swain; tall and overgrown ones like thee never does; yet, if you should chance to reach my years, you may boast to thy great grand boys, thou hast seen *Marshland Shales*."

To George's surprise he saw that all the men lifted their hats as the horse passed them; and as he followed suit he had

---

[1] Dr. Knapp insists George Borrow did not see *Marshland Shales* until 1827.

the uneasy feeling that someone in the crowd was watching
him. The feeling became so strong that, though he was loath
to miss a second of the scene before him, he kept glancing
round to see if there was anybody he knew in the throng.
Each time he did so he had the uncomfortable sensation that
the watcher, whoever he might be, was deliberately eluding
notice.

Marshland Shales was led away and three horsemen swept
into the ring to give a display of trick riding that could not
have been bettered in any circus. Two of them were mere
lads; the third was an immensely tall man with a handsome,
swarthy face and flashing black eyes. George's heart gave a
bound. "Gypsies!" he murmured, craning his neck so that he
might follow their every movement; but just as the tall man
had accomplished the remarkable feat of standing balanced
on one foot on the saddle while his mount galloped round the
ring, a lithe figure ran forward and pulled at his bridle.
The two had a muttered conversation and, to George's amazement, the horseman raised his head and stared full at him
before cantering from the ring. Then the second man turned
and strolled towards him, cracking a whip he held in his
hand:

"What!" he cried, "the sap-engro? Lor! the sap-engro
upon the hill!"

George gazed deep into the man's eyes. He remembered
the woods of Yaxley, the searches he had made along the
roads of England, Scotland and Ireland, the dreams he had
had of just this meeting. "You can't be . . . ?" he stammered.

The man smiled, showing white, even teeth. "Jasper, your
pal! Truth, and no lie, brother."

Brother. The sweet word made George conscious for the
first time of the reason behind his boredom with school, his
solitary wanderings with musket or fishing-rod, his vague dislike
of his class-mates. It had been loneliness. . . .

But Jasper was speaking in his soft, half-whining voice.
"I thought it was you, but to make sure I dodged about,
inspecting you. I believe you felt me, though I never touched
you; a sign, brother, that we are akin, that we are dui palor—
two relations. Your blood beat when mine was near, as mine

always does at the coming of a brother; and we became brothers in that lane.''

"Where are you staying?" asked George eagerly, "in this town?"

Jasper shook his head. "The like of us don't find it exactly wholesome to stay in towns; we keep abroad. Come with me, and I'll show you where we stay.''

The Fair, the horses, the crowds, lost all meaning. George felt he trod on air as he and Jasper walked down the hill, passed through the Close by the Deanery and Cloisters, crossed the bridge and turned east by the Cavalry Barracks to climb the hill leading to Mousehold Heath, the wide, gorse-blazed common that John Crome so loved to paint. There were so many questions that George wanted to ask his long lost friend —but first there was something he must know, the identity of the tall, handsome horseman.

"I suppose he's one of ye?" He knew a certain diffidence about using the word "gypsy".

"Tawno Chikno," replied Jasper, "which means the small one; we call him such because he is the biggest man of all our nation. You say he is handsome, that is not the word, brother; he's the beauty of the world!''

He went on to tell how all manner of women—even to an earl's daughter with "fine diamonds round her neck"—had sighed for love of Tawno, who paid no heed to them, saying he preferred his lawful Romany wife despite her extreme jealousy.

"And is she very beautiful?" demanded George.

Jasper laughed. "Why, you know, brother, beauty is frequently a matter of taste; however, as you ask my opinion, I should say not quite so beautiful as himself.''

By this time they had crossed the heath and turned westwards into a little valley. George stopped, aware of a sudden tingling over his whole body. Before him were the "tilted carts", the low tents, the wood-fires of a gypsy encampment. Little dark children scampered hither and thither, and as he recovered himself and hurried after Jasper the canvas flap of a tent lifted and a lame woman hobbled out, leaning on a crutch. The natural ugliness of her face was accentuated by a malevolent expression, her dirty ragged clothing fluttered in the wind. Waving her crutch at Jasper she let forth a torrent of speech in which George could not distinguish a word. He tossed an answer over his shoulder, and as they passed on turned to George: "What do you think of her? You have seen her now and can judge for yourself—that 'ere woman is Tawno Chikno's wife!"

He led the way to a tent set apart from the others. Inside it sat a middle-aged woman busy with her knitting, but Jasper paid her no attention and motioned George to squat beside the fire. He then asked him what he had been doing with himself in the years since their meeting at Yaxley. George needed no prompting—the most important thing in the world was that Jasper should know every least thing about him. The words bubbled up inside him and tumbled out of his lips as he described Scotland, Ireland, his interest in different languages. At last he paused for breath and, suddenly remembering his mother's polite teachings, inquired, "Where are your father and mother?"

"Where I shall never see them, brother; at least, I hope so."

"Not dead?"

"No, not dead; they are bitchadey pawdel."

"What's that?"

"Sent across—banished."

To George this seemed a most tragic happening and he asked anxiously if Tawno Chikno looked after his friend.

Jasper scowled. "What do you take me for, brother?"

"For about three years older than myself."

"Perhaps; but you are of the Gorgios, and I am a Romany Chal. Tawno Chikno take care of Jasper Petulengro!"

George, fearful lest he had offended, hastened to say he had never heard a sweeter name, and added, "It is something like what you call me."

Jasper's expression lightened. "The horse-shoe master and the snake-fellow, I am the first."

"Who gave you that name?"

"Ask Pharoah."

"I would, if he were here, but I do not see him."

"I am Pharoah."

"Then," said the bewildered George, "you are a king?"

"Chachipen, pal."

"I do not understand you."

"Where are your languages?" mocked Jasper. "You want two things, brother: mother-sense and gentle Romany."

"What makes you think that I want sense?"

"That, being so old, you can't yet guide yourself!"

"I can read Dante, Jasper."

"Anan, brother."

"I can charm snakes, Jasper."

"I know you can, brother."

"Yes," said George, his habit of boastfulness reasserting itself, "and horses too; bring me the most vicious in the land, if I whisper he'll be tame."

Jasper gave him a long, slow look. "Then the more shame for you—a snake-fellow—a horse-witch—and a lil-reader—yet you can't shift for yourself. I laugh at you, brother!"

He told George then that after his parents' banishment he had become head of the family and rich by gypsy standards, since the couple had been forced to leave everything they owned behind them. So wisely had he ruled his relations—they included remote cousins—that many other gypsies, such as Tawno and his wife, had joined him.

"And you are what is called a Gypsy King?" said George in an awe-struck voice.

"Ay, ay; a Romany Kral."

"Are there other kings?"

"Those who call themselves so; but the true Pharaoh is Petulengro."

"Did Pharaoh make horse-shoes?"

"The first who ever did, brother."

"Pharaoh lived in Egypt."

"So did we once, brother."

"And you left it?"

"My fathers did, brother."

"And why did they come here?"

"They had their reasons, brother."

"And you are not English?"

"We are not Gorgios."

"And you have a language of your own?"

"Avali."

George was just going to say how dearly he would like to learn this strange tongue, when the woman in the corner jumped up and started screaming abuse at him, saying that she had no use for stupid Gorgios who didn't believe the Romany folk spoke a proper language of their own. During this tirade she addressed Jasper as her son, which puzzled George until his friend explained that the woman was his mother-in-law.

"Then you are married?" he faltered, more and more impressed by the wonderful creature Jasper had become.

"Ay, truly; I am husband and father. You will see wife and chabo anon."

"We were talking of language, Jasper," said George timidly.

"True, brother."

"Yours must be a rum one?"

" 'Tis called Romany."

"I would gladly know it."

"You need it sorely."

"Would you teach it to me?"

"None sooner."

"Suppose we begin now."

"Suppose we do, brother."

But here the woman shouted that Jasper was a fool, and that she wasn't going to sit by and listen to him giving away Romany secrets. "You'd better be jawing," she screeched at George; "you had better be moving off, my Gorgio; hang you for a keen one, sitting there by the fire, and stealing my language before my face. . . . Do you know that I am dangerous? My name is Herne, and I comes of the hairy ones!"

George thought that "no she-bear of Lapland ever looked more fierce and hairy", but Jasper silenced her with a glare, so he plucked up courage and asked the first question that came into his head: "What do you call God, Jasper?"

"I call God Duvel, brother."

"It sounds very like Devil."

"It doth, brother, it doth."

"And what do you call divine, I mean, godly?"

"Oh I call that duvelskoe."

"I am thinking of something, Jasper."

"What are you thinking of, brother?"

"Would it not be a rum thing if divine and devilish were originally one and the same word?"

IV

Now began a period of such enchantment that George remembered it afterwards as a golden, hazy dream. Together he and Jasper squatted by the tent fire, roved the heath, talked endlessly of everything in earth or heaven but particularly of the Romany language, in which George professed to find the origin of various French, Italian and other words. What really perplexed him was the history of this queer speech and of the gypsies who used it; but even Jasper could give him no clues.

"Whatever we be, brother," he said, "we are an old people, and not what folks in general imagine, broken gorgios; and if we are not Egyptians, we are at any rate Romany chals!"

For long George pondered over that word "Romany". Hadn't he read somewhere that the city of Rome had been built by a vagabond tribe? But if so, where had these wandering people come from to start with? Some day, he promised himself, he would find out; but the present was far too enthralling to allow room for study of the problem. He was entirely absorbed in the company of Jasper and his followers, who had customs and habits different to any he had known. Besides, Jasper mounted him on wild, unbroken horses—was there any sensation to compare with that of a gallop across the heath? And Tawno Chikno boxed with him—was there any thrill so great as that provided by the conquering of the tall, handsome horseman?

Tawno delighted him by calling him Cooro-mengro, the boxer. "I have put on the gloves with him," he said in his gypsy whine, "and find him a pure fist-master; I like him for that, for I am a Cooro-mengro myself, and was born at Brummagem."

The other members of the tribe nodded approval of this praise, and even Mrs. Chikno, who realized she had for once no cause for jealousy, chimed in: "I likes him for his modesty. I never hears any ill words come from his mouth, but, on the contrary, much sweet language. His talk is golden, and he has taught my eldest to say his prayers in Romany, which my rover never had the grace to do."

Jasper's good-looking wife smiled at George. "He is the pal of my rom," she said, "and therefore I likes him, and not less for his being a rye; folks call me high-minded, and perhaps I have reason to be so; before I married Pharaoh I had an offer from a lord—I likes the young rye."

Jasper himself was tremendously proud of George's quickness in learning the gypsy tongue. "We'll no longer call you Sap-engro, brother," he announced, "but rather Lav-engro, which in the language of the Gorgios meaneth Word Master."

No wonder George held his head high and squared his shoulders; no wonder that—like his father before him—he played truant from school when the summer term started so that he could spend every available minute with the gypsies; no wonder he copied their ways so faithfully that he even stained his face and neck with walnut-juice, a happening which brought from Dr. Valpy the acidulated question: "Is that jaundice or only dirt, Borrow?" For the first time in his life George Borrow had found true friendship and was utterly happy.

Alas, the halcyon days on Mousehold Heath came to an abrupt end when Jasper explained to George that it was high time the tribe moved on. Tombland Fair was long past and how could they live, he asked, if they did not follow the music of the fair all round the country, selling the favours they made, telling fortunes, plying the hundred-and-one odd—maybe reprehensible—crafts of the gypsy people? But why, he wheedled, did not George throw in his lot with them?

"Yes," said his wife, "if the young rye chooses to follow us, he shall have my sister. What say you, mother? should not the young rye have my sister Ursula?"

But old Mrs. Herne was the only member of the tribe who had continued to regard George with suspicion. The bare idea of him as a son-in-law sent her into a towering passion, and she immediately bundled all her possessions up and put them on her donkey's back.

"I am going to my people," she screamed. "I am going to Yorkshire, for I can stand this no longer. You say you like him: in that we differs: I hate the gorgio, and would like, speaking Romanly, to mix a little poison with his waters. And now go to Lundra, my children, I goes to Yorkshire. Take my blessing with ye, and a little bit of a gillie[1] to cheer your hearts with when ye are weary. In all kinds of weather we have lived together; but now we are parted, I goes broken-hearted. I can't keep you company; ye are no longer Romany. To gain a bad brother, ye have lost a good mother."

A shiver passed through George—Mrs. Herne looked quite capable of carrying out her threat of poison. The superstitious gypsies slunk away, and even Jasper looked concerned. But neither Mrs. Herne's curses nor thought of his father's wrath caused George to remain in Norwich when the gypsy carts took the road. His love for his mother, the "dame of the oval face" who cherished him so dearly, kept his body in King's Court though nine-tenths of his mind journeyed with Jasper Petulengro, his brother.

The sense of loneliness returned, intensified a thousand-fold because now he knew the meaning of friendship. Every evening he tramped to Mousehold Heath, hope leaping high as he breasted the hill. He walked unseeing past the lovers who strolled with intertwined arms, the small boys aiming catapults at the birds, the evangelists roaring out their messages of salvation from the Ranters' Monticle, until he reached the little valley set between the dark hills. Here hope died, as he had known it would. The grasses waved in the wind, the gorse bushes flamed in the light of the setting sun, but of the gypsies there was no sign. He flung himself down by the blackened patch left by Jasper's tent fire and wept as though his heart would break.

[1] A song.

V

A boy of fifteen who was blood brother to a Petulengro could scarcely be expected to settle down and become a douce scholar: an eminent headmaster of rigid religious principles could scarcely be expected to understand such a pupil. Valpy and George had always been antipathetic; after the departure of the gypsies their mutual dislike flared into open hatred.

There is no doubt that George behaved in a most provoking manner. Conversations with the Petulengro family had reawakened his interest in Defoe, and when Dr. Valpy complained to Captain Borrow of his younger son's idleness—the resultant storm raged for days—he decided to become a buccaneer. This time even his deep-rooted love for his mother failed to shake his resolve; miserably, angrily, he laid plans which soon assumed such grand dimensions that he could not hope to carry them out single-handed.

Unpopular though he was, George had three admirers among his class-mates: John Dalrymple, son of a Norwich surgeon, and Theodosius and Francis Purland, whose father was a local chemist. Fired by George's extravagant tales of foot-pads, smugglers and sea-rovers, they agreed to run away with him to the Caister dunes near Yarmouth, where they would live in caves until a chance came to voyage away with some ship's company. The Purland brothers provided a small sum of money stolen from their father's till. Young Dalrymple purloined a set of horse-pistols and a sack of potatoes. George, as befitted the leader of the expedition, contributed a long list of rules and instructions.

One fine morning they set out blithely on the nineteen-mile walk to Yarmouth. Either the weight of the horse-pistols and potatoes or his sense of moral guilt assailed Dalrymple, for he soon lagged behind the other three, and when they climbed the hill out of Thorpe village and sighted the Thorpe Lunatic Asylum he broke down altogether, threw his burdens on the ground, and fled sobbing back to Norwich. This defection shocked his companions, who pushed on to Acle. Here the Purlands, limping on blistered feet, refused to listen to George's

bright announcement that Yarmouth was but a step farther—
it was really eight miles—and insisted upon sitting down under
the hedge to eat bread and cheese.

Most unfortunately the father of one of their school-
fellows drove past in a gig. He peered at the dusty trio and the
accoutrements of war scattered around them. Surely those
grimy faces were familiar? Had he not seen them before? Ah,
now he had it!—reining in his horse he turned and drove back.

Terror struck Theodosius and Francis dumb, but George
moved forward with a swaggering gait and asked for alms in a
gypsy whine. The gentleman, however, was not to be bam-
boozled. After much pleading and arguing he craftily invited
the trio to dine with him at a nearby inn, and while they were
tucking into a good meal sent his servant with a note to Valpy.
He then held his guests in conversation until a post-chaise
arrived, bundled them inside, and had them driven to Norwich
and retribution.

At some future date George Borrow commemorated the
meeting in a poem entitled, *The Wandering Children and the
Benevolent Gentleman: An Idyll of the Roads*, from which the
following verses are quoted. If they present a truthful version
of the roadside parley one cannot wonder that the gentleman
enlisted Valpy's assistance.

Eldest Child
"Oh, gentleman! sweet gentleman!
  To thee we humbly bow;
Upon poor hungry children three
  Thy charity bestow."

Benevolent Gentleman
"Poor vagrant children, I perceive
  You've run away from home;
But know that from such wickedness
  No good can ever come."

Eldest Child
Sweet gentle Sir! your words are good;
  We hear them thankfully;
But pray bestow with your advice
  One single halfpenny."

Benevolent Gentleman
"Return, poor thoughtless children, home,
   Or evil will ensue;
There's sad temptation in the world
   For children such as you."

Eldest Child
"O clap a stopper on your jaw!
   We hate such stuff and cant;
And keep your counsel for yourself;
   The rhino's what we want."

Benevolent Gentleman
"O what a dreadful thing 'twould be,
   A thing to break the heart,
If all your childish innocence
   For ever should depart!"

The return to Norwich was ignominious indeed. Next morning, after soothing the feelings of the outraged Mr. Dalrymple and Mr. Purland, Dr. Valpy marched into the classroom in a fit mood to wreak vengeance on that dreadful boy, George Borrow. In silence George was hoisted on to James Martineau's[1] back and thrashed so hard that, according to an onlooker, "he had to keep his bed for a fortnight, and would carry the marks for the remainder of his days".

Martineau himself minimized this incident many years afterwards, but not before he had spread abroad a somewhat similar version to that of the onlooker, for in 1893 a feminine acquaintance of his wrote from Hampstead to a friend in Norwich:

"Dr. Martineau, to amuse some boys at a school treat, told us about George Borrow, his schoolfellow. . . . You know what a cruel man that Dr. V. was. He made Dr. Martineau take poor Borrow on his back, 'horse him', I think he called it, and flogged him so that Dr. M. said he would carry the marks for the rest of his life, and he had to keep his bed for a fortnight. . . ."

[1] Dr. James Martineau, eminent Unitarian preacher and theologian.

F

Frances Power Cobbe, who was Borrow's neighbour in Hereford Square, Brompton, during the 1860's, also wrote that Martineau had told her practically the same story, adding:

> "The early connection between the two old men, as I knew them, was irresistibly comic to my mind. . . . I asked Mr. Borrow once to come and meet some friends at our house and he accepted our invitation as usual, but, on finding that Dr. Martineau was to be of the party, hastily withdrew his acceptance on a transparent excuse; nor did he ever after attend our little assemblies without first ascertaining that Dr. Martineau was not to be present."[1]

In face of these two corroborations it seems a trifle strange that when he answered the request of a Mr. James Hooper for information about Borrow's schooldays in 1895, Dr. Martineau wrote:

> "It is true that I had to *hoist* (not 'horse') Borrow for his flogging, but not that there was anything exceptional or capable of leaving permanent scars in the infliction. Mr. Valpy was not given to excess of that kind."

But Martineau never approved of Borrow, calling him in his *Memoirs*, "the writer and actor of romance", and employing the chill phrase, "I have never read *Lavengro*". In his letter to Mr. Hooper, however, he did provide an interesting fact concerning the stories with which George used to regale his class-mates:

> "The plot was woven and spread out with much ingenuity, and the characters were various and well discriminated. But two of them were sure to turn up in every tale, the Devil and the Pope, and the working of the drama invariably had the same issue—the utter ruin and disgrace of these two potentates."

So much for Captain Borrow's fears of his son's Popish leanings!

[1] *Life of Frances Power Cobbe as told by Herself.*

There is no evidence that George was expelled from the Grammar School; but after his punishment he hated everyone connected with it with a bitter intensity and very soon afterwards had what we should nowadays term "a nervous breakdown". Probably the reasons were a compound of his yearning for Jasper Petulengro, his humiliation at being publicly flogged, and his fear of his father's continuous lectures on his appalling behaviour. In *Lavengro* he dramatized this illness:

". . . I grew worse and worse, and was soon stretched upon my bed, from which it seemed scarcely probable that I should ever rise, the physicians themselves giving but slight hope of my recovery; as for myself, I made up my mind to die, and felt quite resigned."

His body was restored to health, he insisted, by the swallowing of a decoction made from roots by some old country crone: his mental state remained low for some time, and he described his feelings in a dialogue between his mother and himself.

" 'What ails you, my child?' said a mother to her son, as he lay on a couch under the influence of the dreadful one; 'what ails you? you seem afraid!'
"*Boy*. 'And so I am; a dreadful fear is upon me.'
"*Mother*. 'But of what; there is no one can harm you; of what are you apprehensive?'
"*Boy*. 'Of nothing that I can express; I know not what I am afraid of, but afraid I am.'
"*Mother*. 'Perhaps you see sights and visions; I knew a lady once who was continually thinking that she saw an armed man threaten her, but it was only an imagination, a phantom of the brain.'
"*Boy*. 'No armed man threatens me; and 'tis not a thing like that would cause me any fear. Did an armed man threaten me, I would get up and fight him; weak as I am, I would wish for nothing better, for then, perhaps, I should lose this fear; mine is a dread of I know not what, and there the horror lies.'

"*Mother*. 'Your forehead is cool, and your speech collected. Do you know where you are?'

"*Boy*. 'I know where I am, and I see things just as they are; you are beside me, and upon the table there is a book which was written by a Florentine; all this I see, and that there is no ground for being afraid. I am, moreover, quite cool, and feel no pain—but, but . . .'

"And then there was a burst of *gemiti, sospire ed alti guai*. Alas, alas, poor child of clay! as the sparks fly upward, so wast thou born to sorrow—Onward!"

Exactly how long this "dark feeling of mysterious dread which comes over the mind, and which the lamp of reason, though burning bright the while, is unable to dispel" lasted we are not told. All we know is that it put an end to George's schooldays, and that by 1819 he was well enough to be articled for five years to Messrs. Simpson & Rackham, solicitors.

George himself had wanted to join the army but Captain Borrow, remembering the disappointment he had suffered over John, pooh-poohed the idea. He had really wanted his second son to enter the Church, but was so upset by George's Yarmouth escapade that he told him in no uncertain terms to choose his own profession. Now George had an acquaintance, Roger Kerrison, who was already apprenticed to Simpson & Rackham, and when he asked this young man's advice was recommended to follow his example.

"It is an excellent profession," said Roger, "more especially for those who never intend to follow it, as I suppose you do not any more than myself. On the death of my father, from whom I expect ten thousand pounds, I propose to go to Newmarket and serve as groom for a year or two in some respectable stable, after which I shall purchase a stud and ride my own horses; and then it will be strange if I can't turn the knowledge I may pick up in the office to some account."

This lordly speech greatly impressed George. True, his own expectations didn't amount to ten thousand pence, but what appealed to him was the phrase, "an excellent profession for those who never intend to follow it". Captain Borrow, cheered by his son's apparent keenness to become a respectable lawyer, gladly agreed to pay his articles, and on the 30th of March George entered the office in Tuck's Court, St. Giles.

Part of the agreement was that he should lodge at the home of Mr. William Simpson—the partners evidently believed in keeping their apprentices under surveillance night and day. By a cruel chance the house was in Upper Close, separated from the Grammar School playground only by a low wall topped by a wood paling. Thus poor George still felt conscious of Dr. Valpy's hawk-like eye and, perhaps to show that gentleman that he was no longer subject to authority, he used to lean against the paling and tell the schoolboys adventurous tales. Apart from this he spoke to few people and took his walks abroad alone, a tall, aloof figure in a tight and sombre black suit.

Mr. Simpson was a genial mentor with a fashionable second wife who loved giving large dinner-parties. He was a small, rotund man immaculately garbed in black broadcloth but with one peculiarity about him—his expensive, highly-polished shoes always creaked as he walked. He was exceedingly kind to his young apprentice, who rewarded him with a tolerant affection; but very soon it was borne in upon him that whatever else George might be fitted for he was a positive duffer at law.

Borrow himself admitted frankly that the hours he spent hunched up at his office desk transcribing documents or studying the works of Blackstone bored him beyond measure. His zest for languages had grown into an obsession. He already knew—or rather, *said* he knew, because he had no scholarly knowledge of any of them—seven languages: Latin, Greek, Irish, French, Italian, Spanish, and the broken jargon of the Petulengro clan. Now that his evenings were more or less free from parental control he began the study of seven more: Welsh, Danish, German, Hebrew, Arabic, Gaelic, and Armenian!

At first he kept his new occupations a secret. Tucked away in the eaves of the Guildhall and festooned with cobwebs, the Corporation Library of Norwich possessed a remarkable collection of old volumes looked at by few of the citizens. George discovered this treasure hoard; what is more, he indulged in the deplorable habit of pencilling notes in the margins of old folios, and these may still be seen in the Public

Library. His favourite volumes were Edmund Lhuyd's *Archæologia Britannica* (1707), a valuable work of Celtic philology; and the *Danica Literatura Antiquissima* (1636), by Olaus Wormius, which fascinated him so much that he took to signing his name "George Olaus Borrow".

George, who preferred learning from the living rather than the dead, became interested in a Welsh groom who was employed by a family in Tuck's Court and led a wretched existence because Roger Kerrison and his fellow-clerks called him "Taffy" and made him a butt for crude jokes. His name was Lloyd, and the teasing of these young bucks preyed on his mind so much that eventually he vowed he would do away with himself rather than survive in such a "nest of porcupines". He was saved from this fate by George, who bargained that he would keep his friends from poking fun at Lloyd, if Lloyd would teach him Welsh pronunciation. There was no need, said George loftily, for actual lessons in Welsh, since he had been twice through Owen Pugh's version of *Paradise Lost* and there was therefore little in Welsh poetry he could not make out with some pondering.

Every Sunday afternoon, spent by George in the bosom of his family, Lloyd called at the house in King's Court and, much to the consternation of Captain Borrow, the most unearthly sounds floated down the stairs from the room still alluded to as "George's study". As if this was not enough, he then imported another peculiar friend, the Jewish Mousha,[1] from whom he was taking lessons in Hebrew, and the poor Captain grew more and more exercised over what he called "this confusion of tongues". Why, oh, why, could not George emulate the example of his elder brother, who had had no fewer than twelve pictures exhibited at the annual exhibitions of the Norwich Society of Artists?

Alas, George had no such intention; moreover, he could never hide his light under a bushel for long, and soon all Norwich knew that "that queer Borrow boy" was to be seen striding up St. Giles's muttering outlandish gibberish to himself. Nor did his misdemeanours stop at such behaviour. At one of Mrs. Simpson's dinner-parties he had insolently

[1] His real name was Levy.

contradicted a rich and venerable archdeacon who was singing
the praises of Ovid, and asserted that the poems of some
unknown Welsh writer called Ab Gwilym[1] put the Roman
writer to shame; while in his position as office doorkeeper he
had kept Sir Edward ——, a noted baronet, cooling his heels
in the other room and ushered a vagabond poet called Parkinson
into his master's presence.

Mr. Simpson, who had shown the greatest patience with his
unruly apprentice, even to swallowing the story that an old
farmer and his wife had presented him with a copy of the
Kiempe Viser,[2] lost his temper over the incident of the
baronet.

"This will never do," he stormed. "You will make me a
bankrupt, unless you alter your conduct. There is scarcely one
of my respectable clients but complains of your incivility.
I speak to you, my poor boy, as much on your own account
as on mine. I quite tremble for you. Are you aware of the
solecisms you commit?"

George shook his head. "I used my best powers of discrimination" he said. "I looked both full in the face, and the
one struck me as being an honest man, whilst the other had the
very look of a slave-driver."

Even the genial Mr. Simpson jibbed at this astonishing
reply, and when he met Captain Borrow during an evening
stroll he told him that though young George was a "very
extraordinary youth, a most remarkable youth indeed!" he
suffered from a "total lack of discrimination", a statement
which worried the old soldier considerably.

"That child with his confusion of tongues!" he fumed to
his wife, who immediately championed her younger son.

"I really think you are too hard upon him. After all,
though not, perhaps, all you could wish, he is not a bad child;
he is always ready to read the Bible. Let us go in; he is in the
room above us; at least he was two hours ago. I left him there

[1] In *Wild Wales*, Borrow said he believed Ab Gwilym "the greatest
poetical genius that has appeared in Europe since the revival of literature.
. . . The great poet of Nature, the contemporary of Chaucer, but worth
half-a-dozen of the accomplished word-master, the ingenious versifier of
Norman and Italian Tales."

[2] Ancient Danish Ballads, collected by Anders Vedel.

bending over his books; I wonder what he has been doing all this time. Let us go in, and he shall read to us."

"I am growing old," answered the Captain decidedly, "and I love to hear the Bible read to me, for my own sight is something dim; yet I do not wish the child to read to me this night, I cannot so soon forget what I have heard; but I hear my eldest son's voice, he is now entering the gate; he shall read the Bible to us this night."

In his bare upstairs room George raised his head from his books. It was a still, summer night; the window was wide open; every word of his parents' conversation came distinctly to his ears. He frowned and twisted uneasily in his chair. Why was it that he could never please his father, never get close to him? Why couldn't the old man realize that the dry as dust legal documents of Simpson & Rackham's office were poor fare to one deep in study of the ancient Welsh bards? He bent again over his desk and the magic verses of Iolo Goch[1] leapt up at him. . . . He took his pen and translated feverishly:

> A promise has been made by me
> Twice of a journey unto thee;
> His promises let every man
> Perform, as far as e'er he can.
> Easy is done the thing that's sweet,
> And sweet this journey is and meet;
> I've vowed to Owain's court to go. . . .

The dawn was breaking above the spires of Norwich when George tumbled into bed, a line of the poem still beating through his brain. "Easy is done the thing that's sweet . . ." "Easy is done the thing that's sweet . . ."

VI

About this time, when he was seventeen or eighteen years old, George Borrow was taken by his Jewish friend Mousha

[1] Contemporary of Owain Glendower, late fourteenth, and early fifteenth, century.

to call upon that remarkable and extraordinary character, William Taylor, the great friend of Southey and the man whose translation of Bürger's *Lenore* was supposed to have inspired Scott to embark on a literary career. "This, madam," declared Scott to Mrs. Barbauld, "was what made me a poet. I had several times attempted the more regular kinds of poetry without success, but here was something that I thought I could do."[1]

Born in 1765, Taylor was sent abroad while still in his teens by his father, a rich manufacturer in Norwich, in order to learn languages. He returned home full of enthusiasm for German literature but nursing a grudge against Goethe because he had failed to acknowledge the present of a book; and when his father sold his business in 1791 he settled down to devote all his energies to literature. He had been brought up among Unitarians, but his extensive study of Voltaire, Rousseau, and Hume led him to break with the faith of his relatives. His sneering remarks on the Church and his extravagant praise of the French Revolution made him an uncommon number of enemies among whom—not surprisingly—were James and Harriet Martineau; while their kinsfolk, the descendants of the Presbyterian Dr. John Taylor, spent a great deal of time explaining that *they* were *the* "Taylors of Norwich" and had no connection with William, whom they regarded as a revolutionary of the most alarming kind.

That Miss Martineau cherished an abiding dislike of William Taylor was made plain by her description of him in her autobiography published in 1877:

"William Taylor was managed by a regular process, first of feeding, then of wine-bibbing, and immediately after of poking to make him talk: and then came his sayings, devoured by the gentlemen and making ladies and children aghast;—defences of suicide, avowals that snuff alone had rescued him from it: information given as certain that 'God Save the King' was sung by Jeremiah in the Temple of Solomon,—that Christ was watched on the day of His

[1] *A Memoir of the Life and Writings of William Taylor of Norwich* (1765–1836), J. W. Robberds, 2 vols., 1843.

supposed ascension, and observed to hide Himself till dark,
and then to make His way down the other side of the
mountain; and other such plagiarisms from the German
Rationalists.''

Certainly Miss Martineau paid tribute to William Taylor's
devotion to his blind mother and kindness to his extremely
unpleasant father, but she promptly added:

''. . . Matters grew worse in Taylor's old age, when his
habits of intemperance kept him out of the sight of ladies,
and he got round him a set of ignorant and conceited young
men who thought they could set the world right by their
destructive propensities. One of his chief favourites was
George Borrow, as George Borrow has himself given the
world to understand. When this polyglot gentleman appeared
before the public as a devout agent of the Bible Society
in foreign parts, there was one burst of laughter from all
who remembered the old Norwich days.''

Doubtless Miss Martineau exaggerated; but several more
restrained writers of the day commented on William Taylor's
unorthodox views and drunken habits, while Dr. Knapp
considered he had a most unfortunate influence upon George
Borrow, and Southey, although remaining a staunch and
life-long friend, wrote to Taylor as early as 1803:

''Your theology does nothing but mischief; it serves only
to thin the miserable ranks of Unitarianism. The regular
troops of infidelity do little harm; and their trumpeters,
such as Voltaire and Paine, not much more. But it is such
pioneers as Middleton, and you and your German friends,
that work underground and sap the very citadel. That
Monthly Magazine[1] is read by all the Dissenters—I call it
the Dissenters' Obituary—and here are you eternally
mining, mining, under the shallow faith of their half-learned,
half-witted, half-paid, half-starved pastors.''

But to the young George Borrow ''godless Billy'', as Taylor

[1] Edited by Sir Richard Phillips.

was nicknamed by his contemporaries, was the kindest, wisest master a boy could ever know. Taylor volunteered to teach him German; Taylor criticized his crude attempts at Welsh and Danish translation; Taylor talked to him by the hour on a variety of subjects so wide that he stood proven as the fountain-head of all knowledge; Taylor wrote of him to Southey:

"A Norwich young man is construing with me Schiller's *Wilhelm Tell* with the view of translating it for the Press. His name is George Henry Borrow, and he has learnt German with extraordinary rapidity; indeed, he has the gift of tongues, and, though not yet eighteen, understands twelve languages—English, Welsh, Erse, Latin, Greek, Hebrew, German, Danish, French, Italian, Spanish, and Portuguese; he would like to get into the Office for Foreign Affairs, but does not know how."

Did William Taylor really exercise an evil influence upon George Borrow? He taught him to drink wine; he introduced him to John Bowring,[1] with whom Borrow was later to quarrel violently; he gave him a deal of sound wordly advice and filled his head with religious doubts; but as Edward Thomas rightly said:

"If Borrow had never met Taylor he would have met someone else, atheist or religious enthusiast, who would have lured him from the straight, smooth, flowery path of orthodoxy; otherwise he might have been a clergyman or he might have been Dr. Knapp, but he would not have been George Borrow."[2]

Intellectually Taylor did George a great service; emotionally he may have done him harm—but it must always be remembered that George was a creature of moods and fancies, capable at times of sudden strange reserves. In all probability Taylor never knew of George's breakdown, of the attacks of melancholy which assailed him without warning. More than once, indeed,

[1] 1792–1872.
[2] *George Borrow: The Man and his Books*, Edward Thomas, 1912.

Taylor rebuked him sharply for neglecting his studies, and he would scarcely have done so had he been aware of the boy's acute depression, for with all his faults he was a kindly, understanding man.

But the companionship of William Taylor and his friends made George conscious of his own limitations. What, after all, had he achieved through his prodigious efforts to learn this language or that? What future could he look forward to, tied as he was to a profession he hated? Would he ever be able to rid his mind of the doubts which hammered through it the day long?—for his eager quest in search of knowledge had brought him no lordly sense of human wisdom but merely a feeling of aching impotence because he could not solve the riddle of his own personality. Who was he? For what was he born? *What was truth?*

What he had read, what he had heard, had destroyed his belief in the God so sincerely worshipped by his parents and he had nothing, absolutely nothing, to put in its place. That shocked him profoundly. Ab Gwilym and the *Kiempe Viser* lost their savour. The masses of notes he had made no longer held any interest. He tossed his German text-books into his desk, avoided Taylor's house at 21 King Street, took to roaming the countryside alone, always alone, a tall, gaunt young man whose thick black hair already showed streaks of grey.

"For what was I born?" cried George Borrow wordlessly. "Are not all things born to be forgotten? That's incomprehensible; yet is it not so? Those butterflies fall and are forgotten. In what is man better than a butterfly? All then is born to be forgotten. . . . Would I had never been born! But was I ever born? Is not all that I see a lie—a deceitful phantom? Is there a world, and earth, and sky?"

So he wrestled with his thoughts as he tramped over Mousehold Heath, until one day he stopped to listen to a Wesleyan evangelist speaking from the Ranter's Monticle. He was a youngish man, quiet voiced, soberly dressed, and he spoke very simply of faith. George listened, almost against his will, staying until the crowd joined in the singing of Wesley's hymn:

"Jesus, I cast my soul on Thee,
Mighty and merciful to save;
Thou shalt to death go down with me
And lay me gently in the grave.

This body then shall rest in hope,
This body which the worms destroy;
For Thou shalt surely raise me up,
To glorious life and endless joy."

George shivered slightly as the last note echoed over the heath. Such faith was not for him, yet as he strode on up the heathery slope he muttered, "Would that my life had been like his—even like that man's!" and melancholy took possession of him. He was alone, helpless, hopeless. If there was a world it held no place for him. Not that it mattered—nothing mattered. His life—if he had ever been alive—had ended the day he sobbed his heart out on this very heath by the remains of a gypsy fire. . . .

Suddenly he stumbled and just saved himself from falling. Was it . . . ? Ah, no, it was a figment of his tired mind, a trick of the evening light, yet it seemed that ahead of him, squatting beside a gorse bush and staring at the red ball of the setting sun was a loved, familiar figure.

"That's not you, Jasper?" he whispered.

And Jasper Petulengro turned his head. "Indeed, brother!"

George peered at him, still unable to believe him real. "I've not seen you for years," he stammered.

"How should you, brother?" asked Jasper calmly.

"What brings you here?"

"The fight, brother."

"Where are the tents?"

"On the old spot, brother."

Thankfulness flooded George's heart. Here at last was truth, real and solid, in the shape of Jasper Petulengro. Eagerly he threw himself down beside his friend and, after asking many questions about the tribe, drew nearer and said thoughtfully, "What is your opinion of death?" (It was all important to know what Jasper, his one true friend, would say about death.)

"My opinion of death, brother, is much the same as that in the old song of Pharaoh, which I have heard my grandam sing:

"Cana marel o manus chivios ande puv,
Ta rovel pa leste a chavo ta romi!

"When a man dies, he is cast into the earth, and his wife and child sorrow over him. If he has neither wife nor child, then his father and mother, I suppose; and if he is quite alone in the world, why, then he is cast into the earth, and there is an end to the matter."

"And do you think that is the end of a man?" asked George fearfully.

"There's an end of him, brother, more's the pity."

"Why do you say so?"

"Life is sweet, brother."

"Do you think so?"

"Think so! There's night and day, brother, both sweet things; sun, moon and stars, brother, all sweet things; there's likewise the wind on the heath. Life is very sweet, brother; who would wish to die?"

"I would wish to die . . ."

"You talk like a gorgio," said Jasper harshly, "which is the same as talking like a fool—were you a Romany Chal you would talk wiser. Wish to die, indeed! A Romany Chal would wish to live for ever!"

"In sickness, Jasper?"

"There's the sun and stars, brother."

"In blindness, Jasper?"

"There's the wind on the heath, brother; if I could only feel that, I would gladly live for ever. Dosta, we'll now go to the tents and put on the gloves; and I'll try to make you feel what a sweet thing it is to be alive, brother!"

The wind on the heath! With that one magic phrase Jasper Petulengro swept the cobwebs of melancholy from George Borrow's mind.

Once again the days danced with enchantment. Parental rebuke, musty old books, the lawyer's stool, the academic companionship of 21 King Street—all were forgotten as

George swaggered off with Jasper to the bowling-green kept by a retired coachman with one leg near the Field of the Chapel, for on this emerald square of turf surrounded by elms once planted to commemorate the Restoration, the best bruisers in all England were gathered to do battle. Cribb, the mighty champion with a face like a lion. Teucer Belcher, son of a famous father, dressed entirely in white from hat to top-coat. Irish Randall, king of lightweights, sprucely clad in brown. Ned Turner, the Welshman, Bulldog Hudson, Scroggins, Purcell—and last and bravest of all, Tom of Bedford, "true piece of English stuff; sharp as winter, kind as spring".

Oh, the wonder and sparkle of the scene! Everything about it shone and glittered under the summer sky, from the jewel-bright patch of grass to the silver trappings of the high-stepping horses, from the polished woodwork of the coaches to the gay apparel of the young bucks, from the elegant beaver hats of the noble lords to the gold rings swinging from the gypsies' ears, from the striped awnings of the booths to the multi-coloured favours flaunted in every lapel. As he followed Jasper through the noisy, shifting crowd George's heart swelled in his breast. This was England, he thought exultantly, the *real* England!

They saw one fight; then another. They listened to the shouts of the countryfolk when one of their number, by a chance never reckoned on by the promoters, defeated a professional pugilist. In the midst of the third fight, when everyone was far too intent upon watching a protégé of Thurtell's trouncing a gallant but untrained lad from Birmingham to notice the darkening sky, a terrific thunderstorm broke overhead. The rain began to fall in torrents and the game young boxer, unable to stand up against this second adversary, lost to Thurtell's man. The crowd stampeded—the fun was over and all they wanted was to hurry to shelter. Careless of whom they trampled underfoot they pressed madly towards their coaches, gigs or horses as the thunder rolled and the lightning flashed.

Jasper plucked at George's sleeve and pointed a finger to the sky. "What do you see there, brother?"

"A strange kind of cloud."

"What does it look like, brother?"

"Something like a stream of blood."

"That cloud foreshoweth a bloody dukkeripen."

"A bloody fortune! And whom may it betide?"

But even as George asked the question an open barouche, drawn by four horses mounted by postilions in scarlet jackets, swept past. In it were seated the victorious boxer and his backer, John Thurtell.

Once again Jasper pointed, this time straight at Thurtell, who was laughing and nodding to George. "*His* dukkeripen!" he said slowly.

As suddenly as it had begun the storm cleared away. The sun shone out again—but on what a different scene! The bowling-green was trodden into a quagmire; the sodden awnings flapped dejectedly; the horses of the few remaining coaches strained and stumbled as they dragged their heavy loads through the mud. The wonder and glitter had gone—if, indeed, they had ever been?

Jasper lifted his head and sniffed the air. "There's a wind on the heath, brother," he said, and set off at a steady lope in the direction of Mousehold.

George followed him, eyes fixed on his lithe body. So long as he had Jasper he could believe in friendship, in life, in himself—ah, but even Jasper had said something a few moments ago . . . ? A sob caught in George's throat as he remembered Jasper's prophecy about Thurtell. "I don't believe in dukkeripens!" he shouted, and pressed on after his friend.

But in his heart he knew that he lied.

VII

The summer died. The Petulengro family departed with a careless wave of the hand from Jasper and the vague promise that he would return next year or the year after. George, who by this time should have grown used to gypsy migrations, was immediately cast down from heaven into a hell out of which even William Taylor's efforts on his behalf failed to raise him.

Despite his pupil's defection Taylor had proved a loyal

admirer of George's ability. When Southey wrote that he was unable to obtain the interest of the Foreign Office, Taylor sent letters to various editors of his acquaintance, eulogizing the German and Scandinavian translations of his "gifted young friend, Mr. Borrow". Thomas Campbell, editor of Colburn's *New Monthly*, and Sir Richard Phillips, owner of the *Monthly Magazine*, asked to see his work, with the result that during the year 1823 several specimens were published. The *New Monthly* printed a mediocre translation of Schiller's *der Taucher*; while the *Monthly Magazine* used an article on "Danish Poetry and Ballad Writing" and a quantity of metrical translations from Danish, Swedish, Dutch, and German poets, including a deplorable version of Bürger's *Lenore*—already so much better done by Taylor himself.[1] All these contributions were signed "George Olaus Borrow".

Most young men of twenty would have been moved to transports of delight by such success: George remained wrapped in his cloak of gloom and besieged by doubts. Suppose he went on studying and translating, translating and studying until he was forty—what then? He would be learned enough, achieve an ephemeral fame; but what manner of use was that to one who yearned for immortality? To gain immortality he must create, not echo, and how could he do so with one leg tied to Simpson & Rackham's office and the other to the little house in King's Court?

It would be foolish to deny that George Borrow had a tendency to melancholia. He had been a strange little boy; he had had a nervous breakdown; he was subject to what he himself called "attacks of the horrors". But was his melancholy innate within him? If so had it been aggravated by the perpetual friction between him and his father? Or was it induced by the father's attitude of disapproval and open preference for the qualities displayed by John, his elder brother?

At this date it is impossible to decide the true answer to these questions; but study of Borrow and his works inclines one to the belief that his fits of depression, which grew more severe and more frequent throughout his youth, had their

[1] According to Dr. Knapp, "in addition to the prose article, we find 674 lines of metrical translation, printed during the year".

origin in his family surroundings. Highly sensitive in character, he had been told from babyhood that everything he did or said compared exceedingly badly with what John would have done or said under similar circumstances. In itself, this was enough to upset any small boy; to George, a child who craved for affection, it brought a sense of his own unworthiness which deepened, as he grew older, into a longing to do something wonderful, something stupendous, which would make his parents realize that their younger son was cast in the heroic mould. His attempts to win their admiration ended in lamentable failure.

Not till long afterwards did George understand how ardently his mother fought on his behalf. He adored his mother, and in youth it seemed to him that he was deliberately being kept from her by his father. Gradually dislike of that father crept unbidden into his mind and by the time he was fully aware of its existence was firmly lodged there. Try as he might, he could not eradicate it—and that worried him mightily, for in the early years of the nineteenth century any lack of filial affection was regarded as a monstrous and unnatural crime. In certain moods he felt himself a pariah; in others he found oblivion in the society of Jasper Petulengro or William Taylor, or in the study of languages; always he was stricken with a mingling of shame and remorse when confronted by his father.

In the spring of 1821 Crome had died, and John Borrow had left for London to study art under Benjamin Robert Haydon, taking with him Captain Borrow's blessing and the handsome sum of £150. Towards the end of 1822 he had journeyed on to Paris, from which city he sent his parents a few remarkably scrappy notes saying vaguely that he was copying pictures in the Louvre. The less John wrote the more anxious and irascible Captain Borrow became. Since his retirement he had developed severe gout—which did not sweeten his temper—and by 1823 was confined to his room.

There he sat, a shrunken figure in a faded regimental coat whose one pleasure was to bawl some reproof whenever George came to see him. Nothing the boy did was ever right. He had been apprenticed—at great cost—to Simpson & Rackham, yet after four years knew but a smattering of law. He had learnt how to make horse-shoes, but was too secretive to tell his parents where he had gained this knowledge. He was an idler, a good-for-nothing, and his ignorance of the Scriptures was shocking.

To do George justice, he was genuinely distressed about his father's frailty and spent most of his free time in attendance on him; but one evening, stung into self-defence, he announced that he was studying Armenian.

"I have ever observed about you a want of frankness, which has distressed me," roared Captain Borrow. "You never speak of what you are about, your hopes, or your projects, but cover yourself with mystery."

George tried to explain that the widow of a clergyman had allowed him to study her late husband's Armenian books and had also—here his gift for self-dramatization expressed itself—drawn his portrait because he "put her in mind of Alfieri's Saul".

"Saul?" said Captain Borrow. "I am afraid she was only too right there; he disobeyed the commands of his master, and brought down on his head the vengeance of Heaven—he became a maniac, prophesied, and flung weapons about him."

"He was, indeed, an awful character," soothed George. "I hope I shan't turn out like him."

"God forbid!" snapped Captain Borrow, "but in many respects you are headstrong and disobedient like him. I placed you in a profession, and besought you to make yourself master of it, by giving it your undivided attention. This, however, you do not do, you know nothing of it, but tell me that you are acquainted with Armenian; but what I dislike most is your want of candour. . . . But what I want to know is—what do you propose to do?"

"To do, Father?"

"Yes! the time for which you were articled to your profession will soon be expired, and I shall be no more. . . . The military pension which I enjoy will cease with my life. The property which I shall leave behind me will be barely sufficient for the maintenance of your mother respectably. I again ask you what you intend to do. Do you think you can support yourself by your Armenian or your other acquirements?"

"I really do not know what I shall do," stammered George. "I think little at all about it; but I suppose I must push into the world, and make a good fight, as becomes the son of him who fought Big Ben: if I can't succeed, and am driven to the worst, it is but dying . . ."

"What do you mean by dying?" bellowed the Captain.

"Leaving the world; my loss would scarcely be felt. I have never held life in much value, and everyone has a right to dispose as he thinks best of that which is his own."

"Ah," said his father witheringly. "Now I understand you; and well I know how and where you imbibed that horrible doctrine, and many similar ones which I have heard from your own mouth; but I wish not to reproach you—I view in your conduct a punishment for my own sins, and I bow to the will of God. Few and evil have been my days upon the earth; little have I done to which I can look back with satisfaction. It is true I have served my king fifty years, and I have fought with—Heaven forgive me, what was I about to say!—but you mentioned the man's name, and our minds willingly recall our ancient follies. Few and evil have been my days upon earth, I may say with Jacob of old, though I do not mean to say that my case is so hard as his; he had many undutiful children, whilst I have only . . . (George); but I will not reproach you. I have also a son to whom I can look with hope, who may yet preserve my name when I am gone, so let me be thankful; perhaps, after all, I have not lived in vain. Boy, when I am gone, look up to your brother, and may God bless you both!"

This speech, with its ponderous sarcasm, its pointed reference to William Taylor, its allusion to John, and its Old Testament analogy, was not calculated to improve the relationship between the father and the younger son. Even allowing for the older man's physical deterioration it was a wounding —one might say an unforgivable—harangue. It was, indeed, a concentrated version of all the speeches Captain Borrow had directed against George since 1806, and George was in no fit state to withstand such an attack. Day after day he sat hunched on his office stool, brooding darkly on suicide, thinking confusedly that since he could not win his parents' love by his manner of living he might do so by his manner of dying. Spasmodically, in an effort to rid himself of the horrors which beset him, he worked furiously at his translations, but always the vision of the old soldier in the regimental coat came between him and the page and, throwing his work to one side, he would stride in the direction of King's Court, half his mind filled with passionate resentment against his father, half filled with pity for the lonely, sick old man yearning for news of a beloved son.

It was to George Borrow's eternal credit that he nursed and tended his father for a full year despite the daily upbraidings he received. From what we can gather he received permission from Mr. Simpson to live at home in order to lift some of the burden from his mother's shoulders. Captain Borrow was now physically helpless, and it was George who washed him, dressed and undressed him, read the Bible and various religious books to him, watched over him at night lest he should wake and require attention. Few thanks came his way. When he was overcome by mental strain and bodily tiredness his father ordered him querulously, "Don't weep, don't weep! Take the Bible and read me something about Jacob and his children." When at last a letter came from John saying that he had received a large sum of money from a Hungarian nobleman for copying an Italian picture he was arraigned for his total lack of ability. When, towards the end of October, all England was shocked by the arrest of John Thurtell for the murder of William Weare,[1] he was told that his friends were felons and gaol-birds.

"Notwithstanding the shock that George Borrow must have experienced by this calamity" (Thurtell's arrest), wrote Dr. Knapp, "no favourable change appears to have been produced in his way of thinking."

Exactly why a friend's arrest on a charge of murder should

---

[1] Thurtell had failed in business, left Norwich, and taken to gambling in London, where Weare cheated him out of £400. He decoyed Weare to Gill's Hill Lane, Elstree, Herts, and killed him there on the night of 24 October, 1823.

have led to any *favourable* change in a young man already sunk in melancholy is hard to determine. What happened in fact was that it threw George into such a mood of despair that after Thurtell's execution in front of Hertford prison on 9 January, 1824, he wrote to his friend Roger Kerrison, then in London:

"I have again been laid up with that detestable complaint which destroys my strength, impairs my understanding, and will in all probability send me to the grave, for I am much worse than when you saw me last. But if ever my health mends, and possibly it may by the time my clerkship expires (30 March), I intend to live in London, write plays, poetry, etc., abuse religion and get myself prosecuted, for I would not for an ocean of gold remain any longer than I am forced in this dull and gloomy town."

George had not long to wait for his release from Norwich. By the beginning of February it was evident that Captain Borrow had only a short time to live. An urgent summons was sent to John, who arrived looking pale and unwell, and in the early morning of 28 February, George was aroused by a cry from his mother, who had awakened to find her husband lying unconscious at her side. She and John rushed for the doctor, but within a few moments the old soldier died. . . .

"There was a deep gasp: I shook, and thought all was over; but I was mistaken—my father moved and revived for a moment; he supported himself in bed without any assistance. I make no doubt that for a moment he was perfectly sensible, and it was then that, clasping his hands, he uttered another name clearly, distinctly—it was the name of Christ. With that name upon his lips, the brave old soldier sank back upon my bosom, and, with his hands still clasped, yielded up his soul."

Strange irony that the arms supporting him were those of George, and not of John.

CHAPTER THREE

"THE BIG WORLD"

(*Lavengro*, Chap. XXIX)

(1824–1832)

I

ONE of the daily sights of Norwich was the departure of the Ipswich Mail, grandly advertised as the "night-coach for London, through in fourteen hours!" Each afternoon a crowd gathered in the courtyard of the Angel Inn to peer curiously at the travellers and pass remarks about the appearance, dress, and baggage of these intrepid folk who treated the stupendous journey as a matter of course.

On Thursday, 1 April, the watchers nudged each other as a lady in deepest mourning, her hands fumbling with a black-bordered handkerchief beneath her heavy crape veil, entered the yard supported by a tall, pale young man. Just behind them, laden down with various packages, stalked an even taller young man with a dark-skinned face which contrasted oddly with his white hair.

Talk buzzed as the taller young man hoisted his boxes and bundles up to the driver. There was that poor Mrs. Borrow seeing her son off to seek his fortune in London town. A queer lad he was too, by all accounts, though there were some who said he was a regular keg of learning. But others knew tales of his drinking with "godless Billy", and hobnobbing with the gypsies on Mousehold, and fighting with that Thurtell who had lost his neck but a month or two back. Maybe his going would be a good riddance; anyway it wasn't right for a lad of—what would he be, twenty or so?—to have that great shock of *white* hair!

The passengers began to take their places as the guard blew several blasts on his horn. Mrs. Borrow, now sobbing violently, strained her younger son to her in a last embrace and sank back upon John's arm. George, determined not to show emotion at this tragic parting, was climbing stiffly up the ladder to his seat on top of the coach when a figure came hurrying through the crowd shouting his name and waving an envelope. Allday Kerrison had come to bid farewell to his friend and to give him a letter for his brother Roger, who had found lodgings for George in London.[1]

Allday had scarcely panted out his good wishes before a neighbouring clock chimed five strokes. The guard blew a final warning, the coachman gathered up his reins, and the horses clattered through the archway into the Market Place. George sat bolt upright on his uncomfortable seat clutching a small green box on his knees. He was so consumed with longing for the mother he had just left that he saw none of the familiar landmarks as the coach swept through Upper Haymarket, Rampant Horse Street, and St. Stephen's, on to the Ipswich road. Not until they were well on the way to Stratton did he recover sufficiently to notice his surroundings.

They were depressing enough, in all conscience. Any signs of spring were hidden by a curtain of rain which was driven across the countryside by a bitter wind. Every raindrop was needle-sharp, and George's fellow-travellers huddled morosely under coats and rugs, cursing the poverty which forced them to journey outside instead of inside the coach, and the muddy, uneven road over which the vehicle jolted and swayed alarmingly.

Yet as George stared at the desolate scene he forgot the agony of farewell. This was adventure! Eagerly he scanned the darkening landscape, and as he espied a bobbing lantern just ahead his spirits rose with a bound. Highwaymen? Footpads? Who knew what exciting happenings might beguile the long hours of the night?

Nobody attacked them except the wind and the rain. They halted at Ipswich—where George would have dearly loved a hot drink but felt it more manly to swallow a pint of remarkably cold ale. They stopped again at Colchester and

[1] *Allday to Roger: 1 April*, 1824: "I will not lose the opportunity of George's going to London, to write to you . . . I do not know how I shall be able to learn Spanish, now George has gone . . . I hope George will succeed in London."

Chelmsford, but at these places George stayed in lonely state on the coach-top, for he had to conserve his slender store of money. He had, indeed, only enough to keep him for a very few weeks, because apart from a sum which would bring his widow an income of £100, Captain Borrow had been unable to leave more than a tiny amount "for the education and maintenance of my younger son during his minority".

But George munched his sandwiches cheerfully, soaking wet and half-frozen though he was. Every now and again he patted the green box on his lap. Within it, neatly tied with red tape, were the translations which were going to bring him fortune. The interminable poems of Ab Gwilym; romantic ballads from the Gaelic, Danish, Swedish, and German; Johannes Evald's play, *The Death of Baldes*; *Faustus: his life, death and descent into hell*, by Friedrich Maximilian von Klinger. How could any young man of twenty fear the future with such potential riches in his possession?

The coach rattled on through the darkness. The wind dropped. The rain increased to a pitiless downpour. The other occupants of the coach-top were reduced to sodden lumps of misery. Only George glowed with exhilaration as he repeated to himself the legend of "that strange melancholy Svend Vonved, who roams about the world propounding people riddles; slaying those who cannot answer, and rewarding those who can with golden bracelets . . ."

> ". . . Svend Vonved binds his sword to his side;
> He fain will battle with knights of pride.
> When may I look for thee once more here?
> When roast the heifer and spice the beer?"
> Look out, look out, Svend Vonved.
> When stones shall take, of themselves, a flight
> And ravens' feathers are waxen white,
> Thou may'st expect Svend Vonved home:
> In all my days I will never come."
> Look out, look out, Svend Vonved."

He loved those verses—to the end of his life he was to use them as a sort of incantation—but even more he loved an original poem of his own, "Lines to Six-foot-three".

A lad, who twenty tongues can talk,
And sixty miles a day can walk;
Drink at a draught a pint of rum,
And then be neither sick nor dumb;
Can tune a song, and make a verse,
And deeds of northern kings rehearse;

Who never will forsake his friend,
While he his bony fist can bend;
And, though averse to brawl and strife,
Will fight a Dutchman with a knife.
O that is just the lad for me,
And such is honest six-foot-three.

Yes, that assuredly was his favourite, fine vigorous stuff
with a heroic ring about it! With its words still warm in his
mind he dreamed happily until somebody trod on his toes
and he came to full consciousness with a start. Gracious, they
were in London! He gazed excitedly about him as several of
the passengers clambered down the ladder. Was this then the
end of his journey? An inquiry of the guard brought the surly
answer that they were merely halting at the Spread Eagle in
Gracechurch Street before going on to the Swan with Two
Necks on the corner of Lad Lane.[1]

A little of George's eagerness deserted him as the coach
swung into the yard of the old balconied inn. The bustle of the
Angel was nothing compared to the confusion which raged
before the Swan with Two Necks. Passengers, porters, ostlers,
and a crowd of curious hangers-on milled around the piles of
luggage, all shouting at the pitch of their voices. Still clutching
his green box, George at last summoned courage to approach
a porter, but as he did so he felt a tug at his arm. "One-and-
ninepence, sir, or your things will be taken away from you!"
said a lisping voice.

He turned to confront the queerest individual he had ever
seen, a man with a rouged, impudent face clad in the remains
of dandified finery. "One-and-ninepence," he repeated, with a
sinister look.

[1] Lad Lane disappeared when Gresham Street was built, but for a long
time a picture of the inn sign remained on the wall of a railway office.
(*Hare's Walks in London,* 1883.)

So this, thought George indignantly, was the kind of greeting London gave her visitors. Involuntarily he clenched his fist and advanced on the man, who slipped quickly away.

The incident had restored his confidence, and as he strode beside the porter he plied the man with questions regarding the names of streets, churches, and buildings. Roger Kerrison had kindly found him rooms at 16 Millman Street, Bedford Row, where he himself lodged, and it seemed to George a mighty long tramp from Lad Lane. Accustomed to Norwich he blinked in amazement at the busy streets, thronged even at this early hour with horse-drawn and pedestrian traffic, at the heaps of garbage lying rotting in the gutters, at the scowling faces which loomed at him out of the clammy mist.

By the time they reached his lodgings George's ever mercurial spirits were sinking rapidly, and when he had paid the porter the excessive sum demanded and lugged his belongings up two steep flights of stairs to a bare little sitting-room they went to zero. Everything about London was so different from what he had expected—the narrowness of the streets, the forbidding appearance of the tall dark buildings, the miserable looks of the passers-by. How could he hope to find his way through the maze of lanes and alleyways which honeycombed this great city? Worse still, how could he win escape from its all pervading atmosphere of dinginess?

Stiff, cold, utterly weary, he sat on a knobbly horse-hair covered chair and stared at the empty grate; but in a few moments his kindly landlady bustled in. He must be dead tired after his long journey, she said, but it wouldn't take her many minutes to get the fire going—and what would he like for breakfast? No doubt he had a real country appetite like Mr. Kerrison's—and while she prepared the meal would he please change out of those horrid wet clothes?

A wave of home-sickness swept George as he nodded dumb acquiescence, but in a trice—or so it seemed—the flames leaped hotly from the empty grate, the soaking garments steamed on a chair-back, and he was facing a gargantuan repast. True, the teapot was cracked, the tablecloth stained, the loaf stale, the eggs musty; and in Norwich he would have grumbled at such things. But as his body absorbed food and warmth so his mind regained equanimity, and before pouring the last dregs of the tea he reached for his precious green box. Which of his treasures should he present to Sir Richard Phillips? (Of course, he would welcome all of them, but perhaps a judicious selection should be made for the preliminary interview.) George fingered the manuscripts written in a queer, angular hand—Ab Gwilym: yes. *Romantic Ballads:* certainly. The translation of the German novel[1]: yes, no, *yes*. Oh, and William Taylor's letter of introduction—unnecessary, of course, for a favourite contributor to the *Monthly Magazine*, but a kindly gesture from a master to the pupil who had outstripped him.

George tucked the papers inside his shirt, relocked the box, prepared for his conquest of London. . . . But the fire lured him and of a sudden he realized how tired he was. He dragged the horse-hair covered chair closer to the blaze, eased his body into its knobbly depths, and planted his feet firmly on either side of the mantelpiece. London, he thought drowsily, there's nothing to fear in London. . . .

II

Sir Richard Phillips,[2] a man of fifty-seven when Borrow met him, had had a variegated career. The son of a Leicestershire farmer he had, after a short and unsuccessful stay in London, opened a small school in Leicester, his "sign" to likely parents being a blue flag hoisted on a pole. Pupils flocked to him, but fortune still proved elusive, so some friends started him in a hosiery shop. Phillips, however, was more interested in politics than stockings and soon launched the *Leicester Herald*, a paper of strong Whig convictions to which many well-known reformers of the day contributed. Unfortunately its proprietor offered copies of Paine's *Rights of Man* for sale

[1] Probably F. M. von Klinger's *Faustus*.
[2] *Memoirs* of the Public and Private Life of Sir Richard Phillips, King's High Sheriff for the City of London and the County of Middlesex, 1808.

and was sentenced to eighteen months in Leicester gaol. Daniel Lambert, the notorious "fat man", must have been a kindly gaoler, for Phillips was allowed the Duke of Norfolk and Lord Moira as visitors, issued the *Leicester Herald* from his cell, and started a second paper called *The Museum*. On his release he dropped the *Herald*[1] but ran *The Museum* from his hosiery shop until the place caught fire.

The insurance money bought another hosiery shop, this time in St. Paul's Churchyard, and marriage with a Welsh girl who won Phillips's heart by making him vegetable pies— he had been a vegetarian ever since eating, unawares, a portion of a favourite heifer on his father's farm. Encouraged by Dr. Priestley, Phillips turned his shop into a "literary repository", and within a remarkably short time won such fame as a publisher that he had to move to larger premises in New Bridge Street, Blackfriars. Many well-known authors of the day went to him, including Maria Edgeworth, William Godwin, and Sydney Owenson (Lady Morgan); but his principal business lay in school text-books and for these he employed a positive army of literary hacks.

Phillips was knighted by George III in 1808, and during his period as sheriff instituted several reforms in London prisons. At some time in his career he went bankrupt, but subsequently repurchased his *Monthly Magazine*, that long-lived and immensely successful journal, and made a second, if more moderate, fortune which enabled him to insert this paragraph in the January 1824 number of his magazine:

"The Editor, having retired from his commercial engagements and removed from his late house of business in New Bridge Street, communications should be addressed to the appointed Publishers (the Whittakers); but personal interviews of Correspondents and interested persons may be obtained at his private residence in Tavistock Square."

This, then, was the man with whom George Borrow sought an interview, a man so utterly unlike his conception of him that from the moment of their meeting his personality was

[1] Later revived as a Tory journal.

unpleasing. Phillips was never a bookman—although he sincerely believed himself to be one. He was a genial, honest, and astute man of business who assessed potential authors in terms of pounds, shillings, and pence. George was a boy entirely ignorant of the world, a quicksilver creature of whims and fancies who had never, despite his odd friendships, his prodigious studies and his youthful wanderings, stood face to face with life.

The two were—and would always remain—poles apart, and neither could be blamed for failing to span the distance which separated them.

Phillips might have retired from the editorship of the *Monthly Magazine*, but he was still financially interested in it and had also started *The Universal Review; or, Chronicle of the Literature of all Nations*.[1] Furthermore, he was anxious to publish a six-volume work under the grand title of *Celebrated Trials, and Remarkable Cases of Criminal Jurisprudence, from the earliest records to the year* 1825,[2] and was on the look-out for a suitable translator who would render his own ponderous book on physics, the *Proximate Causes of the Material Phenomena of the Universe*[3] into German. Young Borrow, therefore, appeared at an opportune moment. He was the very man to hunt up details for William Gifford[4] of the *Universal* and track down records of noted criminals and—hadn't the redoubtable William Taylor given ecstatic praise to his German?—translate the book on physics.

George, whose vivid imagination had pictured a wonderful interview during which the publisher, with tears streaming down his face, acclaimed the author as a genius and begged permission to print all his works forthwith, was hurt, bewildered and angered in turn by Phillips's dogmatic assertions. Poetry? Quite unsaleable and better to burn it at once. Translations from the Celtic or Scandinavian? So much waste of time. A wildly romantic novel (*Dr. Faustus*)? Certainly not, the public would have none of it; but if Mr. Borrow would attempt

[1] In *Lavengro* this is called *The Oxford Review*.
[2] In *Lavengro* this is called *Newgate Lives and Trials*.
[3] In *Lavengro* this is alluded to as a "work of philosophy".
[4] Editor of the *Quarterly Review*, 1809–1824, worked *sub rosa* on the *Universal*, Phillips's son being mentioned as editor.

something like *The Dairyman's Daughter*[1] then he might be disposed to pay the handsome sum of ten pounds for the work. And, by the way, while their mutual friend in Norwich was a great scholar he held some very eccentric views—even contributing an article to the *Monthly* which stated that the Christ had been a soldier in a marching regiment! He trusted that Mr. Borrow entertained no such outrageous notions and hoped he would take dinner in Tavistock Square the following Sunday.

No wonder that George left the house in a daze! "That's a strange man," he said to himself, "he is evidently very clever; but I cannot say that I like him much, with his Oxford Reviews and his Dairyman's Daughters. But what can I do? I am almost without a friend in the world. I wish I could find someone who would publish my ballads, or my songs of Ab Gwilym. In spite of what the big man says, I am convinced that, once published, they would bring me much fame and profit!"

According to his lights Phillips was very good to George. Over the Sunday dinner-table he announced briskly that he wished him to undertake reviewing for the *Universal* and to compile *Celebrated Trials*, for six volumes of which he was prepared to pay £50 altogether! (A paltry offer, but one quite usual in the 1820's.) George stammered his thanks but unfortunately mentioned the publisher's earlier idea of an "evangelical novel" on the lines of *The Dairyman's Daughter*. This was dismissed with an airy gesture, but when George suggested he would be happy to do a good translation from Goethe—"his *Sorrows* for example, or more particularly his *Faust*"—Phillips drew himself up in his chair.

"Sir, Goethe is a drug; his *Sorrows* are a drug, so is his *Faustus*. . . . No, sir, I do not want you to translate Goethe or anything belonging to him; nor do I want you to translate anything from the German; what I want you to do, is to translate into German. I am willing to encourage merit, sir; and, as my good friend (William Taylor) in his last letter has spoken very highly of your German acquirements"—here

---

[1] Published 1811, a glorified and immensely popular tract by Legh Richmond, who also wrote *The Young Cottager*.

Phillips lowered his voice and assumed a solemn expression—
"I have determined that you shall translate my book of
philosophy into German."

"Your book—into German?" croaked George.

"Yes, sir; I am not a drug, sir, in Germany, as Goethe is
here, no more is my book. I intend to print the translation at
Leipzig, sir; and if it turns out a profitable speculation, as I
make no doubt it will, provided the translation be well executed,
I will make you some remuneration. Sir, your remuneration
will be determined by the success of your translation."

"But, sir . . ."

"Sir!" roared Phillips, "you have heard my intentions; I
consider that you ought to feel yourself gratified by my
intentions towards you; it is not frequently that I deal with
a writer, especially a young writer, as I have done with
you."

So George found himself committed to a variety of tasks
for which he had no training and little aptitude. He disliked
reviewing—"works of merit do not require to be reviewed,
they can speak for themselves, and require no praising; works
of no merit at all will die of themselves, they require no killing".
He had no idea where or how to find information for *Celebrated
Trials*, and even when he discovered London's second-hand
bookstalls he was appalled at the outlay involved—the
promised £50 would only materialize when the work was
finished. As for the translation of Phillips's book, it was far
and away beyond his powers, though this he would not admit.
His knowledge of physics was nil; his German, despite Taylor's
eulogies, was by no means thorough; he found it remarkably
difficult to understand the English original, let alone render it
into German—but how could a young man who had stressed
his ability to translate Goethe return his publisher's own
work and cry *cave*?

Night after night George sat in his Millman Street room
poring over Phillips's manuscript. Day after day he laboriously
copied out the lives of famous criminals, or supposed criminals;
but each time he took a batch of work to his master that
gentleman flew into a rage. "Where are Brandt and Struensee
—find them!" And when these errant contributors to

Denmark's rotten state were produced he fumed, "I can scarcely believe my eyes—the most important life and trial to be found in the whole criminal record omitted—what gross, what utter negligence! Where's the life of Farmer Patch? Where's the trial of Yeoman Patch?"

George, walking away from Tavistock Square, used to groan, "What a life! What a dog's life!"

Yet the *Trials* proved an anodyne to a boy passionately dedicated to Ab Gwilym, the *Kiempe Viser*, the ancient Norse and Celtic bards and the memory of a gypsy called Jasper Petulengro. Almost against his will George became interested in the strange and violent lives of Parson Hackman and Martha Reay, Cagliostro, the Gunpowder Plotters, the Cato Street Conspirators, Henry Fauntleroy and the "Modern Macheath", Samuel Denmore Hayward. Details of the trial and execution of John Thurtell fascinated him particularly, since he had known the man, and although he was supposed only to sub-edit the record already written, there was an authentic Borrow touch in the description of the actual hanging. "Why, when his neck broke it went off like a pistol."[1]

George had been fortunate to find work so quickly; the trouble was it was not the right *kind* of work. By that one does not mean that it would have been better for him to starve in a garret while translating more romantic ballads. He was not, and never would be, a poet and his translations had little merit. The discipline to which his irascible employer subjected him and the grinding duties of hack work were probably all to the good. It was the actual choice of work which was wrong. Thanks to his lack of teaching in physics and his imperfect knowledge of German, George found the translation of Phillips's book a labour of Sisyphus—he literally did not understand one word out of five. His little stock of money was dwindling alarmingly and there was no prospect of payment until his stupendous tasks were finished. He was lonelier than he had thought possible, for the gay and comfortably off Roger Kerrison had precious little time to spare. The constant reading

---

[1] In *Romany Rye*, Chap. XLII, Borrow puts a description of Thurtell's execution into the mouth of the jockey.

H

up and copying out of the *Trials*—it was significant that sordid crimes interested him a great deal more than actions committed with some laudable intent—induced in him a ghoulish desire to probe the emotions of the wretched criminals.

III

Once again "the horrors" fell upon Borrow. Within two months of his arrival in London he was haunted by twin bogies far more terrifying than the amorphous doubts which had beset him in Norwich. Always beside him were the rattling skeletons of Ab Gwilym and solitude. He had betrayed the one: the other grinned at him from every corner.

The sudden visit of his brother John on 29 April, lifted him out of his depression—it would never do to allow his brother knowledge of his plight; besides, it was so wonderful to have the solace of one's own kith and kin. John had been asked by the Norwich Corporation to paint the portrait of an ex-Mayor, Robert Hawkes, but had modestly said he lacked the necessary talent and suggested he should ask his master, Benjamin Haydon, to undertake the commission. He had therefore come up to negotiate with that "painter of the Heroic" and took George to call upon him at his home near the Marble Arch.

Haydon, who opened the door grudgingly because he thought they were duns, was delighted to paint a Mayor or anybody else if he received enough money to settle his more pressing debts.[1] At the moment he was at work on a huge painting of "Pharaoh dismissing Moses from Egypt", and confided to John that his brother would make a "capital Pharaoh", a remark which led George to say that his friend Mr. Petulengro would be the ideal model.

"Petulengro?" mused John. "A strange kind of fellow

[1] Haydon's fee was £100. The portrait was hung in St. Andrew's Hall, Norwich, but either from boredom or laziness Haydon provided the figure with his own short legs instead of with Robert Hawkes's long ones. See illustration facing page 33.

came up to me some time ago in our town, and asked me about you; when I inquired his name, he told me Petulengro."

George's heart gave a sudden bound, but to his bitter disappointment John was vague about the gypsy—perhaps deliberately so?—and turned the subject to the wretchedness of poor Mrs. Borrow, who suffered from fits of weeping, and the miserable state of the Captain's little dog, which had pined to skin and bone and taken to sitting on its master's grave. Very much the elder brother, John then read George a lecture because only one letter from him had been received since his departure from London.

With John's return to King's Court George's "horrors" attacked him with intensified ferocity. Once more "everything was a lying dream"—his work, the Millman Street rooms, Sir Richard Phillips, the book on physics—and, in the small hours of the morning, when he pushed aside his papers, snuffed the candle and flung himself exhausted on his bed, sleep was streaked by nightmares. . . .

"They say that light fare begets light dreams; my fare at that time was light enough, but I had anything but light dreams, for at that period I had all kind of strange and extravagant dreams, and amongst other things I dreamt that the whole world had taken to dog-fighting; and that I, myself, had taken to dog-fighting, and that in a vast circus I backed an English bulldog against the bloodhound of the Pope."

Did the tawny head of Jasper Petulengro appear in those nightmares? Somehow we think it did, although Barrow makes no immediate allusion to that symbol of freedom after the brief record of the conversation John held with the gypsy in Norwich. But following in the footsteps of George Borrow from his childhood to his death we become increasingly a-ware of the way in which his mind, during periods of torture, sought out memories of Petulengro and "the people out of Egypt".

The nights were hell: the days a purgatory either of wandering in search of the histories of tragic creatures or of

reading those same histories—macabre occupations which did
him little good, for in every gaol-bird, every gallows' victim,
he saw the strange, ill-fated being of many names . . .
Sap-engro, Lavengro, Romany Rye, Olaus. . . . Oh, God!
George Henry Borrow . . . ! And then there was Bartlett,[1]
Phillips's "pale, shrivelled-looking accountant", who, between
pinches of snuff, assured George he would never do for authorship unless he, too, took to the habit. "There is nothing like
it to get a man through," Bartlett said; a phrase which sent
George's mind scurrying back to Taylor's assertion that snuff
alone had saved him from destroying himself. Was Bartlett
warning him? Did Bartlett know of the dark fears which
beset him?

George had thought of suicide before: now, as he sat in
his candle-lit room, it grew to a monstrous shape in his mind.
He seized his pen, scrawled a few words in a shaking hand on
a piece of paper which he folded and pushed under Roger
Kerrison's door . . .

> "DEAR ROGER—
> Come to me immediately I am I believe dying,
> GEORGE BORROW."

Roger did not come—indeed, his reaction to this note was
to pack his belongings and move hastily to new lodgings in
Lichfield Street, Soho, lest he became involved in any
unpleasantness. In view of his long friendship with the Borrow
family this action seems a trifle heartless, but he did at least
write to his brother Allday and to John Borrow[2] saying that
George had threatened suicide so many times and behaved
in such extraordinary fashion that he found it impossible to
live in the same house with him any longer. In the letter to
John he added that as George was about to return to Norwich
in order to collect some books he strongly advised he should
be kept at home for a time, "lest should he return at once,
as he intends, he again make some attempt to destroy himself,
when he finds that he is alone".

Apart from this letter there is no evidence that George

[1] In *Lavengro* he is called "Taggart".
[2] The letters are dated 26 and 28 May, 1824.

Borrow actually tried to kill himself; but whether he stayed several weeks in King's Court or not, his acute depression did not lift until May 1825 when, according to *Lavengro*, he shook London's dust gladly from his feet and began his famous travels through England.

As he prowled around London in search of material for the *Trials* he was so obsessed with his own misery and with the misfortunes that had befallen the people he read so much about, that when he saw a great crowd gathered at what is now the junction of Oxford Street and Tottenham Court Road he remembered immediately that Oxford Street had been Tyburn Way and pressed forward to see which wretched criminal was being taken to the gallows. To his disappointment he saw a grand hearse, followed by many carriages.

"Whose body is in that hearse?" he asked the man next to him.

"The mortal remains of Lord Byron, the illustrious poet, which have been just brought from Greece, and are being conveyed to the family vault."

Resentment arose in George as the man went on to say what a great and unhappy genius Byron had been. Milton, Otway, Butler—all had been greater men, yet they had lived and died neglected and despised. Why should this lordling, this sprig of fashion, be granted such tribute? How could he have been unhappy, when both in life and death he had the world at his feet? Of course he had written *Childe Harold*— but were not other poets (one called George Borrow among them) every bit as gifted? Besides, Byron had been a renegade, a man who poured abuse on his native land; but as George elbowed his way angrily through the throng the lines from Byron's *Prophecy of Dante* drifted into his head:

> "What have I done to thee, my people?
> Are all thy dealings, but in this they pass
> The limit of man's common malice, for
> All that a citizen could be I was;
> Raised by thy will, all things in peace or war,
> And for this thou hast warr'd with me.—'Tis done:
> I may not overlap the eternal bar
> Built up between us, and will die alone,

Beholding, with the dark eyes of a seer,
The evil days to gifted souls foreshown,
Foretelling them to those who will not hear,
As in the old times till the hour be come
When Truth shall strike their eyes through many a tear,
And make them own the Prophet in his tomb."

"The evil days," George repeated slowly, *"the evil days to gifted souls foreshown . . ."* He forgot his animosity towards Byron as he wrapped the cloak of melancholy about himself. He, too, had translated Dante; he, too, was gifted.

IV

There was a brighter side to Borrow's year in Millman Street. Essentially a countryman, the London scene caught and held him against his will and often he tramped the day long through the busy streets, his eyes and ears absorbing the full flavour of the city—and by that I mean the actual City of London which begins at Temple Bar. In 1939, one hundred and fifteen years after Borrow first knew it, he would —if transported forward to our then brave new world—not only have been bewildered but furious at the changes wrought by time. In 1950, surrounded by empty spaces, he would at least have been able to find his way to Ludgate Hill, where he would have approved his favourite view of St. Paul's:

"Standing so proudly on the most commanding ground in the big city; and I looked up to the mighty dome, surmounted by a golden cross, and I said within myself: 'That dome must needs be the finest in the world'; and I gazed upon it till my eyes reeled, and my brain became dizzy, and I thought that the dome would fall and crush me; and I shrank within myself, and struck yet deeper into the heart of the big city."

George Borrow was a minnow among tritons as a guide to the City of London; yet when he cared he could gather all its romance and history into one paragraph. I, for one, would rather read his description of Cheapside than any other:

"Cheapside! Cheapside! Truly thou art a wonderful place for hurry, noise, and riches! Men talk of the bazaars of the East—I have never seen them—but I dare say that, compared with thee, they are poor places, silent places, abounding with empty boxes. O thou pride of London's east!—mighty mart of old renown!—for thou art not a place of yesterday—long before the Roses red and white battled in fair England, thou didst exist—a place of throng and bustle—a place of gold and silver, perfumes and fine linen!"

Where else do you find that superb sense of England's greatness in medieval times, that shabby sense of the caravanserais which starred the Eastern trade routes, painted in so few words? Where else do you gain such a picture of the very core of London City as in Borrow's account of his walk from Cheapside to London Bridge?

". . . I entered another street, which led up a kind of ascent, and which proved to be the street of the Lombards. . . . I walked rapidly up the street of the Lombards, neither looking to the right nor left, for it had no interest for me, though I had a kind of consciousness that mighty things were being transacted behind its walls; but it wanted the throng, bustle and outward magnificence of the Cheape, and it had never been spoken of by 'ruddy bards!' And, when I had got to the end of the street of the Lombards, I stood still for some time, deliberating within myself whether I should turn to the right or the left, or go straight forward, and at last I turned to the right, down a street of rapid descent, and presently found myself upon a bridge which traversed the river which runs by the big city.

"A strange kind of bridge it was; huge and massive, and

seemingly of great antiquity. It had an arched back, like that of a hog, a high balustrade, and at either side, at intervals, were stone bowers bulking over the river, but open on the other side, and furnished with a semi-circular bench. Though the bridge was wide—very wide—it was all too narrow for the concourse upon it. Thousands of human beings were pouring over the bridge. But what chiefly struck my attention was a double row of carts and wagons, the generality drawn by horses as large as elephants, each row striving hard in a different direction, and not unfrequently brought to a standstill. Oh the cracking of whips, the shouts and oaths of the carters, and the grating of wheels upon the enormous stones that formed the pavement! In fact, there was a wild hurly-burly upon the bridge, which nearly deafened me. But, if upon the bridge there was a confusion, below it there was a confusion ten times confounded. The tide, which was fast ebbing, obstructed by the immense pillars of the old bridge, poured beneath the arches with a fall of several feet, forming in the river below as many whirlpools as there were arches. Truly tremendous was the roar of the descending waters, and the bellow of their tremendous gulfs, which swallowed them for a time, and then cast them forth, foaming and frothing from their horrid wombs."

It was at the highest point of the bridge that George Borrow met the old apple-woman, who sat by her stall reading Defoe's *Moll of Flanders*.[1] She saw no harm in "cly-faking" (thieving), so she told George, despite the fact that her own son had been deported to Botany Bay for it. "She too," she said, alluding to Moll, "was what they call a thief and a cutpurse; ay, and do you think she would have told the world so, if there had been any harm in the thing?"

George was indignant at this bowdlerization of his idol's true meaning, reminded her that Defoe's book was designed to

[1] Mr. Clement King Shorter identifies the apple-woman with a gypsy who kept a bookstall in Norwich market-place when Borrow was eight or nine years old, basing his conclusion on a memorandum written by Borrow's stepdaughter, Henrietta MacOubrey.

show the terrible consequences of crime, and offered her a crown for the volume.

The apple-woman shook her head. "No, dear, I will not sell my volume for two silver crowns; no, nor for the golden one in the king's tower down there; without my book I should mope and pine, and perhaps fling myself into the river; but I am glad you like it, which shows that I was right about you, after all; you are one of our party, and you have a flash about that eye of yours which puts me just in mind of my dear son."

The suggestion that he had gypsy blood was one which went straight to George's heart, and the old woman became one of his few friends in London. Many a time, when "the horrors" clutched him, he sought refuge in her rough philosophy, and it was through her he met the strange Armenian who made a fortune on the Stock Exchange and then, through George's advice, sailed for his native country to spend the lot on rescuing his people from their Persian oppressors.

George made another, very different, friend; the charming young Irish gallant, Francis Arden,[1] whom he met in a Strand hostelry which bore the highly unsuitable name of Holy Lands. It was certainly Arden who introduced him to political argument, London public-houses, theatres, bear-pits, and dog-fights: it may have been Arden who, when an old man, told the American C. G. Leland, the following story:

"One night, when skylarking about London, Borrow was pursued by the police, as he wished to be, even as Panurge so planned as to be chased by the night-watch. He was very tall and strong in those days, a trained shoulder-hitter, and could run like a deer. He was hunted to the Thames, and there they thought they had him. But the Romany Rye made for the edge, and leaping into the wan water, like the Squyre in the old ballad, swam to the other side, and escaped."

This "sky-larking"—if such it was, for while Borrow was inclined to exaggerate more sombre scenes, Mr. Arden was

[1] Called "Ardry" in *Lavengro*.

definitely given to exaggerating brighter ones—was short-lived. In January 1825 the *Universal Review* came to an end, and with it all the high hopes raised by the grandiose advertisements which had been appearing in the *Monthly Magazine*:

"A selection of the most remarkable Trials and Criminal Cases is printing. Mr. Borrow, the editor, has availed himself of all the resources of the English, German, French, and Italian languages. . . ."

"Sir Richard Phillips has placed his notable work, the *Proximate Causes of the Material Phenomena of the Universe*, in the hands of Mr. Borrow, who is translating it into the German language. . . ."

Sir Richard had no mind to lose a second fortune, and when he saw the sales of the *Universal* dwindling he decided to sell out his remaining interests in publishing and retire to modest comfort in Brighton. Before he left London, however, he had a succession of stormy interviews with poor George, who had had the temerity to ask for payment for his reviews.

"Sir," said Phillips, "what do you want the money for?"

"Merely to live on," answered George, "it is very difficult to live in this town without money."

"How much money did you bring with you to town?"

"Some twenty or thirty pounds."

"And you have spent it already?"

"No," said George, "not entirely; but it is fast disappearing."

"Sir," roared Phillips, "I believe you to be extravagant; yes, sir, extravagant! You eat meat; you should eat bread and cheese."

"So I do, sir, when I am disposed to indulge; but I cannot often afford it—it is very expensive to dine on bread and cheese, especially when one is fond of cheese, as I am. There is drink, sir; with bread and cheese one must drink porter, sir."

The vegetarian Phillips threw up his hands in horror. "Then, sir, eat bread—bread alone. As good men as yourself have eaten bread alone; they have been glad to get it, sir. If with bread and cheese you must drink porter, sir, with bread alone you can, perhaps, drink water, sir."

Then there were endless troubles over the *Trials*. This massive work—the combined six volumes totalled no fewer than 3,600 pages!—displeased Phillips mightily, and he mortified George by cutting or altering all the cases he particularly liked, and complaining bitterly of the prominence he had given to the life of *Gentleman Harry*—"that life of Harry Simms has long been the greatest drug in the calendar!" he thundered.

The final, most stupendous, row occurred after George had handed in his translation of Phillips's book, and that gentleman had promptly given it to some German friends to read. Not surprisingly, for the bewildered George had simply translated it literally, word for word, they could make neither head nor tail of the first chapter and refused to read further. Phillips immediately sent for George and before his eyes tore the manuscript into little pieces and stamped on them.

"Sir," he shouted, "you know nothing of German; I have shown your translation to several Germans: it is utterly unintelligible to them!"

George was stung into asking if they had read the original in English.

"They did, sir, but they did not profess to understand English."

"No more do I," flashed George, losing his temper completely, "if that Philosophy be English."

This retort marked the end of his association with Phillips. According to George he was treated most scurvily, being paid for his reviews with two bills, one payable in twelve, the other in eighteen months, which he eventually got cashed at a 30 per cent discount. Phillips did, however, pay him the full £50 for the *Trials* and was, indeed, not so black as his protégé painted him in *Lavengro*. He was a business man who demanded value for money and this, alas, the earnest but untrained youth had been unable to give him.

V

One surmises that most of the £50 went to settle out-standing debts with the Millman Street landlady, for by February 1825 George was in very low water again. But he was *free*, free at last to do the work his soul craved, to conquer the world with his *Romantic Ballads*, his Ab Gwilym, his *Dr. Faustus*. Characteristically his quicksilver spirits soared. Since coming to London he had often heard of Mr. John Murray,[1] the publisher, who "lived at the western end of the town", and when the kindly, snuff-taking Bartlett gave him a hint that "Glorious John" might look with favour on his work, George took to haunting Albemarle Street. . . .

"I went to the house where Glorious John resided, and a glorious house it was, but I could not see Glorious John. I called a dozen times, but I never could see Glorious John. Twenty years after,[2] by the greatest chance in the world, I saw Glorious John, and sure enough Glorious John published my books, but they were different books from the first; I never offered my ballads or Ab Gwilym to Glorious John. Glorious John was no snuff-taker. He asked me to dinner, and treated me with superb Rhenish wine. Glorious John is now gone to his rest, but I—what was I going to say?—the world will never forget Glorious John."

But in 1825 "Glorious John" was far beyond Borrow's reach; indeed several lesser publishers were also, and he was fortunate to place *Dr. Faustus* with the firm of W. Simpkin & R. Marshall, who promised to publish the book in April[3] but wisely—as it turned out—said they would pay nothing until the following September.

Winter softened into spring as George hawked his Ab Gwilym and his *Romantic Ballads* round London. The publica-tion of the *Trials* in March merely jerked him back into the

[1] John Murray II (1778–1843).

[2] Really fifteen years after: Murray published *The Zincali: or the Gypsies of Spain* in 2 vols., April, 1841.

[3] *Faustus: His Life, Death, and Descent into Hell.*

depths, for it reminded him of the flattering notices about his
translated poems which had appeared in the *Monthly Magazine*
before his break with Phillips.

In the issue of 1 September, 1824, an announcement had
read:

"We have heard and seen much of the Legends and
Popular Superstitions of the North, but in truth, all the
exhibitions of these subjects which have hitherto appeared
in English, have been translations from the German. Mr.
OLAUS BORROW, who is familiar with the Northern
Languages, proposes to present these curious reliques of
romantic antiquity directly from the Danish and Swedish;
and two elegant volumes of them, now printing, will appear
in September."

On 1 December more gracious praise was given:

"We have to acknowledge the favour of a beautiful
Collection of Danish Songs and Ballads, of which a specimen
will be seen among the poetical articles of the present month
(p. 432). One or more of these very interesting translations
will appear in each succeeding number."

Thanks to George's unfortunate remark about Phillips's
book all contracts were hastily cancelled, and only one other
poem was published in the March 1825 issue. This was *The
Deceived Merman*, an exceedingly poor version of a Danish
ballad later made famous by Matthew Arnold as *The Forsaken
Merman*.

George's failure to interest any publisher in his *Romantic
Ballads* caused him to pin his faith on *Dr. Faustus*, to which he
wrote an eloquent preface saying that "although scenes of
vice and crime are here exhibited, it is merely in the hope
that they may serve as beacons, to guide the ignorant and
unwary from the shoals on which they might otherwise be
wrecked".

The "scenes of crimes and vice", however, scandalized the
public. Norwich Corporation ordered the book to be burnt,

and were highly indignant at the description it contained of the people of Frankfort:

> "They found the people of the place modelled after so unsightly a pattern, with such ugly faces and flat features, that the devil owned he had never seen them equalled, except by the inhabitants of an English town called Norwich, when dressed in their Sunday's best."

Perhaps fortunately for George's future *Dr. Faustus* had low sales and few reviews, and a paragraph in the *Literary Gazette* led the reading public to shun it[1]:

> "This is another work to which no respectable publisher ought to have allowed his name to be put. The political allusion and metaphysics, which may have made it popular among a low class in Germany, do not sufficiently season its lewd scenes and coarse descriptions for British palates. We have occasionally publications for the fireside—this is only fit for the fire. . . ."

The condemnation heaped on the book in which he so fiercely believed was the last straw to George Borrow. Despondent and hungry—for he had but a handful of silver left—he wandered about London, hating the city a little more each day. He avoided Arden and other friends, but paid many visits to the old apple-woman. The vagabond in him itched for the open country; but how was he to reach it? He could not write home for money since his mother had little enough for herself. He had quarrelled with Phillips and antagonized other publishers by his arrogant assertion of genius. Even his Armenian friend, who had begged him to translate a book, had disappointed him by taking his advice at the worst possible moment and removing himself and his fortune to Armenia.

On a bright May day [2] George drifted disconsolately to the Southwark side of London Bridge, his mind full of wild,

---

[1] The readers of 1825 were a douce and decorous lot, very different from the readers of the twentieth century.

[2] Probably 12 May, which was the date of Blackheath Annual Fair.

impossible plans. Vaguely, without any sense of direction, he walked on until he came to Greenwich, where the old wounded sailors were taking the air outside the Hospital, "once the favourite abode of Queen Elizabeth, the refuge which a grateful country had allotted to them. Here they can rest their weary bodies; at their ease talk over the actions in which they have been injured; and, with the tear of enthusiasm flowing from their eyes, boast how they have trod the decks of fame with Rodney, or Nelson . . ."

George turned to the right and climbed the hill to Blackheath, where he found a great fair in progress and was asked by one of the "thimble and pea" tricksters to act as his "bonnet" or cover-man should any lordling complain he had been cheated when the thimble was lifted from the table to disclose a pea instead of a golden sovereign. Forty to fifty shillings a week were the wages offered—very tempting to one whose total wealth was down to eighteenpence—but one example of the trickster's methods was enough for George, who strode on across the heath until he came upon several men sitting drinking from a cask.

"Here he comes!" cried one, and as the startled George looked up he saw Jasper Petulengro coming towards him, a mug of ale in his hand and a song on his lips.

> Here the Gypsy gemman see,
> With his Roman jib and his rome and dree—
> Rome and dree, rum and dry
> Rally round the Rommany Rye."

Jasper, the blood brother, the friend who never failed! The tears sprang to George's eyes as he took the gypsy's sinewy hand.

"Sit down, brother, and take a cup of good ale. *Aukko tu pios adrey Rommanis*—here is your health in Romany, brother."

"Your health in Romany, brother," echoed Tawno Chikno.

"The Romany Rye. . . . The Gypsy gentleman!" cried the others.

As casually as if they had parted only yesterday Jasper began to talk, boasting of his fights in the ring which had brought him £50; but as he spoke his bright black eyes flickered over George, noting his miserable appearance. "How much money have you got in your pocket, brother?" he asked suddenly.

George told him, adding defensively that he had been "writing lils in the Big City".

This interested the gypsies, and Jasper said jestingly he might write about them.

"Not he," sighed Tawno, "he'll have quite enough to do in writing his own lils, and telling the world how handsome and clever he was; and who can blame him? Not I. If I could write lils, every word should be about myself and my own tacho Rommanis—my own lawful wedded wife, which is the same thing. I tell you what, brother, I once heard a wise man say in Brummagem, that 'there is nothing like blowing one's own horn', which I conceive to be much the same thing as writing one's own lil."

But presently Jasper drew George to one side and suggested they should walk together. For the first time in their friendship George felt hurt—why had Jasper shown him up by asking how much money he had? Was it just that he might boast of his own winnings?

"What is the use of having money unless you let people know you have it?" said Jasper softly. "It is not everyone who can read faces, brother; and unless you knew I had money, how could you ask me to lend you any?"

"I am not going to ask you to lend me any."

"Then you may have it without asking."

George's anger left him. Who but Jasper would thrust £50 into his hand without a thought of repayment? He refused, however, to accept any money at all. He would either starve in the Boro Foros (Big City) or somehow earn sufficient to take to the woods and fields.

"Come with us," coaxed Jasper. "We shall stay on t'other side of the hill for a fortnight, and as you are fond of lil writing, you can write the lil of him whose dook gallops down that hill every night, even as the living man was wont to do long ago. Jemmy Abershaw, one of those whom we call Boro-drom-engroes, and the gorgios highwaymen. I once heard a rye say that the life of that man would fetch much money; so come to the other side of the hill, and write the lil in the tent of Jasper and his wife Pakomovna."

George hesitated. Every bone in him ached to go with Jasper, to live as he lived, lawless, unafraid, eternally on the move. Pride alone stopped him. The gypsies liked him certainly —but they liked him as a young gentleman with a proper home, not as a beggar with eighteenpence in his pocket. He gave no reason, simply thanked Jasper, wrung his hand and turned back towards London, the words of the gypsy drinking song jigging in his brain.

> Here the Gypsy gemman see,
> With his Roman jib and his rome and dree . . .

London, he thought, I must get out of London—and suddenly, from a bookshop window, a card stared out at him. "A NOVEL OR TALE IS MUCH WANTED", it read.

VI

According to *Lavengro* George Borrow wrote this "much wanted" novel in ten days and called it *The Life and Adventures of Joseph Sell, the Great Traveller*. He had paper, ink, pens and candles in his rooms; he expended his eighteenpence on bread, which he washed down with water; he wrote like one possessed. On the tenth day he marched triumphantly to the bookshop (which, he says, had previously refused the Ab Gwilym translations), slammed his manuscript on the counter, and marched home again with £20. An improbable, yet not impossible, story. Many other authors have achieved similar feats under the spur of necessity—and they had not the immediate and exhilarating memory of Jasper Petulengro to aid them.

George Borrow did not realize that years after his death various learned and literary gentlemen were to quarrel violently over *Joseph Sell* and spend a deal of time and energy trying to

I

track down this elusive adventurer. Their search was vain; not even the popular fiction collections of the day such as *The Literary Magnet, The Phantasmagoria, or Sketches of Life and Literature, Watts' Literary Souvenir, The Forget Me Not, The Amulet,* or *Tales of the Wild and Wonderful* yielded a clue. Theories were then produced in abundance—one gentleman even going so far as to say that "in Norfolk, as elsewhere, a 'sell' is a word in current slang used for an impostor or a cheat, and doubtless Borrow meant to make merry with the credulous"; while the devoted Dr. Knapp trotted out so many dates and so many vindications of his hero that the brain reels when studying them.

Exactly why all this stir and fret arose over *Joseph Sell* is puzzling, because anybody who has read and loved Borrow's works is fully aware of the vagaries in which he liked to cloak the truth. The fact remains that the episode of *Joseph Sell* and the seven years following it have been more argued about and written up than any other period in Borrow's life; and the extraordinary thing is that the writers—who freely admit his exaggerations, his games with time, his occasional puckish desire to mislead—forget their mutual hatreds over *Sell* in a chorus of belief concerning the remaining forty-five chapters of *Lavengro* and the whole forty-seven chapters of *The Romany Rye*. They insist that the wanderings described in these chapters all took place between May and September 1825, *because Borrow said so*; they further insist that the seven years between the autumn of 1825 and his first interview with the British and Foreign Bible Society towards the close of 1832 are shrouded in mystery, because Borrow alluded to them as *"the veiled period"* in his life.

There is no evidence that Borrow wrote *The Life and Adventures of Joseph Sell*; but then there is no evidence that he did not. The title means nothing—his books prove that he made a habit of changing titles and proper names. The devotee of Ab Gwilym would scarcely feel proud of a piece of writing churned out in a handful of days and might well have published it under a pseudonym. All that is known is that Borrow was in desperate financial straits in the beginning of May yet was able, on or about 22 May, to pay his Millman Street landlady in full, dispatch a trunk containing his books, papers and most of his clothes to Norwich, and leave London for Amesbury in Wiltshire with a certain amount of money in his pocket. The inference is that he wrote *something* which brought him in several pounds.

Again, the fact that Borrow dates all his adventures in the remaining chapters of *Lavengro* and the whole of *The Romany Rye* May to September 1825, does not by any means prove that they were packed into those few months. We know from other incidents which are supported by outside evidence that the creative part of his mind, which loved a good story, thought nothing of ante- or post-dating events by so much as a decade. (Had he been born in a later age he would have been an adept at jig-saw puzzles.) We also know that by the time he settled down to write *Lavengro* and *The Romany Rye* he was a figure romanticized in the public eye by his *Bible in Spain*, a figure—dare it be said?—strangely reminiscent of the sombreroed, cloaked silhouette advertising *Sandeman's* port which has dominated London's Underground stations for so long.

No man so innately romantic as Borrow could be expected to resist the temptation to keep such splendid guise, to hint at some sad mystery behind it. He truthfully described his parentage, childhood, youth and early struggles in authorship in fifty-eight chapters of *Lavengro*. Who shall blame him if he deliberately telescoped the events of the next seven years in an effort to hide the unpalatable truth that he failed to make a living until 1833?

The present writer does not pretend to the scholarly knowledge possessed by Borrow's earnest biographers. After the study of Borrow's life and works and the reading of those same biographies she ventures, timidly, to put forward yet another theory.

Borrow's *The Zincali: or The Gypsies of Spain* was published by John Murray in two volumes on 17 April, 1841. Seven hundred and fifty copies were printed, and it is doubtful whether they were all sold. On 10 December, 1842, Mr. Murray published *The Bible in Spain* in three volumes, the first edition being a thousand copies. This book had such a success that it ran into seven editions during the year 1843 and carried two further editions of *The Gypsies of Spain* "on its back".[1]

With pardonable swagger—after all, the man had genius— Borrow had scattered through both these books references to supposed earlier travels. He was, he said, familiar with "the principal capitals of the world", including Paris, Constantinople, Shiraz, and Havana. He had, during the so-called "veiled" years, travelled not only Europe but "India and China to the frontiers of Tartary". Having sampled life in Hungary and Turkey he had moved on to his meetings with Baron Taylor in such different places as Bayonne, Seville, Niznhi-Novgorod, Stamboul, and "in the brilliantly lighted hall, or in the desert amongst Bedouin *kháimehs*". In the wilds of Jutland he had "heard the ballad of Alonso Perez de Guzman chanted in Danish by a rustic". He had "lived much among the Hebrew race, and was well versed in their ways and phraseology; lived in habits of intimacy with Gypsies in various and distant lands; and seen the legitimate children of most countries of the world".

It was but natural that those entranced by Borrow's very real adventures in Spain and Portugal should have believed his references to earlier journeys to be equally true—and any doubting Thomases were speedily convinced by Lieut.-Colonel Elers Napier's account of his talks with Borrow in the *patio* of *La Reina* in Seville and in the ruined *Itálica*[2]:

"The 'Unknown' " (he wrote) "was rather startled when I replied in Hindee, but was delighted on finding I was an Indian, and entered freely, and with depth and acuteness, on the affairs of the East, most of which part of the world he had visited."

The Colonel was even further impressed by the knowledge of Romany displayed by Borrow when they met some gypsies:

" 'Where in the name of goodness did you pick up your acquaintance and the language of these extraordinary

---

[1] *See* Bibliography at end of book.
[2] *Excursions Along the Shores of the Mediterranean*, published, 1842.

people?' 'Some years ago in Moultan,' he replied. . . .
But the 'Unknown' had already said more than he perhaps
wished on the subject. He dryly replied that he had more
than once owed his life to Gypsies, and had reason to know
them well; but this was said in a tone which precluded all
further queries on my part. The subject was never again
broached, and we returned to the *fonda*."

There was also the ecstatic, if misguided, review of *The
Bible in Spain* in the February 1843 number of *Tait's Edinburgh
Magazine*:

"We find Mr. Borrow in Paris, a spectator of, if not an
actor in, the Revolution of the Barricades (July 1830); in
the Peninsula, in Norway, in Russia, among the Bohemians,
the Tartars, the Turks—everywhere, and last of all in
Barbary—a kind of Wandering Jew!"

To do Borrow justice his original intention was to write
Lavengro as strict autobiography—he said so many times in
letters to Mr. John Murray and it was advertised as such in
Murray's advance notices. But even as he was working on the
first volume he was acclaimed as the far travelled hero of
The Bible in Spain, and it was at this point that he began to
talk about "the veiled period" in his life, to say that nothing
would induce him to reveal his experiences between 1826 and
1833.

Richard Ford, Mr. Murray's literary adviser at the time,
did his best to persuade him otherwise, as may be seen from
these extracts from his letters.

February, 1844.

"I have often thought of the eight years over which you
propose to drop a curtain. This is worth reconsideration.
No doubt it will excite a mysterious interest, but then it is
open to any construction that the *necios y tontos* (stupid
people) may put on it. I should be inclined to give some
incidents of the interval and not stall a curtain over so long
a period. I am inclined to think that it must be too curious
to be lost to mankind."

December, 1844.

"I shall be most curious to hear you tell your own story of your recent adventures (Borrow had been to the Levant); but first let us lift up the curtain over those seven years."

March, 1845.

"I rejoice to hear that *Lavengro* progresses. *Paso á paso se va léjos.* (Step by step you can go a long way.) Lift up the hem of the curtain over those said seven years."

Borrow remained adamant. What is more he crossed out the word "autobiography", and when *Lavengro* was at last published in 1851 he began his preface: "I have endeavoured to describe a dream . . ." *The Romany Rye*, published in 1857, was described merely as a sequel to *Lavengro*, and ended at Horncastle Fair in August 1825, after which Borrow wrote as a final sentence; "I shouldn't wonder if Mr. Petulengro and Tawno Chikno came originally from India. I think I'll go there."

Did he really go to India, to all those other places mentioned so casually in *The Bible in Spain*?

One cannot believe that he did. Quite apart from the fact that there is no record of any passport being issued to him before 1833 the so-called "veiled period" has such a number of large holes in it that any idea of prolonged travel is ruled out; while the information which has been garnered from the correspondence of his family and friends is curiously void of any reference to journeyings abroad.

The writer is convinced that George Borrow was in England from 1825 to 1833 and that his reason for refusing to discuss this was a very simple one—he did not wish to "lose face" with his public. (In their different ways most authors have a similar dislike of doing so.) Besides—and one feels this bit deep with Borrow—any full account of those years would reveal the glaring fact that he was, in the material sense, a dead failure until he was almost thirty. The lapses of time which cannot be accounted for were, the writer is sure, spent in some of the wanderings described in the later part of *Lavengro* and in *The Romany Rye*; and it is more than likely that he had at least a nodding acquaintance with casual wards and prisons during his vagabondage.

By September 1825 Borrow was back in Norwich, for about the middle of that month he wrote to W. Simpkin & R. Marshall saying that as their bill would become due for payment in a few days he would be willing to take thirty copies of *Dr. Faustus* in lieu of the money. "The book has been *burnt* in both libraries here," he added, "and, as it has been talked about, I may, perhaps, be able to dispose of some copies in the course of a year or two."

At this time he had some money. During his summer wanderings, so he recounts in *The Romany Rye*, Jasper Petulengro had slipped a leather purse containing fifty guineas into his pocket by sleight of hand and beseeched him to buy a horse with it, explaining that he could sell the animal again at a horse fair for a handsome sum, repay the original price and keep the profit. When George demurred, Jasper said the deal was to protect himself, since if a gypsy offered such a horse to a dealer the man would immediately accuse him of having stolen it. George, therefore, bought the horse and sold it several weeks later, probably at Horncastle Fair, for a considerably larger sum. That this transaction took place seems proved by Jasper's words when he visited his old friend at Oulton Broad in 1842:

"I suppose you have not forgotten how, fifteen years ago, when you made horse-shoes in the little dingle by the side of the Great North Road, I lent you fifty cottors (guineas) to purchase the wonderful trotting cob of the inn-keeper with the green Newmarket coat, which three days after you sold for two hundred?"

If Petulengro was right in his dates, however, the horse was bought in 1827, and the money George certainly possessed two years earlier must have come from another source, possibly from his smithying in Mumper's Dingle. Anyway, he decided that he could afford to stay for a while with his mother and brother and at last achieve his cherished ambition to publish his *Romantic Ballads*. Simon Wilkin, a Norwich publisher, agreed to issue five hundred copies if the author could guarantee the production costs, and Allan Cunningham, the Scots poet

—whom Borrow had met while in London—wrote as preface some verses beginning:

> Sing, sing, my friend, breathe life again
> Through Norway's song and Denmark's strain.

In a fever of excitement George dashed round collecting subscribers and it says much for the kindness of Norwich citizens towards the man who had ridiculed them in *Dr. Faustus* that the list rose to two hundred and included, besides that of the Bishop, Dr. Bathurst, many well-known names such as Gurney, Gurdon, Harvey, Rackham, Hare, and Woodhouse. Each subscription was for ten and sixpence and George gleefully announced that the total "amply paid all expenses". The book was published in the spring of 1826, three hundred copies being sent to John Taylor, a London publisher who added his imprint and said he would sell them off at seven shillings.

Cunningham wrote a letter of glowing praise when he received his advance copy. "You cannot imagine," he said, "how much these ballads have stirred me up, 'Like fire to heather set'; and though I think so well of myself as to believe that all the rest of mankind will not feel so warmly as I do, if they feel but half your fortune is made." He went on to give George wise and detailed advice as to the necessity of distributing complimentary and review copies and added, "Walter Scott must not be forgotten. All this is expensive, but . . . if you wish to thrive, you must e'en do it. Write to Taylor and make your own arrangements. I told him he might look for a communication from you."

Unfortunately George, exhilarated by sight of his beloved poems in print, entirely ignored his friend's kindly words. He never wrote to Taylor; he sent out no copies for review. He *may* have sent one to Sir Walter Scott and received no acknowledgment, because it was about this time that he developed his life-long animosity towards that great man. The poems, which scarcely deserved Cunningham's eulogy, won no recognition and the three hundred copies mouldered on booksellers' shelves.

Characteristically, George blamed everybody except himself

for this catastrophe. In a fine fury with Scott, the book trade, and the muddle-headed British public he accepted the invitation of Haydon to sit for a figure in some "heroic painting" he was at work on, and left Norwich for London, taking rooms in 26 Bryanston Street, Portman Square, from which address he wrote to Haydon:

"I should feel extremely obliged if you would allow me to sit to you as soon as possible. I am going to the South of France in little better than a fortnight, and I would sooner lose a thousand pounds than not have the honour of appearing in the picture."

This note, preserved in Haydon's correspondence, was the foundation of several legends concerning Borrow's travels in France and Spain and led to the idea (since disproved) that he was a Foreign Correspondent to the *Morning Herald*; but there is no evidence whatever that George ever left England's shores that summer of 1826. He was, we know, determined to win fame and fortune through his translations, and in the Borrow Museum, Norwich, are innumerable papers bearing proof of his industry in this direction during the "veiled period". He also spent a great deal of time hammering at publishers to take the results of his work and was forced, by his lack of success, to undertake a great deal of ill-paid hack work.

How long Borrow stayed in Bryanston Street is not known; but the failure of the *Romantic Ballads*, the disinterest of publishers in his projects, and the departure of his brother John to a job in the *Real del Monte Company* in Mexico, combined to bring about a return of his melancholy. He still had a little money; he may have made a little more—what more likely than that he again took to the roads of England and sought solace in the company of Jasper Petulengro and the mysterious Isopel Berners?

But *The Romany Rye*'s adventures with these strange folk and many others too are told further on in this book. In this chapter the writer is concerned only with cold—very cold—fact.

Early in 1827 George Borrow was back in Norwich and stayed there for practically a year, judging by letters which passed between his mother and brother—the burden of their song was, "Poor George, he has no luck. He works hard and remains poor!" Idleness was the last fault of which he could be accused. Not only did he undertake many a hack job he would fain have forgotten in later years, but he set himself to the study of yet more languages, pathetic remnants of his methods remaining to this day. For George, as has been said before, was no philologist. He had a remarkable ear aided by a phenomenal memory, which allowed him to pick up a tongue quickly when it was spoken to him by a native; when he studied it through grammars he had to resort to a laborious copying-out of easy words in two columns, the first being in English, the second in whatever language he happened to be studying. From these parallel columns—and how infinitely painstaking the process must have been—he progressed by slow degrees to a working knowledge which enabled him to read and speak, albeit carelessly, whatever speech was dearest to him at the time.

Like a flame in his heart was his absolute conviction that through translation success would come; yet every so often, when "the horrors" came to gnaw and bite at him, he realized the falseness of that conviction and fled to his second man, who found all comfort in living as "the people out of Egypt" did. And again the scholar, the first man within him, recoiled from gypsy vagabondage and panted after academic recognition.

There was the young George Borrow of "the veiled period". A being haunted by the heritage and upbringing that warred within him; a creature who fought continually not only against his dual personality but against the "shadowy third" that most unaccountably held possession of his soul.

The "shadowy third" had a name, although he did not know it—genius.

VII

Norwich—London—the open road; they formed a triangle along the lines of which George Borrow sped repeatedly and in vain, seeking always the fulfilment of his dreams. No wonder that afterwards he wished to forget that empty odyssey; no wonder that during it he steeped himself in the *Memoirs of Vidocq*[1], that enchanting gentleman who was principal agent of the French Police until 1827 and then, incongruously, proprietor of a paper-mill at St. Mandé.

In 1829 a new star of hope beamed bright on Borrow's horizon. It will be remembered that while he was still a lad "godless Billy" had introduced him to Dr. John Bowring, who had made a great impression on him. . . .

> (He was then) "an individual, apparently somewhat under thirty, of middle stature, a thin and weaselly figure, a certain obliquity of vision, and a large pair of spectacles. This person, who had lately come from abroad, and had published a volume of translations, had attracted some slight notice in the literary world, and was looked upon as a kind of lion in a small provincial capital. After dinner he argued a great deal, spoke vehemently against the Church, and uttered the most desperate Radicalism that was perhaps ever heard, saying, he hoped that in a short time there would not be a king or queen in Europe, and inveighing bitterly against the English aristocracy, and against the Duke of Wellington in particular, whom he said, if he himself was ever president of an English republic—an event which he seemed to think by no means improbable—he would hang for certain infamous acts of profligacy and bloodshed which he had perpetrated in Spain. Being informed that the writer was something of a philologist, to which character the individual in question laid great pretensions, he came and sat down by him, and talked about languages and literature. The writer, who was only a boy, was a little frightened at first."[2]

John Bowring's dazzling memory had remained with George Borrow, and when, in 1827 and 1828, his *Ancient Poetry and*

[1] The English translation of these *Memoirs* was published in 4 vols., by Whittaker, Treacher & Arnot, London 1828–9, and was often, and erroneously, attributed to George Borrow.

[2] *The Romany Rye*, Appendix, Chap. XI, written more than thirty years after the meeting it describes. In the interim Borrow had quarrelled violently with Bowring, hence the acid tinge to the wording.

Romances of Spain and *Servian Popular Poetry* appeared, the idea came to his admirer—Ah, here is the collaborator for whom I have waited so long, a man who shares my enthusiasm for the old bards of different countries, a man whose passion for translation equals my own!

Up to a point George was right. Bowring was a great linguist, an ardent worshipper at the shrines of ancient poets who mirrored the history of their people in song, and he had in him a touch of the lawless vagabond. Beyond that point, however, George was wrong. Even nearer to Bowring's heart than song or legend were politics, national or international, and he put translation into what must be confessed was probably its right place—a secondary one. Indeed, being something of an opportunist, he went farther and used translation simply as a means to an end.

A curious, immensely gifted and energetic man, this John Bowring. Born in Exeter, where his father was a highly respected citizen, he, like George, learnt his French from a refugee priest. Unlike George he was able, through parental indulgence to what was regarded as a potential asset, to learn other languages thoroughly under able masters. A position was found for him in a London mercantile house for which, from 1811 onwards, he travelled extensively in Spain, eastern Europe and Russia. His Liberalism led to his imprisonment in Calais in 1822, when he was arrested by the French on a charge of inciting the Liberal element in that country against the Bourbon Government; and he won considerable *réclame* through Canning's prompt action in obtaining his release. On his return to England he gave up commerce in favour of literature and helped Jeremy Bentham start the *Westminster Review* in 1824, afterwards obtaining the Governmental job he had long set his heart on in his joint appointment with Mr. Villiers[1] as "a commission to investigate the commercial relations between England and France".[2]

In 1829 Bowring visited Denmark in order, so he said, to *Scandinavianise*. A Press report announcing that he was again

---

[1] Afterwards Earl of Clarendon, the Ambassador to Spain who greatly helped George Borrow.

[2] *Autobiographical Recollections of Sir John Bowring*, London, 1877.

in London after this exploration of Danish literature sent
Borrow's spirits soaring skywards—why not enlist the aid
of this mighty one on the side of his cherished but universally
neglected project, the publication of his translation of the
Kiempe Viser?

The years in the wilderness had left their mark. The Borrow
of 1824 would have demanded superbly that Dr. Bowring
should see the beauty of his favourite work: the Borrow of
1829 trailed a humble red herring before his real request. . . .

> "17, Great Russell Street, Bloomsbury,
> *December* 6th, 1829.
>
> "MY DEAR SIR,—Lest I should intrude upon you when
> you are busy, I write to inquire when you will be unoccupied.
> I wish to shew you my translation of the *Death of Balder*,
> Ewald's most celebrated production,[1] which, if you approve
> of, you will perhaps render me some assistance in bringing
> it forth, for I don't know many publishers. I think this will
> be a proper time to introduce it to the British public, as
> your account of Danish literature will doubtless cause a
> sensation. My friend Mr. R. Taylor[2] has my *Kiempe Viser*,
> which he has read and approved of; but he is so very deeply
> occupied, that I am apprehensive he neglects them; but I
> am unwilling to take them out of his hands, lest I offend
> him. Your letting me know when I may call will greatly
> oblige,—Dear Sir, your most obedient servant,
>
> GEORGE BORROW."

This naïve epistle brought a prompt invitation from
Bowring to call upon him, and at the meeting he suggested
it might be possible to collaborate in a Danish Anthology.
The ecstatic George scurried homewards to set down details
of a work which, had it ever been printed, would have been
of colossal size. There were to be four volumes: the heroic
and supernatural songs from the *Kiempe Viser* with copious
notes; the historical and romantic ballads, also from the
Kiempe Viser; modern Danish poetry; and lastly a volume
principally devoted to translations from Ölenschlæger.

[1] Published after Borrow's death, by Jarrold & Son, Norwich, 1889.
[2] Richard Taylor, Red Lion Court, Fleet Street.

George then began to bombard Bowring with visits and letters, explaining that the first volume was already complete, and that he would work like a galley-slave to produce the remaining three. Doubtless this rather shocked Bowring, who had never intended such a mighty project, and certainly never envisaged all the actual translation being done by Borrow alone. He said plainly and firmly that two volumes were quite sufficient, and entered into negotiations with Mr. Richard Taylor, who printed the following prospectus in January 1830:

It is proposed to publish, in Two Volumes Octavo
Price to Subscribers £1 : 1 : 0., to Non-Subscribers £1 : 4 : 0.

THE SONGS OF SCANDINAVIA
translated by
Dr. Bowring and Mr. Borrow.

Dedicated to the King of Denmark, by kind permission of His Majesty.

The First Volume will contain about One Hundred Specimens of the Ancient Popular Ballads of North-Western Europe, arranged under the heads of Heroic, Supernatural, Historical, and Domestic Poems.

The Second Volume will represent the Modern School of Danish Poetry, from the time of Tullin, giving the most remarkable lyrical productions of Ewald, Ölenschlæger, Baggesen, Ingemann, and many others.

Whether the subscribers did not materialize, or whether the failure of a Gibraltar firm in which Bowring had an interest caused him to withdraw any financial support is not known, but the two volumes never appeared. Much later—as may be found in *The Romany Rye*—Borrow abused Bowring and accused him of all manner of chicanery: at the time he flew to him for help over various other projects. Would Bowring speak to some editor and ask if he would commission an article on Welsh poetry? Would Bowring use his influence with the British Museum and induce the authorities to allow

him to transcribe the Exeter Manuscript in Anglo-Saxon?
Would Bowring get him a job actually in the Museum?

Bowring was a kindly man and did all he could, although
his efforts proved fruitless. One can imagine, however, that
his patience wore a trifle thin as George's requests grew more
urgent and extravagant. It was one thing to persuade a Mr.
Gruntvig that Borrow would be an excellent translator of
his Norman-Saxon manuscript: it was quite another to
recommend him to Royalty, as was asked in this long and
somewhat wild letter . . .

> "7, Museum Street,
> Friday Evening,
> *May* 21, 1830.

MY DEAR SIR,—As at present no doubt seems to be
entertained of Prince Leopold's accepting the sovereignty
of Greece, would you have any objection to write to him
concerning me? I should be very happy to go to Greece in
his service. I do not wish to go in in a civil or domestic
capacity, and I have, moreover, no doubt that all such
situations have been long since filled up; I wish to go in a
military one, for which I am qualified by birth and early
habits. You might inform the Prince that I have been for
years on the Commander-in-Chief's List for a commission,
but that I have not had sufficient interest to procure an
appointment. One of my reasons for wishing to reside in
Greece is, that the mines of Eastern Literature would be
acceptable to me. I should soon become an adept in Turkish,
and would weave and transmit to you such an anthology
as would gladden your very heart. . . . I hope this letter
will not displease you. I do not write it from *flightiness*,
but from thoughtfulness. I am uneasy to find myself at
four and twenty drifting on the sea of the world, and likely
to do so.—Yours most sincerely,

> G. BORROW."

Needless to say, no military commission in Greece was
forthcoming, but George returned to the attack in the middle
of September, saying that he was very unwell and adding:

"My complaints are, I believe, the offspring of ennui and unsettled prospects. I have thought of attempting to get into the French service, as I should like prodigiously to serve under Clausel in the next Bedouin campaign."

And a year later he wrote from Norwich at enormous length setting forth an astonishing list of claims he wished Bowring to place before the Secretary at War.

"You might say when you recommend me that, being well grounded in Arabic, I might be an acquisition to a corps in one of our Eastern colonies. I flatter myself that I could do a great deal in the East . . . There is much talk at present about translating European books into the two great languages, the Arabic and the Persian. Now I believe that with my enthusiasm for those tongues I could, if resident in the East, become in a year or two better acquainted with them than any European has been yet, and more capable of executing such a task . . ."

One can hardly blame John Bowring for giving up answering George's letters and turning his attention to politics! Like many other men possessing an element of greatness, the temperamental George was, at times, an intolerable nuisance to his friends.

VIII

George returned to Norwich an embittered and despondent man. Despite the lyric praise of Cunningham he nursed in his heart—"Get out of bed, George Borrow, and be sick or sleepy no longer. A fellow who can give us such exquisite Danish Ballads has no right to repose"; despite the tremendous amount of time and energy he had expended over *The Songs of Scandinavia*, the cruel world had once more pricked the rosy bubble of his dreams. There was nothing for it but to go on drifting, to help his mother with the household chores, to sit in the cobwebby Guildhall library laboriously learning more languages that, in all probability, he would never use, to receive admonitory letters from John and write humble ones back.

It was a dreary existence coloured only by occasional successes with newspaper articles and an acrimonious, long drawn out correspondence with the Army Pay Office regarding some back-pay of his brother's which had been stopped on orders from Colonel Lord Orford when John went to Mexico. The sum amounted to about a hundred pounds, but it might well have been a hundred thousand so vigorously and tenaciously did George fight to win it. When he was at last successful, in the autumn of 1832, he showed remarkable forbearance when John sent a surly acknowledgment: "I am glad you got the half-pay . . . You never tell me what you are doing; *you can't be living on nothing*."

The truth was that George had suddenly developed "prospects"—such miraculous ones that he could scarcely believe his good fortune. In some way he had made the acquaintance of the Rev. Francis Cunningham of Lowestoft, who greatly admired his linguistic ability and who determined that the British and Foreign Bible Society—for which he had founded a Paris branch—should avail themselves of Borrow's services without delay. As well as addressing an urgent appeal to the Society himself, he enlisted the aid of his brother-in-law, that same Joseph Gurney who had long ago reproved George for allowing fish to gasp to death on the river bank at Earlham. Gurney, famous as leader of the Society of Friends, had great influence with the Bible Society, and their Secretary replied to his letter saying that they were on the lookout for just such a young man as Mr. Borrow and would he please come to an interview in London in December.

To George this news was wonderful indeed. True, in his youth he had been a professed atheist, but since then he had passed through a fiery crucible and was genuinely ready to swear complete allegiance to the Bible Society's ideals. He was, perhaps, ready to swear to any ideals if the swearing would introduce him to the travel for which he longed. Mr. Shorter puts the matter aptly and deliciously:

"Verily I believe that it would have been the same had it been a society for the propagation of the writings of Defoe among the Persians. With what zest would Borrow have

J

undertaken to translate *Moll of Flanders* and *Captain Singleton* into the languages of Hafiz and Omar! But the Bible Society was ready to his hand, and Borrow did nothing by halves. A good hater and a staunch friend, he was loyal to the Bible Society in no half-hearted way, and not the most pronounced quarrel with forces obviously quite out of tune with his nature led to any real slackening of that loyalty. In the end a portion of his property went to swell the Bible Society's funds."[1]

There was an added reason behind George's exaltation. During the summer of 1832 he had paid frequent visits to Oulton Hall, owned by a family called Skepper, and had grown deeply attached to a widowed daughter of the house, Mary Clarke, who had lived with her parents since the death of her husband, a Naval Officer, within a few months of their marriage. Nine years older than Borrow, Mary Clarke was a serious minded young woman and a devout Church worker— indeed, it is pretty certain that it was she who introduced George to Francis Cunningham. She was attracted by George's quick bright mind and fine physical presence, while he was strangely touched by her interest in his career. Apart from his mother and Isopel Berners, whose real relationship to him he always wrapped in mystery, Mary Clarke was the only woman who had ever offered him companionship: in return he vowed to justify her faith in his abilities.

December came, bringing with it the sad knowledge that he did not even possess the coach fare to London. Another man would have borrowed the money from his mother or a friend; but not George. Without a word to anyone about his deplorably impecunious state, he *set out to walk to London*, accomplishing the journey of one hundred and twelve miles in twenty-seven hours! His total expenses were fivepence halfpenny—a pint of ale, a half-pint of milk, a roll of bread and two apples.[2] And as he strode along he sang the song of *Svend Vonved*. He was not just a young man going to keep an important interview: he was a crusader in search of the Holy Grail.

1 *George Borrow and his Circle.*
2 *See* MS. Autobiography; also *Memoirs of Caroline Fox*; Ritchie's *East Anglia*; and Rev. Wentworth Webster in *Journal of Gypsy Lore Society.*

CHAPTER FOUR

"OH! THE BLOOD GLOWS IN HIS VEINS!"
(The Romany Rye, Appendix, Chap. II).

(1832–1835)

I

THE British and Foreign Bible Society was founded in 1804, its object being to "circulate the authorized version of the Bible without note or comment", and its committee including William Wilberforce, Zachary Macaulay and Granville Sharp. Their laudable purpose did not exactly please the official printing firms from whom they bought sheets[1] since all finished copies of the Society's Bibles bore the ominous words "Sold under cost price". The original idea of selling Bibles printed only in English was quickly abandoned. Nuremberg was the first Continental centre to be established, several others followed, and in 1812 an eager emissary, John Paterson of Glasgow, struggled his way to Moscow while Napoleon's armies were sweeping into Russia. One of the last Europeans "to behold the old Tartar wall and high brick towers"[2] so soon to be engulfed in the flames, he went north to St. Petersburg where—with typical Scots tenacity—he presented a plan for a St. Petersburg Bible Society office to Prince Galitzin even as the Tsar was hastening to join his armies and Moscow was burning.

The plan included a memorial to the Tsar for his gracious interest in the Society's work, and Canton relates that

"The plan and memorial were examined by the Czar on the 18th (of December); with a stroke of his pen he gave his sanction—'So be it, Alexander'; and as he wrote, the

[1] The King's Printers (Holders of a Patent), and the Universities of Oxford and Cambridge (Holders of Licences to print).

[2] *The History of the British and Foreign Bible Society*, William Canton (pub. Murray, 1904–1910).

last tattered remnants of the Grand Army struggled across the ice of the Niemen."[1]

On his triumphant return to St. Petersburg in 1815 the Tsar authorized the Society to translate the Bible into modern Russian. Greatly heartened, the Society cast longing eyes eastwards to Manchuria and China. In 1821 their agent, Dr. Pinkerton, engaged a M. Stepan Vasilievitch Lipoftsov, who belonged to the Asiatic Section of the Russian Foreign Office and had spent twenty years in China, to translate the New Testament into Manchu. By 1822 five hundred and fifty copies of the *Gospel according to St. Matthew* had been printed in St. Petersburg and these, with the exception of a hundred sent to London, were stored with the types in the vaults of the Society's Russian bankers.

In November 1824, however, there occurred the terrible Neva floods—still spoken of with bated breath in the strangely different Leningrad of our day. The finished copies, on silky Chinese paper, were reduced to pulp: the soaked, rusted types lay abandoned in a cellar. But the Society were undeterred. Lipoftsov continued his translation, and by 1826 the whole New Testament in Manchu was complete although the actual printing of it remained in abeyance.

Six years later a missionary called William Swan stopped in Petersburg on his way to his Siberian station, and prowled around the Baron Schilling de Canstadt's famous Chinese Library and Oriental Museum.[2] To his surprise and delight he came across a manuscript of the *Old* Testament translated into Manchu in Pekin. Understandably enough, the scholarly Mr. Swan forgot all about Siberia, sent an urgent message to the Bible Society in London, and sat down there and then to transcribe the manuscript.

Thus it was that in December 1832 the Bible Society were eagerly searching for someone with a working knowledge of Manchu who would supervise the setting-up and printing of

---

[1] *See* Canton's *History of the Bible Society.*

[2] After Schilling's death this superb collection was moved to the Library of the Imperial Academy of Science. So late as 1936 the writer saw several items from it in a Soviet Museum in Leningrad.

both the Old and New Testaments in that language *in St. Petersburg.*

Their quest was no easy one. To begin with few people in England knew Manchu, then the court and diplomatic language of China: to end with those who did would rather have voyaged to the moon than to the savage and fearsome Russian capital. The Committee were on the point of despair when their Secretary, the Rev. Andrew Brandram, received this letter from the Rev. Francis Cunningham:

"MY DEAR FRIEND, — A young farmer in this neighbourhood has introduced me today to a person of whom I have long heard, who appears to me to promise so much that I am induced to offer him to you as a successor to Platt and Greenfield. He is a person without University education, but who has read the Bible in thirteen languages. He is

By kind permission of the British and Foreign Bible Society

The Rev. Andrew Brandram

independent in circumstances, of no very exactly defined denomination of Christians, but I think of certain Christian principle. I shall make more enquiry about him and see him again. Next week I propose to meet him in London, and I could wish that you should see him, and, if you please, take him under your charge for a few days. He is of the middle order in society, and a very produceable person . . ."

The placing of Borrow's scholarship on a par with that of T. Pell Platt, Fellow of Trinity College, Cambridge, who was honorary libriarian to the Society for eight years, and of William Greenfield, a well-known linguist who was head of their editorial department at the time of his death in 1831, shows the profound impression George made on the Rev. Cunningham; though had that worthy divine known of Jasper Petulengro and Mumper's Dingle perhaps he would not have written that charming description, "a very produceable person". Fortunately, he was unaware of gypsy rovings and desperate struggles, and as Andrew Brandram studied the letter he heaved a heartfelt sigh of relief. Here, at last, was the very man the Society wanted!

II

On the 3rd or 4th of January 1833 the Committee of the Society sat in solemn conclave at their Earl Street[1] office. After a deal of argument they were of half a mind to engage the young man they were about to interview as their supervisor in St. Petersburg, despite their interest in a Mr. John Hattersley, who had already translated versions of the Bible into Berber and Arabic.

Presently the candidate was ushered into the room, a very large young man with a foreign habit of gesticulating with his hands. His speech was cultured, his dress neat, but about him there was a something—well, it was difficult to explain, but the only word to describe it was *untamed*. Perhaps the contrast

[1] Afterwards removed to 146 Queen Victoria Street.

between his prematurely white hair and the bright darkness of his eyes had to do with it? The gentlemen at the table shuffled their papers uneasily and began their questioning.

The answers to their routine inquiries were satisfactory enough. Name, George Borrow, Age, twenty-nine. Son of the late Captain Thomas Borrow and his wife Ann Perfrement. A loyal Churchman—judicious probing of his knowledge of Church matters left nothing to be desired. It was his ardent wish to devote his life to the spreading of the Gospel in distant lands.

"And what," asked the Committee, "did Mr. Borrow consider his especial qualifications for such a post?"

George Borrow squared his shoulders. "I am a philologist," he said simply, and lest this statement should be doubted he at once began, with a wealth of gesture and in a deep sonorous voice, to recite translations of the Scriptures in a succession of unknown tongues. Seldom can such a torrent of uncouth speech have shattered the decorum of that Board Room. Under its force the gentlemen sat, stupefied yet fascinated, until the last bell-note quivered into silence.

Finally somone murmured that it was all most interesting, but had Mr. Borrow any—er—other proof of his capabilities as a linguist?

Certainly! With a flourish he drew from his capacious pockets a series of shabby, dog-eared volumes and slapped them on to the table.

The gentlemen peered, blinked, turned them over with fastidious fingers. *Celebrated Trials and Remarkable Cases of Criminal Jurisprudence, from the earliest records to the year,* 1825, *VI vols.; Faustus, His Life, Death and Descent into Hell, translated from the German; Romantic Ballads from the Danish of G. Öhlenschlager, and from the Kiempe Viser, and Miscellaneous Pieces from the Danish of Ewald and Others.*

The gentlemen coughed and wriggled in their chairs. Really—Dr. Faustus and criminal jurisprudence! Hurriedly they suggested that Mr. Borrow should withdraw while they discussed the matter. An hour later they recalled him, having apparently conquered their aversion to Dr. Faustus, and said they wished him to stay in London for a few days at their expense. As the Rev. Joseph Jowett, the editorial secretary, bowed him out, he asked courteously if Mr. Borrow had had a comfortable coach journey from Norwich.

"Oh," said George, "I walked!"

One imagines that there were many conferences and much shaking of heads in the Society's office during the next week. But George came through the preliminary examination in Arabic and other languages with flying colours and about the middle of January returned home by coach with ten pounds for his expenses, instructions to study Manchu, the cautious promise of a permanent post if his progress proved satisfactory, and a crate-load of Manchu dictionaries from the Society's library. Doubtless the shrewd Jowett realized George's impecunious state, for he kindly gave him the proof corrections of a Mexican (*Nahuatl*) translation of St. Luke to do and paid him a fee.

Absorbed though he was in his Manchu studies the ever-eager George sent a copy of this Gospel with an enthusiastic letter to his brother John, which brought forth the damping reply:

"I have just received your letter of the 16th, February, together with your translation (!) of St. Luke. I am glad you have got the job, but I must say that the Bible Society are just throwing away their time . . ."

One feels glad that this characteristic epistle did not arrive until after George had left England.

Nobody except George Borrow, of course, would have tackled a language like Manchu with such superb confidence. Yet on 9 June he wrote triumphantly to Mr. Jowett, "I have mastered Mandchou"; with the result that on 5 July, after a further examination during which he was asked to translate a Manchu hymn into English, he was formally offered the St. Petersburg appointment at a salary of £200 a year and expenses. Mr. Jowett was, however, a trifle disturbed by the swaggering style of George's letters and added a personal postscript:

"Excuse me if, as a clergyman, and your senior in years

though not in talent, I venture, with the kindest of motives, to throw out a hint which may not be without its use. I am sure you will not be offended if I suggest that there is occasionally a tone of confidence in speaking of yourself, which has alarmed some of the excellent members of our Committee. It may have been this feeling, more than once displayed before, which prepared one or two of them to stumble at an expression in your letter of yesterday, in which, till pointed out, I confess I was not struck with anything objectionable, but at which, nevertheless, a humble Christian might not unreasonably take umbrage. It is where you speak of becoming *useful to the Deity, to man, and to yourself.* Doubtless you mean—*the prospect of glorifying God*; but the turn of expression made us think of such passages of Scripture as Job xxi, 2; xxxv, 7 and 8; Psalm xvi, 2 and 3."

Borrow seems wisely to have adapted himself to the phraseology current in Earl Street, for when Mr. Jowett next wrote he said:

"The spirit of your last letter was truly Christian, in harmony with the rule laid down by Christ Himself, and which in one sense He so wonderfully exemplified, that 'He that humbleth himself shall be exalted'."

Now all was flurry and bustle in the little King's Court house. Mrs. Borrow, overjoyed that her ugly duckling had at last turned out a swan, bedewed his garments with happy tears as she washed and ironed them with loving care. George dashed hither and thither returning borrowed books, saying good-bye to friends—did he, we wonder, pay a visit to "godless Billy", and did that mentor's lip curl in a cynical smile when he learnt of his erstwhile pupil's venture?—and doubtless journeying to Oulton to take farewell of Mrs. Clarke. Many people, including John Venning, a Norwich merchant who had spent a long time in Russia, loaded him with letters of introduction and much sound advice. On 25 July he said a tearful good-bye to his mother and took coach for London—his seven years Odyssey had begun!

Think what it must have meant to George Borrow, after the long years of frustration, to win this sudden achievement of heart's desire! Yet in his delirious excitement he remembered the little elderly woman sitting in the empty house at Norwich. A few hours before he sailed from Customs House Wharf for Hamburg he wrote to her:

> *London, July 30th, 1833.*
>
> "MY DEAREST MOTHER,—I have paid in for you at the bank the sum of £17, which is, I believe, about what you advanced me. I have been paid £30 to defray my expenses from London to St. Petersburg, and I dare say it will cost me nearly that to get there, as the fare to Hamburg alone is seven guineas! My salary commences from the time I set out on my journey, which is to-night; for we must be on board before twelve o'clock, as the steamer starts at one in the morning . . . Mr. Venning's packet has arrived with letters to several of the Princes, so that I shall be protected if I am seized as a spy; for the Emperor[1] is particularly cautious as to the foreigners he admits. It costs £2 : 7 : 6 merely for permission to go to Russia, which alone is enough to deter most people!"

Poor George's elation was not proof against sea-sickness. The weather was appalling, and for three full days the packet *Tourist* wallowed her way across the North Sea while he lay groaning in his stuffy second-class cabin. Two Copenhagen Jews, Weil and Valentin, ministered to him but, so he wrote to his mother:

> "On landing I was so exhausted from sickness and from want of sleep, that my old complaint, the *horrors*, came instantly upon me, and a physician had to be sent for, who gave me laudanum, which soon recovered me."

In the company of his new friends he visited Altona, where he met some deeply read Jews able to quote from both the Babylonian and Jerusalem *Talmuds*, but Borrow was shocked

[1] Tsar Nicholas I.

to find that these wise men were not strict Jews. "I prefer a superstition," he wrote sternly, "especially when founded on such a mountain of learning as the Jewish is, to heartless infidelity, with which those of this place are too much tainted." He also went for a day to Bremen, which he found more to his liking than Hamburg, where "the dancing-saloons, which I am informed are most infamous places, are open to the public this (Sunday) evening".

On 7 August Borrow left by coach for Lubeck. The road through Holstein was terrible, rough masses of unhewn rock alternating with quagmires of mud. The rain descended in torrents, sending Borrow into such a fury that he blamed not only the state of the road but the behaviour of the elements as well upon the ill-nature of the King of Denmark! After a more pleasant journey from Lubeck to Travemünde he embarked on the Russian steamer *Nikolai*.

What a vastly different voyage this from the London–Hamburg misery!

"On board this vessel" (George wrote) "I passed my time so agreeably amongst a moderate number of genteel, well-bred, and intelligent passengers, that I was almost sorry when we reached Petersburg, which we did after a passage of only seventy-two hours, during which the sea exhibited the smoothness of a mill-pond, and the wind was invariably favourable."

No chameleon was more susceptible to environment than was George Borrow. In the same way that he had once stained his face with walnut-juice when first acquainted with the Petulengro clan, so he became, on the instant of his engagement with the Bible Society, a Church man—a militant one to boot. During the brief voyage to St. Petersburg he became a man who, under his breath, chanted the incantation of every *mujik*, "Russia, my Russia, Holy Russia!" So, two years later when he crossed the Spanish border at Badajoz, he was to become the proud, cloaked horseman, Don Jorge.

Doubtless his instinct for self-dramatization urged him to identify himself afresh with different races, sects, countries, or individuals. Yet the thing went deeper than mere mimicry. Once George Borrow embraced anything from a mode of dress to a faith he held it close to his heart for always. Conversely, when he conceived a sudden hatred he remembered it for the rest of his days. He hated all Hamblys because of his father's early brush with one of that name. He hated all Valpys because the Rev. Edward had humiliated him. He hated the Orford family because Colonel Lord Orford had quibbled about his brother's army allowances. He hated the parson at Oulton because the poor man had complained about his dog. For reasons equally remote or puerile, he hated all connections of the Bowring, Curzon, Peto, and Martineau families, and the Holy Catholic Church.

Men of logical mind have condemned Borrow for his violent likes and dislikes, his "posturing" as they call it. Why? Surely he had only retained what they had long since lost; the direct, uncompromising mind of childhood? Anybody who was kind to him earned his lasting gratitude: anybody whom he felt instinctively was against him his lasting hatred. That child-like side of Borrow, indeed, was more in affinity with the Russians, among whom he spent his first years abroad, than with all the "people out of Egypt" he met during his lifetime.

III

George Borrow saw the Kronstadt guard-ship riding high on the waters of the Finnish Gulf; the writer only remembers a fortress looming out of the mist after voyages starred by innumerable glasses of tea and motherly admonitions that home would soon be reached.

It is a hundred and twenty-eight years since Borrow entered St. Petersburg: it is fourteen years since the writer last saw that city, but maybe because she shares with Borrow what she calls a childlike and most people nowadays a *nostalgie de la boue* frame of mind, she can picture his arrival. . . .

There were the white steps of the *Angliskaia Naberzhnaia* and beyond them the *Ulitsa Galernaia* gleaming in the sunlight. The officials in the little wooden Customs shed did not keep him long. After all, he thought with pride, they see I have "letters to the Princes": for their part the guards sprawled their legs under the rickety table and thanked heaven that here was at least one mad foreigner who did not expect them to live up to their fearsome reputation for cross-examination. The ubiquitous *droshky* drivers, bundled into the sheepskin coats they wore winter or summer, tugged at the bridles of their drooping, straw-hatted horses extolling the merits of their particular vehicles. Ragged children darted along the quay holding out cabbage leaves filled with fruit. The sellers of sunflower seeds proffered their wares in little sacks. Merchants, beggars, prostitutes, tradesfolk, housewives, grouped like the chorus from some colourful Russian opera, stood watching the *Nikolai's* passengers and talking, talking, talking until the hot air seemed to quiver with sound.

Borrow climbed into the *droshky* of his choice, leaning back with careless abandon on its dirty, moth-eaten cushions, feasting his eyes on the tall buildings sharp-etched against an azure sky, the lazy barges that floated, so many brown birds, on the shimmering waters of river or canal, the great palaces fringing the wide, arrow-straight streets. Even the grim sentinel so unsuitably named after St. Peter and St. Paul excited his admiration; but when the *droshky* wheeled into the Nevski Prospect he sat forward with a gasp of sheer wonderment. Never had he imagined such beauty! Here was the mighty Neva sweeping seawards, carrying the proud ships on her breast. On her banks the polished granite quays shone bright as silver. Along the three miles of the Prospect grand carriages rolled smoothly over the fitted wooden blocks that formed the roadway. On the pavement in front of the gracious houses with their pillars, their porticoes, their marble steps, strolled officers of the Imperial Guard in glittering uniforms, Don and Kuban Cossacks in long, tight-waisted black coats, brilliant sashes and high fur hats, priests whose sombre robes were relieved only by a flash of gold as the sun struck the crosses on their chests, Ukrainians, Tatars, men from those mysterious lands behind the Ural Mountains, all in their national dress.

So suddenly that Borrow first thought it a trick of the sunlight the scene changed. The houses were no longer stone but wood, with low shaggy eaves from beneath which glassless windows peered like inquisitive eyes. Along the Prospect, like clumps of exotic flowers, were gay booths selling everything imaginable from skeins of wool dyed scarlet or emerald to pearly slabs of cured white salmon. Around these swarmed such a mass of humanity that to begin with Borrow felt he was looking at some vast, multi-hued body from an unknown world; presently he became aware that each particle of the body was different. Jews in greasy *caftans*, men whose trousers were topped by flapping, grimy shirts and tucked inside *vilinki* (the felt boot still worn by the Russian peasant), men in flowing robes which betrayed their desert origin, men whose embroidered coats flaunted the Imperial dragon of China.

The *droshky* had to move at snail's pace through the press —for the crowd straggled right to the river bank. To Borrow, seated lonely in his chariot, strange faces were upturned. Here was the blond hair and long head of a Scandinavian; there the flat, high-cheekboned countenance of the Mongol; here the merry, dark eyes of a man from the Caucasian foothills; there the oblique gaze of the Tatar; here the sharp glance of a trader from Baghdad; there the sad scrutiny of a mountain dweller unhappy in this sea-girt city.

In the capital built by Peter the Great to prove the immense progress of his country George Borrow became fully alive for the first time in his thirty years. His desire must have been to leave his modest hotel and explore every by-way of the city, listen to every tongue spoken within her boundaries. Greatly to his credit he sallied forth the morning after his arrival to pay his respects to the estimable Mr. Swan, whom he found "one of the most amiable and interesting characters I have ever met with". Mr. Swan introduced him to a Mr. Schmidt, a gentleman engrossed in preparation of a Mongol grammar, and the following day Mr. James Venning, son of the kindly Norwich merchant, presented him to Prince Galitzin, afterwards arranging for him to lodge in the *Barona Shabo*,

221 *Ulitsa Galernaia*, a house belonging to an Englishman called Egerton Hubbard.[1]

In London Borrow's human contacts had been few and somewhat unfortunate: in Petersburg he showed an unexpected capacity for firm and enduring friendship. Mr. Swan, with whom he worked daily for several months, formed a high opinion of him and wrote to Jowett: "I willingly bear testimony to his diligence in transcription. I have collated with him all he has done, and hope he will succeed in the objects of his visit." His Britannic Majesty's Minister Plenipotentiary, the Hon. J. D. Bligh, went out of his way to help him. Nikolai Gretch, author of the famous Russian Grammar, and his son Alexis, editor of a literary review known as the *Northern Bee*, were entirely captivated by him. Freidrich von Adelung, nephew of the renowned German philologist and himself a scholar of repute, lent him Oriental books and manuscripts. Baron Schilling, whose collection of Far Eastern literature was unique, gave him the run of his library.

Borrow's letters home reflected his new-found happiness. "Petersburg is the finest city in the world. London, Paris, Madrid, and other capitals which I have visited, are not worthy to hold a candle to it." "There is in this place a singular mixture of Europeanism and Orientalism highly interesting to the attentive observer. The beard twelve inches long and the peculiar dress of the lower and middle ranks of the Russians, contrast wonderfully with the close shaven chins and common-fashioned habilments of the upper classes and foreigners." "Notwithstanding I had previously heard and read much of the beauty and magnificence of the Russian capital, I confess that what I have beheld has surpassed my expectation. There cannot be a doubt that it is the finest city in Europe, being pre-eminent for the grandeur of its public edifices and the length and regularity of its streets."

Now if Borrow had really visited "Paris, Madrid, and other capitals" he had hitherto kept uncommonly quiet about it; but surely he was entitled to this little exaggeration and to the

[1] In the 1840's the house was pulled down in order to build a bridge across the Neva from the *Angliskaia Naberzhnaia* to *Vasilii Ostrov* (Basil Island).

touch of affectation which caused him to date all his correspondence according to the Russian calendar, adding the magic
addition in brackets "Old Style".[1]

The important thing was that "tall George", as he was
called affectionately by Nikolai and Alexis Gretch, had come
into his own, and the friend who did more than anyone else
to foster this sudden strength of character was undoubtedly
that charming and lovable cynic, John Hasfeld.[2]

The Petulengro-Borrow relationship was an emotional affair
with a tang of the supernatural about it: the Hasfeld-Borrow
friendship was a sound and solid one with roots set deep in
ordinary earth. Hasfeld was a Dane, born in 1800, who had
entered his country's Foreign Service and eventually been
sent to Petersburg as "Royal Interpreter" about the year
1830. Whether this post did not carry sufficient salary, or
whether his gregariousness demanded other outlets is not
known, but by the time he met Borrow he held a strange
variety of jobs. In the winter, when the Court was in Petersburg, he netted a handsome income from lecturing in Russian
on English to large classes of noble youths. He drew 1,200
roubles a year for teaching in an army cadet school where he
showed an almost acrobatic agility in turning from Danish to
Swedish, German, English, Russian, or French. He was also
—heaven knew why—a member of the Russian Marine Corps,
which brought him in another 800 roubles.

Extraordinarily talented, a worldly-wise cosmopolitan to
his finger-tips, he only betrayed his nationality in his cups,
when he was wont to sing lustily:

> *"Han kan ikke döe, unden at han först skriver:*
> *Nu drikker jeg den sidste Draabe af Kruset!"*[3]

John Hasfeld was the closest friend George Borrow ever
had. He was also the best, for he understood Borrow's mercurial nature. He had the greatest respect for his abilities and

[1] Twelve days behind our reckoning; thus 13 August, in Europe was
1 August, in Russia, and so on.
[2] This spelling is copied from his own signature. Probably originally
Hatzfeldt or Hasfeldt.
[3] "Neither can die without first writing to the other:
  Now drain the last drop in the jug!"

a tolerant understanding of his weaknesses. When Borrow showed him the panegyric he had written to the Bible Society concerning the son of William Glen, Persian scholar and missionary in Astrakhan, he merely quirked an ironic eyebrow at the phrase "he hopes that at some future period he may tread in the steps of his father and proclaim a crucified Saviour to the Oriental heathens", and dragged his friend off to have a drink, knowing full well that the extravagant words sprang not from insincerity but from a crusading spirit. For Borrow's attacks of "the horrors"—he had at least two of these in 1834, one caused by fever and the other by the belated news of his brother's death in Mexico on 22 November, 1833—he prescribed a bottle of Port Wine a day and, by way of convalescence, a roistering night in St. Petersburg's quayside taverns.

Most important of all, it was Hasfeld who drew from Borrow's heart the rare bud named genius and nursed it to full flower.

Borrow's letters to Hasfeld—and he wrote many between his departure from Russia in 1835 and the Dane's visits to him at Oulton in 1852 and 1857—have vanished in the mists of time; but a few of Hasfeld's letters were found among Borrow's papers after his death and in reading them we feel instinctively that their writer knew that most elusive of creatures, the *real* George Borrow.

Who else but Hasfeld could have written to the evangelical missionary sternly bent on the spiritual conquest of Spain:

". . . I have not written as often to you as I have thought about you, for otherwise you would have received a couple of letters daily, because the sun never sets without you, my lean friend, entering into my imagination. I received the Spanish letter a day or two before I left for Stockholm and it made the journey with me, for it was in my mind to send you an epistle from Svea's capital, but there were so many petty hindrances that I was nearly forgetting myself, let alone correspondence. I lived in Stockholm as if each day were to be my last, swam in champagne, or rested in girls' embraces. You doubtless blush for me; you may do

K

so, but don't think that conviction will murder my almost shameless candour, the only virtue which I possess, in a superfluous degree. In Sweden I tried to be lovable, and succeeded, to the astonishment of myself and everybody else. I reaped the reward on the most beautiful lips, which only too often had to complain that the fascinating Dane was faithless like the foam of the sea and the ice of spring. Every wrinkle which seriousness had impressed on my face vanished in joy and smiles; my frozen heart melted and pulsed with the rapid beat of gladness; in short, I was not recognizable. Now I have come back to my old wrinkles, and make sacrifice again on the altar of friendship, and when the incense, this letter, reaches you, then prove to me your pleasure, wherever you may be, and let an echo of friendship's voice resound from Granada's Alhambra or Sahara's deserts. . . .

"I have received a letter from my correspondent in London . . . He informs me that my manuscript has been promenading about, calling on publishers without having been well received; some of them would not even look at it, because it smelt of Russian leather; others kept it for three or six weeks and sent it back with 'Thanks for the loan'. They probably used it to get rid of the moth out of their old clothes. It first went to Longman & Co's, Paternoster Row; Bull of Hollis Street; Saunders & Otley, Conduit Street; John Murray of Albemarle Street, who kept it for three weeks; and finally it went to Bentley's of New Burlington Street, who kept it for SIX weeks and returned it; now it is to pay a visit to a Mr. Colbourn, and if he won't have the abandoned child, I will myself care for it. . . . Thank God, I shall not buy bread with the shillings I perhaps may get for a work which has cost me seventy nights, for I cannot work during the day . . ."

Hasfeld's deep attachment to Borrow formed the theme song to most of his letters.

"Today I was thinking 'Where can he have gone?' when my comforter, the red-bearded *artelstchik*, came in bringing the 'rum runes' of friendship. I was so rejoiced to behold thy tall tracks that I rushed at the letter as the eagle darts upon his prey, quickly broke the mysterious fastenings on the seal, and read with tears in my eyes how very very far my friend is from me."

And again he wrote:

"There is no one who has taken your place in my friendship. Men in general are a bore to me; the world is a bore. Nothing diverts me; I eat and drink because I am hungry and thirsty, but satisfaction have I none; I cannot purchase it, for it is not to be found in all the bazaars of the Nevski Perspective."

Hasfeld's presence always acted like a tonic upon George Borrow, and it is no exaggeration to say that if he had not tended his friend continually through the summer of 1834, "the horrors" brought about by news of John's death in Mexico, combined with a minor but painful eye trouble and a number of worries connected with his work might well have resulted in Borrow's complete breakdown.

It was in June that Mrs. Borrow's pathetic letter reached her son.

". . . I am sorry to hear you have been so unwell, and particularly 'the horrors'. I am afraid you do not live regular. When you find yourself low, take a little wine, but not too much at one time; it will do you the more good; I find that by myself.

"My dear George, take care of your *health*, for you are now my *only hope*. It grieves me to tell you, but I must. Our dear John is no more! He died the 22nd, November (1833) rather suddenly . . . I hope and trust in God his soul is at rest. Poor fellow! When I first heard it my heart sank, but the Lord supported me . . . Do not grieve, my dear George. I trust we shall all meet in heaven. Put a crape on your hat for some time."

John's death shocked Borrow profoundly. His brother's

conscious air of superiority, his pitying letters, his petty reproofs and spiteful digs—all these were swept away and George remembered only that beautiful bright being "with the rosy, angelic face, blue eyes and light chestnut hair" who had been to his infant self the epitome of all virtues.

"MY DEAR, DEAR MAMMA" (he wrote), "I have received your melancholy letter, which has given me the severest stroke I ever experienced. It quite stunned me, and since reading its contents I have done little else but moan and lament—though doing so is of no use. O that our darling John had taken the advice which I gave him nearly three years since, to abandon that horrid country and return to England! though it is probable that that would not have saved him; for I think from his departing so suddenly that his constitution was undermined and gave way at once. Peace be to his soul! a noble, better, kinder being never walked God's earth. Would that I had died for him! for I loved him dearly, dearly. Perhaps his was the best lot, for the pain he felt is nothing to the pangs which torment me when I think of him. . . ."

The letter went on to reassure Mrs. Borrow as to his state of health, and here we detect the heartening influence of Hasfeld:

". . . I learn how to cure my disorders by experience. The 'horrors', for example. Whenever they come I must drink strong Port Wine, and then they are instantly stopped . . . How came you, my dear mother, to think I live irregularly? I have three meals a day . . ."

After adjuring Mrs. Borrow to keep a maid, for "what am I working for here and saving money, unless it is for your comfort? for I assure you that to make you comfortable is my greatest happiness, almost my only one", Borrow added a sad little postscript, "I have got the crape".

From the moment of his arrival in Russia Borrow had sent his mother regular remittances; now he redoubled his efforts to provide her with extra comforts, but on his return to England in 1835 that indomitable woman proudly showed him her bank-book—she had saved almost all the money he had paid into her account.

IV

It would have been easy for Borrow to draw his salary, enjoy the linguistic feast temptingly spread before him, and keep the Bible Society quiescent by means of a series of vague, conciliatory epistles. St. Petersburg was a far cry from London. The Society, befogged by such various happenings as the Neva floods, the whimsical behaviour of M. Lipoftsov, the edict of the surly Tsar Nicholas ordering the closing down of the Russian Bible Society, and the extraordinary stories of Russia brought home by their indignant missionaries, despaired of doing anything immediate in that lamentable country and only expected their Mr. Borrow—who, certain members of the Committee said nastily, should never have been engaged —to keep the Russian door ajar lest, at some far future date, the opportunity should occur to push it wide open.

The Committee members had no cause for worry. George Borrow was the best agent in Russia they ever had, and it was due entirely to his efforts that the whole New Testament was printed in the Manchu language.

Mr. Swan had rightly testified to Borrow's diligence. From August to December 1833, the two worked together, and although at first Borrow was eager to begin transcribing the Old Testament manuscript recently discovered he gave up this task after (so he wrote to the Society), finishing the Second Book of Chronicles, and wisely confined his energies to working with his colleague on the New Testament.

From the very beginning, however, he ran into difficulties so prodigious that the wonder is he did not throw up his task forthwith. In a nutshell, he made unwelcome acquaintance with the Russian proverb, "The Heavens are wide and the Tsar is high". Mr. Schmidt, with his airy assurances that official permission to print the Testament in Manchu was simple to obtain, proved entirely wrong, a fact which Borrow first found out when he interviewed Lipoftsov. This gentleman possessed to the full the evasive qualities of his race. Professing to know no other European tongue save Russ, he poured out a torrent of liquid speech on the unfortunate head of his visitor, who at that time possessed only the slightest knowledge of the language.

In halting phrases, Borrow reminded Lipoftsov that the Bible Society had paid him a large sum of money for his version of the New Testament in Manchu and that they now looked to him for aid in seeing the manuscript through the press. He added the *douceur* that Professor Abel Rémusat of Paris, greatest authority on Oriental translations in Europe, declared it to be the most "idiomatic, clear and faithful" translation he had ever read.

Lipoftsov hunched his shoulders and gazed blandly at the strangely un-English-looking Englishman. But yes, assuredly he was most grateful to Mr. Borrow's kind employers for entrusting him with a task of such magnitude and expressing themselves satisfied with the result. But no, he had the merest acquaintance with this M. Schmidt, who was agitating in such a commendable but mistaken manner. Certainly, it was his sworn duty to instruct Mr. Borrow in the intricacies of Manchu; as for obtaining the *imprimatur* for so important a volume as had been mentioned, well—here Lipofstov's hands were outheld in a gesture of supplication—"the Heavens are wide and the Tsar is high!"

There is really so small a change between the Russia of 1833 and the Russia of 1951. Then as now that huge, amorphous body THE STATE, dictated mens' lives. Lipofstov dwelt in terror of the Tsar's secret police: his 1951 prototypes dwell in terror of the Kremlin agents.

Lipoftsov's past was stainless: since he was now a member of the Russian *Tsenzurny Comitet* (Board of Censors), he was naturally anxious that his present should shine clear as crystal in the eyes of authority. This Mr. Borrow might be consumed by a passion to immolate himself upon a Manchu altar "in the noontide of his mortal life": he himself was a man of seventy who had skirted many excursions and alarums before listening to Nicholas I's pronouncement that he "would make a clean sweep" of all his brother Alexander's Biblical activities. Charmingly, beguilingly, the old gentleman talked himself out of any useful co-operation.

Borrow was therefore left, at the very start of his mission, with the aid of Mr. Swan—already overdue in his departure for Siberia—and Mr. Schmidt, who needed a violent prod in the ribs before he so much as lifted his head from his Mongolian Grammar. And Borrow was a stranger in a strange land—that needs remembering.

Was it the fierce flame of evangelism within him which drove him to surmount the obstacles that towered dizzily in his path? At risk of offending the descendants of those who sponsored him one feels emphatically that gratitude and sheer tenacity of purpose were his inspirations—plus a romantic longing to "wander, Testament in hand, to Kiakhta if not Pekin, with side-glances at Tatar hordes". Backed by Hasfeld, who knew a great deal more about the Russian character than he did, Borrow set about the dual task of wooing the Government and completing Swan's transcription of the New Testament into Manchu.

By January 1834 the transcription was despatched to London. By February Borrow—who by this time had mastered not only the Russian language but the Russian intricacies of mind—wrote ecstatically to Mr. Jowett that the Asiatic Department of the Russian Foreign Office had been graciously pleased to permit the printing of the Manchu Scripture.

The Committee in Earl Street were overjoyed. Here at last was their opportunity to spread the Gospel among their poor Far Eastern brethren. Brandram and Jowett tumbled over each other to send their good Mr. Borrow hearty congratulations; neither of them—despite their careful scanning of his lengthy letters—understood one-tenth of the difficulties he had conquered.

Borrow had early realized that the prodigious amount of labour involved in transcription was but a small part of his job; that he must stand or fall by his powers of persuasion with a government which looked askance at all other governments in general and European ones in particular. Carelessly, as though the winning or losing of a game was a mere bagatelle, he professed his willingness to play his Russian friends at chess. He seldom won—that was not to be expected—but his fame percolated by slow and tortuous ways to the ears of the very man he wanted, His Excellency M. Bludoff, Minister of the Interior.

His Excellency's initial reaction was to smile, move one or two pawns, and reflect how foolish these English were; his second to guard his king and send a haughty message that while he could not receive Mr. Borrow, since the matter in question was none of his concern, he would use his influence in presenting his rather unusual request to the correct quarter. He then sat back and dismissed Mr. Borrow from his mind.

But Borrow's knowledge of chess was growing apace. His next move was to approach Mr. Bligh, the British Minister, and beg him to inform M. Bludoff that the Bible Society were prepared to sign an undertaking not to sell or give away one single copy of the Manchu Testament in any part of the vast Russian Empire. Furthermore, the Imperial Government should have the right to supervise the packing and despatch of all printed copies to China and Chinese Tartary.

Mr. Bligh sought an official interview with M. Bludoff. A fortnight later Borrow received an order to present himself at the Asiatic Department of the Foreign Office, where he was cautiously informed that if he guaranteed to edit the work himself under the censorship of M. Lipoftsov, permission to print *might* be granted. Another fortnight elapsed, during which the Russian officials hid themselves securely behind enormous bundles of red tape. Borrow, whose efforts to curb his natural impatience had led to an attack of "the horrors", valiantly swallowed the last of Hasfeld's Port Wine and again visited Mr. Bligh.

That very evening M. Bludoff was engaged to dine with Mr. Bligh. The meal must have been an excellent one, for towards midnight Borrow received a message bidding him to call upon the Minister of the Interior the following morning. M. Bludoff, now a strangely affable mandarin, reiterated his Department's inability to move in the matter but graciously handed Borrow a letter to the Director of Worship, saying he was sure this document would have the desired effect. (Had he spoken plainly he would have said he had appreciated playing chess with such a worthy opponent.)

Borrow scurried to the office of the Director of Worship, cooled his heels in a waiting-room for the better part of a day, and was then told abruptly to call at the Asiatic Department of the Foreign Office early the next week.

To a man of Borrow's temperament this final delay was the last straw. He walked homewards enveloped in gloom, sure that all his efforts had been in vain, that the subtle M. Bludoff had merely sent him back to the starting-point. The following Monday he entered Lipoftsov's office with dragging steps, scarcely heeding that old gentleman's voluble greetings. Suddenly he became aware that Lipoftsov was waving a paper under his nose. He glanced at it vaguely—then snatched at it. *There, in black and white, was the permission to print the Manchu Testament!*

Borrow left the Asiatic Department treading on air. Was he in snow-covered St. Petersburg watching the *troikas* spinning across the frozen Neva? Ah, no, he was five thousand miles away on the frontier of Chinese Tartary, in the little town of Kiakhta. . . .

There it lay on the fringes of the desert, a huddle of wooden buildings clustering round the palaces of its rival mandarins, one a Tatar, the other a Chinese—for while Kiakhta belonged officially to Russia the Manchu Emperors were reluctant to relinquish their ancient sovereignty over this market renowned from earliest times, this fabled meeting-place on the great trade route linking Occident and Orient. In summer Kiakhta grilled in the fierce desert heat: in winter it was swept by the icy desert wind. The year round its buildings were smothered in dust, infested by every insect that had ever pestered man. Each morning the caravans swayed in from the Gobi; each evening they swayed in from Pekin. All day, all night long, the heavy air vibrated with the clack of many tongues; and in the tea-houses set high above the market-place squatted the merchants of the East, hands crossed over paunched bellies, heads nodding to the rhythm of the story-teller's legends, eyes glancing obliquely at the dignified camels, the resentful mules, the delicately-stepping Chinese donkeys that moved in slow, endless procession, laden with silks and spices, pigs' bristles and gold dust, bundles of furs and bricks of fragrant tea.

Such was the Kiakhta of the 1830's[1] to which George Borrow longed to go. He saw himself striding down its sandy roadways like some prophet of old, distributing copies of the Manchu Testament, a vision which entranced him so much that in his letters to Mr. Brandram and Mr. Jowett telling them the splendid news of the printing permission, he wrote:

"This town is the emporium of Chinese and Russian trade, Chinese caravans are continually arriving and returning, bringing and carrying away articles of merchandise. There are likewise a Chinese and a Tartar Mandarin, also a school where Chinese and Tartar children along with Russian are educated. Your sagacity will at once perceive what great advantage this town is capable of being turned to in the cause of God. . . . In a word, were an agent for the Bible Society to reside at this town for a year or so, it is my humble opinion, and the opinion of much wiser people, that if he were active, zealous and likewise courageous, the blessings resulting from his labours would be incalculable. It would be by no means a difficult thing to make excursions into Tartary, and to form friendships among the Tartar hordes, and I am far from certain that with a little management and dexterity he would be unable to penetrate even to Pekin, and to return in safety, after having examined the state of the land. I can only say that if it were my fortune to have the opportunity, I would make the attempt, and should consider myself only to blame if I did not succeed. . . ."

The Committee in Earl Street were deeply impressed by this "noble offer". Naturally, however, they regarded the actual printing as the immediate and all important matter. Politely but firmly they shelved Kiakhta until some vague

[1] Russian Kiakhta is now called Troitsokosavsk, in the Buriat-Mongol Republic. Almost adjoining it is Chinese Kiakhta, known as Mai-mai-Chên.

future date when "such a scheme would be found to lie within the range of safe and prudent speculation". Borrow never shelved it. All through his stupendous task the name danced before his eyes.

V

George Borrow's mood of wild optimism soon gave way to one of despair. Everybody and everything in Petersburg combined to put obstacles in his path. The type fount which had lain for ten years in the bankers' vaults proved, when examined, to have stuck together in one solid mass, and it took him weeks of hard labour to prise apart and clean each separate letter. He then had to choose and sort out more type kindly provided by Baron Schilling. As we already know, he had an attack of fever followed by "the horrors". Ill and wretched, he crawled from paper-makers to printers, arguing, wheedling, beating down absurdly high estimates, even representing himself as a German because "all Russians thought the English were made of gold". The news of John's death and the long delay in getting the Bible Society's credit note through were additional worries, and when he eventually succeeded in persuading a German printer called Beneze to set up the type—for Russian type-setters were hopelessly lazy—he found that neither Beneze nor his compositors could master the intricacies of the Manchu alphabet.

Through the heat of the summer Borrow worked alongside his printers; but no sooner had they become fairly efficient than they demanded shorter hours and higher wages, and he had to resort to bribery and corruption in the shape of bottles of vodka. Long afterwards, indeed, Hasfeld wrote to him: "I well remember how you toiled over your Manchu Testament; how thin you grew, and how you almost killed Beneze and his lads!"

Somehow the work went on despite constant set-backs, for while Lipoftsov was a brilliant Manchu scholar he was very much aware of his position as official censor, and Borrow had to keep the peace between him, Beneze, and a "Tartar pundit" called Ali Makisha, who had been engaged in an advisory capacity at the princely salary of some six shillings a week.

The only heartening interludes were two letters from home in September.

"There has been a Bible meeting all this week" (wrote Mrs. Borrow), "and your name was sounded through the Hall both by Mr. Gurney and Mr. Cunningham. They said you had left home and your dearest friends to go to a foreign land to translate and edit the Manchu. They hoped your fellow-citizens would offer up their prayers to Almighty God for health and strength to enable you to get through your great work. Mr. Cunningham held up your last letter in his hand and said it was most interesting—and much more. All this is very pleasing to me. God bless you!"

Even more significant to Borrow was the warm praise from Mrs. Clarke of Oulton:

". . . You were mentioned at many of the Bible meetings this year, and dear Mr. Cunningham spoke so nicely of you at our Oulton gathering held in a malt office near Mutford Lock where you left the coach to come to us just two years ago, and, as I am not afraid of making you proud, I will tell you one of his remarks. He mentioned you as one of the most extraordinary and interesting individuals of the present day. I believe you have done far more than any of them expected."

One can imagine Borrow reading and re-reading these letters, drawing from them the consolation he so badly needed: one can also imagine the dismay he felt when he received this chilly communication from Mr. Jowett:

"Now you are sufficiently aware that the publication of the Manchu Scriptures is a work in which our Committee have taken a very lively interest. You may, therefore, readily conceive of their disappointment at receiving so very few notices of your progress . . . You ought to reflect that the Committee who stand between you and the public, should be enabled to give an answer to the question, 'What is Mr. Borrow doing?' And it should also be considered that the Society lives in the public estimation by the knowledge of its difficulties, trials, and hopes, as detailed in the Reports of its agents.

"You can have no difficulty in furnishing me with such monthly information as may satisfy the Committee that they are not expending a large sum of money in vain. . . ."

Anger and wounded pride struggled within Borrow as he read the immensely long letter which gave, in page after page, details of his sins of omission. Anger won, thanks to that ominous question, *"What is Mr. Borrow doing?"* Doing, forsooth! Had not his life for the past nine months been one long series of titanic battles with Russian officials, German paper-makers, Esthonian printers? Had he not worked thirteen hours a day beside the compositors? Had he not worn himself out, mentally and physically, in the Society's service? Hot with rage, he reached for pen and paper—but as he glanced at the calendar on his desk he paused. Dear heaven! The date was past the middle of October. Now when . . . when had he last written to Jowett and Brandram?

Prolonged rummaging among the mass of books, manuscripts and notes which littered his room elicited the startling information that, except for brief financial requests addressed to the Treasurer, he had sent no news to the Society since the beginning of May! Engrossed in his task he had been oblivious to the passage of time.

This discovery cooled Borrow's wrath sufficiently to enable him to compose two lengthy and excellent epistles to Mr. Jowett: it did not, however, obliterate memory of that unjust, unforgivable question.

"Would it have answered any useful purpose" (he demanded) "if, instead of continuing to struggle with difficulties and using my utmost to overcome them, I had written in the following strain—and what else could I have written if I had written at all?—'I was sent out to St. Petersburg to assist M. Lipoftsov in the editing of the

May 3 1835 St petersburg.

My dear Sir.

I write a few hasty lines for the purpose of informing you that I shall not be able to obtain a pass-port for Siberia, except on the condition that I carry not one single Mantchou Bible thither. The Russian Government is too solicitous to maintain a good understanding with that of China to encourage any project at which the latter could take umbrage. Therefore pray inform me to what place I am to despatch the bibles. I have had some thoughts of embarking the first five parts without delay to England, but I have forborne from an unwillingness to do any thing which I was not commanded to do. By the time I receive your answer every thing will be in readiness, or nearly so, to be forwarded wherever the Committee shall judge expedient. I wish also to receive orders respecting what is to be done with the types. I should be sorry if they were to be abandoned in the same manner as before, for it is possible that at some future time they may prove eminently useful. As for myself, I suppose I must return to England, as my task will be speedily completed. I hope the Society are convinced that I have served them faithfully, and that I have spared no labour to bring out the work, which they did me the honor of confiding to me, correctly and within as short a time as possible. At my return; if the Society think that I can still prove of utility to them, I shall be most happy to devote myself still to their service. I am a person full of faults and weaknesses as I am every day reminded by bitter experience, but I am certain that my zeal and fidelity towards

Facsimile of letter from George Borrow in St. Petersburg to the Rev. Joseph Jowett

those who put confidence in me are not to be shaken. Should it now become a question what is to be done with these Manchou Bibles which have been printed at a considerable expense? I should wish to suggest that Baron Schilling be consulted; In a few weeks he will be in London, which he intends visiting during a summer tour which he is on the point of commencing. He will call at the Society's House, and as he is a nobleman of great experience and knowledge in all that relates to China, it would not be amiss to interrogate him on such a subject. I again repeat that I am at command. In your last letter, but one, you stated that our noble President had been kind enough to declare that I had but to send in an account of any extraordinary expenses, which I had been put to in the course of the work, to have them defrayed. I return my most grateful thanks for this most considerate intimation which nevertheless I cannot avail myself of, as according to one of the articles of my agreement my salary of £200 was to cover all extra expenses. Petersburg is doubtless the dearest capital in Europe, and expenses meet an individual, especially one situated as I have been, at every turn and corner, but an agreement is not to be broken on that account.

I have the honor to remain
Revd and dear Sir
Your obedient humble servant
George Borrow.

Revd Joseph Jowett.

Facsimile of letter from George Borrow in St. Petersburg to the
Rev. Joseph Jowett

Mandchou Testament. That gentleman, *who holds three important situations under the Russian Government, and who is far advanced in years*, has neither time, inclination, or eyesight for the task, and I am apprehensive that my strength and powers unassisted are incompetent to it' (praised be the Lord, they were not!), 'therefore I should be glad to return home. Moreover the compositors say that they are unaccustomed to compose in an unknown tongue from such scribbled and illegible copy, and they will scarcely assist me to compose. Moreover the working printers say (several went away in disgust) that the paper on which they have to print is too thin to be wetted, and that to print on dry requires a two-fold exertion of strength, and that they will not do such work for double wages, for it ruptures them.'

"Would that have been a welcome communication to the Committee? Would that have been a communication suited to the public? I was resolved 'to do or die', and, instead of distressing and perplexing the Committee with complaints, to write nothing until I could write something perfectly satisfactory, as I now can; and to bring about that result I have spared neither myself nor my own money. I have toiled in a close printing-office the whole day, during 90 degrees of heat, for the purpose of setting an example, and have bribed people to work whom nothing but bribes would induce to do so.

"I am obliged to say all this in self-justification. No member of the Bible Society would ever have heard a syllable respecting what I have undergone but for the question, *'What has Mr. Borrow been about?'* "

With Borrow's second letter he enclosed a testimonial from Lipoftstov—who apparently used dead European languages even if he eschewed live ones:

"Testifico—
Dominum Borrow ab initio usque ad hoc tempus summa cum deligentia et studio in re Mantshurica laborasse."

He also referred again—and how one admires his courage in doing so at such times—to Kiakhta:

The Nevski Prospect, St. Petersburg

By courtesy of Mr. Cherry Kearton

The Retiro, Madrid

"True it is that this undertaking would not 'come within the limits of safe and prudent speculation'. But is it possible for a plan to come within the limits of safe speculation, which has in view the conversion of the Tartar? . . . I speak Russ, Mandchou, and the Tartar or broken Turkish of the Russian steppes, and have also some knowledge of Chinese, which I might easily improve at Kiakhta. . . . I have formed many acquaintances amongst these most singular people (the Tartars) . . . Notwithstanding the superstition and fanaticism of these men I am much attached to them; for their conscientiousness, honesty and fidelity are beyond praise . . . How lamentable that such people should in the all-important matter of religion have embraced error instead of truth; what ornaments they would prove at the present day to Christianity, if, instead of Mahometanism, Christianity had originally come in their way! Of a surety they would reflect much more lustre on the religion of Christ than millions whose deeds and behaviour are more worthy of the followers of the impostor than of Him 'in whose mouth was found no craft or subtlety'. . . ."

These two letters entirely changed the Committee's view of their Mr. Borrow. For the first time, indeed, they understood the full significance of his lone and desperate crusade. By Christmas, 1834, the four Gospels were through the press; by July 1835, the Society published an official report that gladdened Borrow's heart:

"The printing of the Mandchou New Testament in St. Petersburg is now drawing to a conclusion. Mr. G. Borrow, who has had to superintend the work, has in every respect afforded satisfaction to the Committee. They have reason to believe that his acquirements in the language are of the most respectable order; while the devoted diligence with which he has laboured, and the skill he has shown in surmounting difficulties, and in conducting his negotiations for the advantage of the Society, justly entitle him to this public acknowledgment of his services."

L

VI

How different was the spring of 1835 to the spring of 1834. Not only was the printing of the Testament scheduled for completion by July, but a beloved work of Borrow's own was also in the press. This was *Targum, or Metrical Translations from Thirty Languages and Dialects*, which had as pendant a pamphlet called *The Talisman*, containing verses from Pushkin and Mickiewicz besides some ancient Russian ballads.

As Borrow strode along the Nevski Prospect he thought St. Petersburg had never looked so beautiful as now, shining serenely beneath a milky sky. A little soft wind blew in his face and with it came that magic tinkling sound which meant the ice was splintering on rivers and waterways. He stopped at a booth to buy a handful of Easter cakes and sat on the parapet munching them, his head full of plans. In August, when he had despatched the finished sheets of the Testament to the binders, he would journey south to Moscow and Nizhni-Novgorod,[1] return to superintend the packing of the books and then . . . Kiakhta!

The August visit came true. In a jolting diligence Borrow travelled the long road to Moscow, peering through clouds of dust at the mighty forests, the immense sweeps of grain, until he reached the ancient capital of Russia. . . .

"In it there is a wonderful building called the Kremlin, situated on a hill. It is partly palace, partly temple, and partly fortress. In one of its halls are I don't know how many crowns, taken from various kings whom the Russians have conquered. But the most remarkable thing in the Kremlin is a huge bell in a cellar or cave, close by one of the churches; it is twelve feet high, and the sound it gives when struck by an iron bar, for there are no clappers to Russian bells, is so loud that the common Russians say it can be heard over the empire."[2]

It was from Moscow that Borrow visited the suburb of

[1] *Now Gorki.*   [2] *Wild Wales*, Chap. XCIX.

Maryna Roshtcha, at that time a favourite camping-ground for the *Tsygany*, or Russian gypsies. Many of their women-folk, so he stoutly averred in a letter to the Society,[1] had married noblemen; but a number of their sisters were "low and profligate females" who haunted the local taverns, while the men were astute horse-copers.

Interesting as was his account of the *Tsygany*, far more so was the light it threw upon the Borrow of 1835, a light which cast the shadow of the "colossal clergyman" of later years. There was no tramping across the heath, no staining of the face with walnut-juice, no jingling in the pocket of eighteen-pence. *Mr.* Borrow drove out in a hired *calèche*, accompanied by a *valet de place*. He did not wander among the gypsies, but stood up in his carriage and spoke to them in the dialect once learnt from Jasper Petulengro, whereupon the gypsies gathered around him and shouted—in the oddest mixture of Russian and Romany—"Oh, how we love you!"

". . . I visited this place several times during my sojourn in Moscow" (went on his letter to the Society), "and spoke to them upon their sinful manner of living, upon the advent and suffering of Jesus Christ, and expressed, upon my taking leave of them, a hope that they would be in a short period furnished with the word of eternal life in their own language. . . ."

From Moscow Borrow rode to Nizhni-Novgorod. There, between the frowning walls of another Kremlin and the grey swirl of the Volga river, he made contact with more gypsies also with that Baron Taylor whom he claimed to have already met in Bayonne in 1826.

But nothing he saw in Moscow or Novgorod lessened his allegiance to St. Petersburg, and to that city he returned thankfully towards the end of August.

Now in the spring of the same year the Society, fired by Borrow's enthusiasm for the conversion of the Tatars, had given him permission to apply to the Russian Government for

[1] Afterwards printed in the *Athenæum*, 20 August, 1836.

a pass to journey across Asiatic Russia to Kiakhta. "The steppes of Tartary should flourish as the gardens of the Lord!" and Mr. Borrow should set forth on his perilous and noble mission laden with his Manchu Testaments. Exactly how Mr. Borrow proposed to cover some five thousand miles of a country so terrible that thirty years later the most experienced and well-equipped explorers gave up the expedition as impossible he did not explain, nor did he vouchsafe any details as to the transport of several hundred books. Such petty trifles were none of his concern—*he was going to Kiakhta*.

Tsar Nicholas I—"I think I see him now, with his grey cloak, cocked hat, and white waving plumes, striding down the Nevsky Prospect, and towering a whole head over other people"[1]—held the opposite view. Seriously alarmed by the activities of various foreigners in different parts of his realm, he issued a *Nolo*, or edict, forbidding the issue of any passports to Asiatic Russia.

Doubtless it gave the urbane M. Bludoff exquisite pleasure to communicate news of this veto to George Borrow: what was truly astonishing was the Englishman's calm acceptance of it. Perhaps nobody except Hasfeld realized Kiakhta had become such an obsession with Borrow that his heart believed him already there. The Russian route might be barred: the sea route to China remained open. Now that his work in Petersburg was all but over he would soon go home to England and see the Committee in Earl Street. Beyond any shadow of doubt they would send him to China, and Pekin was a mere nine hundred miles from Kiakhta.

So it was that Borrow gloried in the Petersburg spring and revelled in the September evenings when he and Hasfeld plighted eternal friendship over what Dr. Knapp insists were "jugs of ale",[2] but the writer suspects were bottles of Port Wine and vodka. "*Bozhe Tsarya Khrani!*" they cried: "*Gamle Norge!*", "Old England!" and once again they drank the *Bororskäl*:

> "*Han kan ikke döe, unden at han först skriver:*
> *Nu drikker jeg den sidste Draabe af Kruset!*"

[1] *Wild Wales*: Chap. XCIX.
[2] *Borrow: Life, Writings and Correspondence*, Vol I, Chap. XIX.

England or Norway; "God Preserve the Tsar" or the "last drop in the jug"—what mattered the toast so long as two friends, arms intertwined, were able to stagger down the Neva quays? Hasfeld handed Borrow a real Jewish *shekel*: Borrow gave Hasfeld copies of his precious *Targum* and *Talisman* to present to Pushkin and Zhukovski[1] (the Russian translator of Homer). Together they giggled over the Russians' pompous description of Borrow in the safe-conduct pass issued from Petersburg to Lubeck—stature, *tall*; hair, *grey*; face, *oval*; forehead, *medium*; eyes, *brown*; nose and mouth, *medium*; chin, *round* . . . these solemn pronouncements ending in a most undignified quarrel between the Russian and German languages, one of which declared his eyebrows to be *blond* and the other *grey*. Together they avowed their joint belief in Till's *Owl Glass*[2]; together they swore they would exchange letters at least once a week.

On 9 September Borrow sailed past the Kronstadt lightship on his way to England; but in his mind he believed himself on the way to Chinese Tartary. The belief remained long after hope had faded—like his master Defoe, Borrow could be a magnificent liar on occasion, and always maintained that he had travelled all over China and the Far East—even to Kiakhta. . . . "Did it never strike you," wrote Hasfeld years afterwards to the author of the *Bible in Spain*, "how much you resemble *Don Quijote de la Mancha*? To my notion, you might readily pass for his son."

---

[1] Both Pushkin and Zhukovski sent notes of thanks.
[2] *Wunderliche und seltsame Historie Tillens Eulenspiegels, eines Bauern Sohn, aus dem Lande zu Braunschweig gebürtig.*

CHAPTER FIVE

"THE MOST HAPPY YEARS"
(Preface to the *Bible in Spain*)

(1835–1840)

I

PERHAPS the ill-nature of Denmark's king again affected George Borrow; perhaps, when he stepped ashore at Trava-munde, he realized he had said a final good-bye to the Russian people he loved so well; perhaps he mourned the parting from the lovable, laughing Hasfeld who swore that Borrow's Tatar servant, Mahmoud, "only needed to give you horse meat to have merited a diploma", and accused his friend of having lived on a cheap but sustaining diet of pike soup for over six weeks, thereby "coming near to exterminating the whole breed".

At all events Borrow's spirits sank lower and lower as his coach rumbled across the desolate heaths of Holstein. He remembered how he had written to his mother during his last attack of "the horrors" that he dreaded returning to a life of study, for "it is very hard to dig holes in the sand and fill them up again, as I used to do". He remembered a phrase in one of Mr. Jowett's letters warning him against excessive paraphrase in his Manchu Testament—"The passion for honorificabilitudinity is a vice of the Asiatic languages, which a Scripture translator, above all others, ought to beware of countenancing."[1] He remembered his brother's death—"Would that I had died for him! for I loved him dearly, dearly."

By the time he landed at Customs House Wharf on 19 September, his gloom was so complete that the rapturous welcome given him by the Bible Society Committee was received in apathy. Their Mr. Borrow had done such magnificent work in Russia! At any moment permission would be granted for Mr. Borrow's voyage to China—here a group of

[1] Letter of 31 December, 1834.

Reverend gentlemen gathered round to ask Mr. Borrow's ideas about distribution of the Testaments in that country, while Messrs. Brandram and Jowett beamed from the background on their strangely whitened sheep. Mr. Borrow gazed lugubriously at his questioners: there was only one word in his mind and he dared not use it—*honorificabilitudinity*.

The Committee were still congratulating each other on their Mr. Borrow's abilities, and Messrs. Brandram and Jowett were still holding a portentous and private conversation about the Manchu Empire, when it was discovered that the lion of the afternoon had vanished. Ah, well, poor boy! (Heads nodded in sympathy.) It was only natural he wished to hasten to his recently bereaved mother. A trifle temperamental . . . ? Yes, yes, but a sound agent! The important factor was that the young man had brought back with him—and no doubt about it—one thousand copies of the New Testament in Manchu. Happily unaware that the Pekin Government had decreed Mandarin Chinese as the only official language, the Committee discussed the transhipment of Mr. Borrow to the China coast—after all, that Manchu Testament had cost them upwards of £2,000!

And George Borrow? He sat, huddled in a coat of indubitably Russian sheepskin, oblivious to the dank autumn mist and the rain which spattered his face, atop the Norwich-bound coach. His fellow-passengers edged away from him, tried to get the Russian smell out of their nostrils by exclaiming about various landmarks. Borrow paid them no heed: he was wrestling, as once he had wrestled by a dying fire on Mousehold Heath, with his immortal soul. Then he had rejected a gypsy life because of his mother: now he rejected Kiakhta because of a woman from Oulton Broad who had written to him in Petersburg—"I must tell you that your letter chilled me when I read of your intention of going as a Missionary or Agent, with the Mandchou Scriptures in your hand, to the Tartars, that land of incalculable dangers . . ."

In Petersburg Borrow had cherished Mrs. Clarke's letters. Apart from those of his mother, they were the only truly comforting ones he received. In answer to them he had poured out all his hopes and fears for the future, and—since he never did things by halves—as he wrote he knew a feeling akin to worship of this stately, kindly woman, so far above him in every way, who showed such deep faith in his abilities. But in Petersburg Kiakhta had been a flame in his heart and Mrs. Clarke an idol occupying a niche in his mind. On his homeward journey the flame had flickered low without the Russian winds to fan it; and as he neared England the idol had moved from its niche to the forefront of his mind. On his arrival in London he had been handed a letter which gave the sorrowful news of the death of Mrs. Skepper, Mrs. Clarke's mother, and hinted at the writer's devout thankfulness that dear Mr. Borrow would soon be with her to help her bear this terrible blow.

Borrow honestly believed that his longing to go to Kiakhta sprang from evangelical fervour; but he was, in truth, no proselyte. Indeed, his religious zest was strangely akin to that expressed by Dr. Keate of Eton in his dictum: "Blessed are the pure in heart—if you are not pure in heart, by God, I'll flog you!" Mr. Shorter, who wisely pointed this resemblance, might well have added that if the word "loyal" were substituted for "pure in heart" one had a glimpse of Borrow's real feeling for Mrs. Clarke. Also, surely, of Borrow's real feeling for the Bible Society? The Society gave Borrow the chance to prove himself when they sent him to Russia. *But if it had not been for Mrs. Clarke* would he ever have won an introduction to that Society or been inspired by a desire to serve them?

So the conflict between George Borrow and his soul went on to the roll and sway of the coach until Ipswich was reached and the cramped travellers descended gingerly from their perch to seek food and warmth in the inn. Resolutely Borrow strove to push it from his brain and concentrate on the coming reunion with the mother he loved so well—but although he did not fully realize it the battle was already over, his loyalty to Mrs. Clarke had won.

At the little house in King's Court a tremendous welcome awaited him. Fires blazed in every room; the dining-table was ready laid; in the kitchen the little maid stooped, scarlet-faced, to baste the goose for the last time; neighbours ran in and out with tasty tit-bits. Mrs. Borrow sat in the parlour, her chair drawn close to the window, shushing everybody who entered lest she miss the first sound of her son's approach. Presently she heard footsteps ringing loud on the stones of the courtyard, a voice singing, "Look out, look out, Svend Vonved!" and the tears poured down her cheeks. George, her George, was home!

Such a prodigious amount he ate, the poor starved boy, and such wondrous adventures he had to tell. How proud she was of him, this big son who had worked miracles in foreign parts; how touched when—after the maid had cleared away and the neighbours had gone—they drew their chairs to the fire and he told her of his determination that she should have every comfort whatever it cost. This was her moment to prove from her bank-book how little she had spent out of all the money he had sent her, to explain that the small income from her investments was ample for her needs, to tell him how endlessly kind Mary Clarke had been in visiting her, to say how much she hoped that someday he and Mary Clarke might become more than friends.

Long after his mother had gone to bed George Borrow sat by the glowing fire. *Mary Clarke*, said his mind, *Mary Clarke*.

II

By 23 September Borrow had despatched to Mr. Brandram a full report of his visits to Moscow and Nizhni-Novgorod. By the beginning of October he was staying at Oulton Hall, then the home of Mr. Edmund Skepper, Mrs. Clarke's father. On 9 October, backed up by Breame Skepper, Mrs. Clarke's brother, he "told of his missionary experiences" at a local Bible Society meeting with such eloquence that, so he informed Mr. Brandram, "some of the most vicious characters in the neighbourhood have become weekly subscribers to the Branch Society". On 26 October he wrote to Mr. Jowett, "I am weary of doing nothing, and am sighing for employment"[1]; and on the same day Mr. Brandram sent him a most significant letter:

"I fear you will have been disappointed at not hearing from me. Shortly after your departure (for Norwich) we

[1] Borrow's salary of £200 a year still went on.

passed a resolution that you should go to Portugal; but when it came for confirmation my heart misgave me. I had in imagination set you down at Oporto . . . the more I turned it in mind the less did it appear that the door was sufficiently open to warrant the step . . .

"What do you think yourself? What do your imaginings lead you to think of China? Supposing yourself arrived on its shores, from all the information you have picked up, do you imagine that you could make any progress in distribution? Favour us with your thoughts. Experimental agency in a Society like ours is a formidable undertaking. May God direct us!"

Here was the chance for which Borrow had worked so hard in St. Petersburg. Had it come before he left that city how rapturously it would have been received! But the victory won by Mrs. Clarke atop the Norwich coach had been cemented by his stay at Oulton, which had acquainted him with all her worries. Without hesitation he answered Mr. Brandram that while he fully appreciated the "benevolent and excellent heart unwilling to fling me into an undertaking which you supposed might be attended with peril and difficulty", he wished to make it clear that he was most anxious to go to Portugal and to extend the journey into Spain. The religious friends with whom he had discussed the project were enthusiastic, while he himself hoped, "with the blessing of God", to write a small book on his Iberian travels which, if looked upon with favour by the Society, might help to recoup them for his expenses.

The mission to China and the suggestion that he should translate the Testament into Armenian (he had long tried to convince Brandram and Jowett that this was necessary) were relegated to the future in a short paragraph: ". . . On my return I can commence the Armenian Testament, and whilst I am editing that, I may be acquiring much vulgar Chinese from some unemployed Lascar or stray Cantonman whom I may pick up upon the wharves; and then—to China . . ."

And this vague, one might say careless, reference came from the man on whose heart Kiakhta had been written in letters of fire a brief two months earlier!

Moreover, the letter to Brandram was quickly followed by Borrow's personal appearance in Earl Street, and so eloquent were his descriptions of what he could accomplish in the Peninsula that at a committee meeting on 2 November, this minute was recorded:

> "RESOLVED that Mr. George Borrow be requested to proceed forthwith to Lisbon and Oporto for the purpose of visiting the Society's correspondents there, and of making further inquiries respecting the means and channels which may offer for promoting the circulation of the Holy Scriptures in Portugal."

The fact that Spain was not mentioned in this cautious announcement troubled Borrow not one whit. *"Je ne demande pas mieux!"* he shouted exultantly. The dusty Tatar outpost was blotted from his mind and in its stead stretched the "wilds of the Alemtejo", those mysterious regions beyond the Tagus which led to "the land of old renown", the "land where the Guadalete flows!" Once again he was the crusader setting forth with the colours of the Society in his hat, and although he wrote his mother on the eve of his departure from London in the *London Merchant* on 6 November, that he would be home in four or five months,[1] his dreams envisaged no such quick return.

Nobody will ever know exactly what passed between George Borrow and Mary Clarke during that October stay at Oulton. The writer inclines to the belief that when Borrow sailed for Lisbon his attitude towards her was still a combination of gratitude and worship, but suddenly gilded by a sense of his own importance as a man on whom another human being relied absolutely for advice and guidance in affairs both spiritual and material. All his life he had been regarded as *unreliable*—even Brandram and Jowett occasionally showed distrust in his judgments while his mother, despite her pride in his achievements, asked doubtfully from time to time whether her dear George could maintain his present success. Mary Clarke betrayed no such lack of confidence. She told

[1] Actually eleven months.

him he was the only person in the world whose opinion she valued, and then proceeded to pour into his ears such a pathetic and intimate tale of woe that his faith in himself swelled visibly as he listened.

It would be wrong to suggest that Mary Clarke had any bad influence over Borrow. After her marriage to him in 1840 she proved an excellent wife to a very difficult man. Without her he might never have written *Lavengro*, *The Romany Rye*, and *Wild Tales*; without her he might have travelled the Far East even to Kiakhta and given the world something as good, if not better, than those books. There can be no doubt, however, that the idea of marriage occurred to her long before it entered Borrow's head—in the late autumn of 1832, to be exact.

Even had Borrow wished to evade her (and all the evidence points the other way) he would have found it impossible to do so. Mary Clarke was a very clever woman: he was never a clever man. The fact that she was nine years his senior scarcely counted: what counted was that she possessed a far older mind and a strong will which she was accustomed to imposing upon those around her. She had worn down family opposition to her marriage with that gay, debt-ridden, consumptive Naval officer, Henry Clarke. On his death she had returned to her parents' home and proceeded to run them and it with remarkable efficiency. By the time she met Borrow she was a trifle bored by the decorous retirement thought proper to a widow of her day and was also conscious that her fortieth birthday lay less than four years ahead. His good looks were spectacular; about him was an aura of romance; he was young, eager, malleable, greatly gifted. Mary Clarke promptly lost her heart but kept her head. This was the man she wanted, the man she meant to have; but first he must achieve a certain measure of success.

Mary Clarke never understood Borrow—genius was something outside her comprehension. She was astute enough to realize that if he remained in England he would continue to drift, so she placed him deftly in the path of the Rev. Andrew Cunningham. The rest was easy, so easy that when the Society's esteemed "agent in foreign parts" wrote her a rhapsody on the Tatar hordes she flew into something akin to panic. She had no desire for a *hasty* marriage; but if her dear George went to this outlandish place filled with cut-throats it seemed most unlikely there would ever be a marriage at all. She was still searching wildly for reasons against his journey to Kiakhta when Fate played prettily into her hands.

On Mrs. Skepper's death her husband was persuaded by their only son, Breame, to make a singular will which gifted the Oulton property to his male heir.[1] This, his daughter Mary stoutly asserted, he had no right to do, for Mrs. Skepper had brought Mr. Skepper £9,000 and with this sum had purchased a five-per-cent mortgage on the whole estate. Mrs. Clarke's head for business never proved more valuable than in the subsequent family wrangles; but the idea that she genuinely sought Borrow's advice on these financial affairs is ludicrous— on any such subject she could have talked him under the table in five minutes. The extraordinary behaviour of her father and brother merely provided a lever whereby she could prise the Kiakhta notion from Borrow's mind. At the same time—and we feel sure she was one of the "religious friends" with whom he discussed Mr. Brandram's proposal—she was anxious he should accept the Portuguese offer since she felt that a short sojourn there would consolidate his position with the Bible Society.

Mary Clarke deserves full credit for being the only person who ever talked Borrow out of a pet project—but how she regretted doing so when the "four or five months" stretched into eleven and her dear George swooped eagle-wise upon his native land only to disappear again for four more years! She had thought of Portugal as a nice, civilized European country where English business-men made fortunes out of port: she had forgotten its proximity to Spain, that proud land which was to prove her bitter rival.

III

The times were scarcely propitious for a protracted stay in the Peninsula. Portugal was exhausted after an eight years

[1] The Will was dated 6 October, 1835.

civil war between the supporters of the child Queen, Donna Maria da Gloria,[1] and the followers of her uncle, Dom Miguel, who had only abandoned his claims in May 1834. Spain was in even worse state, being in the very midst of a civil war waged by the soldiers of the Queen Regent Maria Christina (mother of another infant Queen, Dona Isabel II),[2] against the forces of her brother-in-law, Don Carlos. To add to the general confusion neither country had fully recovered from the Napoleonic campaign, and there seemed precious little hope of Borrow fulfilling the grand promise he had made to Brandram of visiting "institutions for infantine education".

The voyage of the *London Merchant* was not without incident. One of the crew, crawling sleepily from his hammock, pointed to the mast and said: "I dreamt that I fell into the sea from off the cross-trees." Shortly afterwards the Captain ordered the topsails to be taken in as a squall was brewing, and the same sailor fell to his death. "I shall never forget," wrote Borrow, "the look of agony he cast us as the ship hurried past him."

Perhaps this tragedy darkened Borrow's first impression of Lisbon, for when they dropped anchor off Belem on the evening of 12 November, he stared without interest at the lovely Manueline tower rearing from the Tagus to mark the spot whence Vasco da Gama set forth in 1497. Even sight of the Geronimo Monastery behind the tower failed to rouse him from apathy, although he knew Manuel I had ordered it to be built as a monument to Portuguese seafaring supremacy and that behind its long Gothic façade the great explorers rested after all their wanderings. The following morning the Customs officials at the *Cais do Sodre* subjected him to "much ill-usage and robbery"; the city looked "huge and ruinous, still exhibiting . . . the vestiges of that terrific visitation of God, the earthquake, which shattered it some eighty years ago"; his lodgings proved "dirty and expensive"; Mr. Wilby, the merchant to whom he bore a letter of introduction, was away. "I had scarcely pressed the soil one hour," wrote Borrow passionately, "before I heartily wished myself back

[1] Daughter of Pedro IV, Emperor of Brazil.
[2] Daughter of Ferdinand IV, by his fourth marriage.

in Russia, a country which I had quitted about one month previous, and where I had left cherished friends and warm affections."

Fortunately a good rest sent his ever-mercurial spirits soaring. He acquired an excellent servant called Antonio; he explored the city from the *Castelo São Jorge*, that very seal of Lisbon which frowns from her highest hill in grim reminder of Roman and Moorish conquests, to the English cemetery, where he kissed the cold tomb of Fielding,[1] "the most singular genius which England ever produced"; from the *Rua do Alecrim* (Street of Rosemary) which runs, switchback fashion, from the *Square of the Inquisition* (now the *Rossio*) to the *Cais do Sodre*, to that "source of free waters", the *Aqueduct das Aguas Livres*, which spans the valley of Alcantara and brings to Lisbon the blessing—unknown to the capital of her Spanish neighbour—of the cool, tinking sound of many fountains.

"Lisbon" (said George Borrow) "is unquestionably the most remarkable city in the Peninsula, and, perhaps, in the south of Europe. . . . I boldly say that there is no monument of man's labour and skill, pertaining either to ancient or modern Rome, for whatever purpose designed, which can rival the waterworks of Lisbon; I mean the stupendous aqueduct whose principle arches cross the valley to the north-east of Lisbon, and which discharges its little runnel of cool and delicious water into the rocky cistern within that beautiful edifice called the Mother of the Waters from which all Lisbon is supplied with the crystal lymph . . ."[2]

It was from Lisbon that George Borrow set forth upon the Portuguese and Spanish journeys immortalized in his *Bible in Spain*. From that same city, one hundred and fifteen years later, the writer set forth to follow in his footsteps. Naturally,

[1] Fielding died in Lisbon, October, 1754.
[2] The writer asked the *Companhia das Aguas, Avenida da Liberdade*, for a pass to the Aqueduct. Not only was the visit arranged, but the visitor was congratulated upon being the only foreigner to express an interest in the Aqueduct for over twenty years. (June, 1949.)

both countries had undergone many changes since Borrow's day; but if one travelled simply, with his book as a constant companion, one found many points of similarity along certain of his routes. The robbers and bandits had vanished from the Alemtejo and the plains of Old Castile: the gypsies were still omnipresent. The northern provinces of Portugal still reminded one of the Old Testament: the sprawling hinterland of Spain still showed pitiable signs of another civil war. The wild beauty of the Peninsula had not altered: over it still hung the heavy shadows of the Bourbons, the Braganzas, the Inquisitors; and the farther one followed Borrow the more one realized the truth of his opinion that Europe ended at the Pyrenees.[1]

Borrow enjoyed exploring Lisbon, but every time he turned from her hill-tops to gaze at the coast-line of the Alemtejo across the Tagus he knew a fresh impatience to be off on his travels. He was obliged, however, to await the return of Mr. Wilby in order to present Mr. Brandram's letter of introduction. (Mr. Brandram's second letter, to the Rev. E. Whiteley, Chaplain at Oporto, was apparently never used. It contained several telling phrases—"We have some prospect of his eventually going to China"; "With Portugal he is already acquainted, and speaks the language"[2]; "I recommend him to your kind attentions, and I anticipate your thanks for so doing, after you shall have become acquainted with him. Do, not, however, be too hasty in forming your judgment." A postscript ran: "Mr. Borrow will direct his attention to Schools, and is authorised to be liberal in *giving* New Testaments.")

It was on the suggestion of a Captain John Rowland Heyland, whom he had met aboard the *London Merchant*, that Borrow decided to visit Cintra, the "glorious Eden" of Byron. Heyland rode with him the fifteen or so miles from Lisbon, and the two stayed a few days at an inn close to the sombre palace of Dom João I, who inlaid the ceiling of one of the

---

[1] Borrow's three tours of the Peninsula were as follows:
  (a) Lisbon, Mafra, Alemtejo, Badajoz, Madrid: Nov. 1835–Oct. 1836.
  (b) Cadiz, Lisbon, Seville, Madrid, Salamanca, Corunna, Oviedo, Toledo: Nov. 1836–Sept. 1838.
  (c) Cadiz, Seville, Madrid, Gibraltar, Tangier: Dec. 1838–March 1840.
[2] The earlier visit to Portugal was probably imaginary.

Bull Fight, Madrid

By courtesy of Mr. Cherry Kearton

Toledo and the Tagus

great salons with mosaic magpies as a warning to his wife's ladies to hold their chattering tongues. Curiously enough, out of all the places visited by Borrow this first one, Cintra, seemed to the writer least touched by the passage of time. Borrow rode a fine horse up the winding mountain road bordered by sub-tropical trees to the Castle of the Moors and the Pena Palace; she rode a humble donkey. Borrow had a linguistic competition with the Inn landlady, who had been—and was to become again—a governess in London; in 1949 the same Inn (now the Hotel Centrale), belonged to Mme de Bon Jésus, once a cook—and what a cook!—in London, who proudly displayed a notice, ENGLISH TEAS PROVIDED, and enjoyed nothing better than bouts of verbal fisticuffs with Spanish, French, Dutch, or English guests.

From Cintra Borrow rode down to the plain of Colhares and the sweet small bays of *Praia das Maças*, craning his neck to look back at the lofty peak of Cintra, with its "mingled scene of fairy beauty, artificial elegance, savage grandeur, domes, turrets, enormous trees, flowers, and waterfalls, such as is met with nowhere else beneath the sun"; the writer made the same journey in the open-sided tramcar which clanks its way through the rich vineyards to the Atlantic coast. Another expedition took him to Mafra, that huge palace-monastery strangely reminiscent of the Escurial; the writer found Mafra just as Borrow found it—except that its monks were no longer forced to "beg their bread, serve under the banners of Don Carlos in Spain, or prowl about as banditti".

Borrow returned to Lisbon from the Cintra Littoral full of enthusiasm for the "free and unembarrassed manner in which the Portuguese peasantry sustain a conversation, and the purity of the language in which they express their thoughts, and yet few of them can read or write. . . ." Nor, to his surprise, had he met with antagonism from the few priests with whom he had talked. Eagerly he poured out to Mr. Wilby his ideas about sending colporteurs laden with Testaments into the highways and by-ways and was chagrined when that gentleman declared emphatically that the poor colporteurs would all be murdered at the instigation of the village priests who, while doubtless charming to converse with, were extremely

M

jealous of any threat to their power. Far better, said Mr. Wilby, to distribute most of their stock among Lisbon booksellers and hire a few needy Portuguese to hawk the remainder round the streets.

The indignant Borrow gave way partially, and with bad grace. Hugging twenty Testaments and two Bibles to his bosom he dashed down to the Lisbon quays, was infuriated to learn that the public ferry-boat would not leave until the evening owing to the tides, and hired a youth with a small boat to take him and his servant across the Tagus to Aldea Gallega. It was a foolish move. A storm raged in the estuary; the youth proved to be a half-wit who chanted Dom Miguel's forbidden song, "*Quando el Rey chegou*", to the detriment of his seamanship; throughout the twelve-mile crossing the cockle-shell boat was in danger of being engulfed by the waves. Late in the evening Borrow staggered ashore to be greeted by tremendous crowds and beating drums. A lodging? Yes, in the only inn. Food? No, because this was the eve of the Feast of the Conception of the Virgin and all Aldea Gallega was bent on celebration.

After much stumbling and groping through the darkness Borrow found a wine-house full of drunken soldiers, was charged three whole crowns for a meal there, and had a long wrangle with an old muleteer who at last agreed to guide him to Evora. The inn was filthy and cold; Antonio had to share his room, beneath which was a stable crammed with mules and their *almocreves*. Outside the window was a large and odoriferous pigsty. "How could I sleep?" demanded Borrow. "The hogs grunted, the mules screamed, and the *almocreves* snored most horribly." By four o'clock he was dressing; by four-thirty he had sent the protesting Antonio scurrying out into the cold to rouse the aged muleteer and his nephew; by five he was riding under a bright moon in the direction of Evora.

It has been said too many times that George Borrow's passionate, insensate hatred of the Holy Catholic Church sprang from his Peninsular experiences. It is a totally untrue statement. Borrow was brought up from infancy to detest "all Popery", and we know from James Martineau and others

that his "tall" schoolboy yarns always ended with an indictment of Roman Catholicism. Beliefs learnt in childhood bite
deep, and Borrow's stay in Petersburg did nothing to allay
his suspicions of the Pope and all his works. By the time he
reached Portugal very little was needed to change his rooted
dislike of Rome into violent loathing—and that little was
provided by his uncomfortable night in Aldea Gallega. Absurd?
Yes, but then Borrow's sudden passions had their absurd side.
Certainly, in the next five years he was to suffer a host of
insults and indignities from the Spanish priesthood; the fact
remains that he regarded the Feast of the Conception of the
Virgin as a sort of heathen orgy in which the very animals
joined, and that from the moment he left Aldea Gallego he
maintained an uncompromisingly hostile attitude towards the
Holy Catholic Church. Since "Gallega" is a Portuguese version
of Galicia and since the half-witted boat boy had been a
Galician, he extended his hatred to embrace every inhabitant
of that Spanish Province.

Borrow's ride through Alemtejo, with its white sandy soil,
its desolate heaths, its great forests with their towering cork
trees, its wandering herds of cattle and goats with their perpetually tinkling bells, was enlivened by his guide's startling
tales of robbers—particularly of one called Sabocha, whose
exploits had become legendary. Every inch the missionary,
Borrow left New Testaments and tracts beside the dead fires
of the "sons of plunder"; and had the good fortune to be
overtaken by Dom Geronimo de Azevedo, Government
Secretary at Evora, a charming and much-travelled man who
promised to introduce the Bible into the schools under his
jurisdiction. With this new friend Borrow sampled the famous
dish of Pengões (rabbit roasted with sweet sauce), stayed
overnight at Vendas Novas, and began next day the long,
slow climb through wooded hills where the fat reddish pigs
rooted for *bolotas* (sweet acorns from the *azinheiras* tree), and the
olive groves shone silver in the winter sun. Presently the road
forked eastwards to Elvas and Badajoz, south-east to Evora.

The brilliant talk of Dom Geronimo, the fairy-like beauty
of Monte Almo with its green slopes and foaming streams, the
multi-coloured scarves worn by the goat-herds, scarcely served

to console Borrow, who kept looking back at the white ribbon
zigzagging along the side of Montemor—the road that led to
Spain.

It was night before they reached Evora, that ancient
home of the Portuguese Kings set in a fertile upland plain.
Borrow found lodging in a *posada* (now a garage) opposite
the great Convent of San Francisco and, fortified by Dom
Geronimo's generous offer of help, set off early the following
morning to distribute his Testaments among schools and booksellers. He met with sad disappointment. There were no
schools—though people to whom he spoke said vaguely one
might open soon. The old town with its confusion of arches,
belvederes, minarets, and carvings, its host of churches and
palaces, irritated him by its air of apathy. The *posada* was full
of Spanish smugglers and their rusted pieces of iron, copper,
or brass. Everybody in the place, from the cold-faced Governor
sitting in the magnificent library of the massive Cathedral
to the swarthy peasants who crept along the narrow streets
wrapped in their scarves, exemplified the quality expressed
in the Portuguese word *soudade*. When asked if they were
Constitutionalists they raised dull eyes and said "yes" without
conviction: when tackled about their faith they shook their
heads in brooding melancholy. They were obsessed by witchcraft, wore sprigs of rosemary in their hats to ward off the
evil eye, and only showed interest at the mention of money.

Even Borrow's evangelical zeal wilted when confronted
with Evora. It was, he considered, frowning at the delicate
Temple of Diana once built by the Romans, a pagan town.
He was wrong, as he would have discovered had he enquired
the history of the long, low white building[1] in the Cathedral
square. Here for centuries the Inquisitors had lived and
tortured their victims, and it was their memory, not Diana's,
that lay heavy over Evora.

Dom Geronimo proved a delightful host but a broken reed
when it came to practical assistance. The only sympathetic
character was an aged shopkeeper in the market, who said he
had been greatly persecuted by the Church and would therefore
take half Borrow's Testaments and try to sell them. There

[1] Now the *Hotel Alentejano*.

was nothing to do but accept his offer and retire to sit by the fountain near the south-west Gate of the Moors, where all visitors to the town came to water their horses, and lecture "the children of Portugal upon matters relating to their eternal welfare".

Borrow felt sure his "utter fearlessness" in telling the Evora muleteers that the Pope was "an arch-deceiver" was the reason they did not attack him. Knowing these people, the writer feels it far more likely that they had no least idea what he was talking about and regarded him as some sort of mild lunatic. However, despite glowing epistles to Brandram and Jowett, Borrow soon gave up the attempt to convert Evora and for the remainder of his stay made plans for a journey into Spain. With superb effrontery he actually wrote to Dr. Bowring asking for letters of introduction to Lord Howard de Walden, British Minister to Portugal, "and letters something similar for Madrid, which I should like to have as soon as possible". (These came eventually, under cover of a stiff, cool note.)

Curiously enough, the only regret Borrow expressed on leaving Evora was that he had not witnessed the Feast of St. John, held there every midsummer. The writer, who happened to arrive in Evora during the Feast, could not help wondering what a man who thought the Feast of the Conception of the Virgin a pagan orgy would have made of the terrific jamboree going on on the *Rossio de San Braz*. Only one thing about it would have appealed to him—the presence of the gypsies from all over the Peninsula.

IV

On 6 January, 1836, George Borrow rode down the hill from Elvas mounted on a "sorry mule without bridle or stirrups . . . covered with sores, wall-eyed, and with a kind of halt in its gait". Before him lay the plain of Estremadura and beyond it rose the mountains, and as he gazed at the cloud-circled peak of proud Albuquerque his eyes filled with tears.

Spain, beautiful romantic Spain at last, after all the tribulations of the past few weeks! His mind went back to the series of vexations which had pursued him since leaving Evora. The *calèche* with the drunken muleteer in which he had driven back to Aldea Gallega; the delay in Lisbon while he waited for interviews with this authority and that; the exorbitant charges of hotel-keepers, tradesmen, servants; the gruelling return journey through the Alemtejo; the shot from a Portuguese soldier's rifle which had just missed him near Arrayolos; the surly guards at the fort of Elvas. Some day, of course, he would return to force the true Gospel down Portuguese throats —but now, Estremadura!

He urged his wretched beast to a canter and splashed through the boundary brook of La Caya. Even as he gained the farther bank a beggar asked him for alms in the sonorous, magnificent tongue of Spain: *"O Señor Caballero, que me de usted una limosna por amor de Dios . . . !"* and he cried ecstatically: *"Santiago y cierra España!"* as he flung the man a coin and rode on across the many-arched bridge over the Guadiana river into Badajoz. How different were the Customs House officials to those of Lisbon; how friendly the people in the streets; how welcoming the proprietor of the *Three Nations posada*! Eagerly he strode round the city, head upturned to the Spanish sun, his excited mind busy with thought of the three-day coach journey to Madrid which he would start on the morrow.

In reality Borrow did not leave Badajoz until 16 January, for on his return to the *posada* he found it crowded with his friends, the "people out of Egypt".

"It was at Badajoz that I first fell in with those singular people, the Zincali, Gitanos, or Spanish gypsies. It was here that I met with the wild Paco, the man with the withered arm, who wielded the *cachas* (shears) with his left hand; his shrewd wife, Antonia, skilled in hokkano baro, or the great trick; the fierce gypsy, Antonio Lopez, their father-in-law; and many other almost equally singular individuals of the Errate, or gypsy blood. It was here that I first preached the gospel to the gypsy people, and commenced that translation of the New Testament in the Spanish gypsy tongue, a portion of which I subsequently printed at Madrid."[1]

The memory of Jasper Petulengro still held sway. Without another thought for the real object of his mission to Madrid, Borrow squatted before the *posada* fire with his Gitano friends. When he left Badajoz only his luggage travelled by coach; he rode to the Castilian boundary accompanied by Antonio Lopez, who had provided him with a raw-boned *burra*. What a journey it was! Full of wild men, wild animals, wild weather. What a thrill Borrow knew when "the gypsies crowned him their king, near the ruins of Merida, at a barbarous festival, where they strewed the ground with sweetmeats and danced upon them, performing at the same time other wild and uncouth ceremonies". How he revelled in the nights spent with groups of wandering gypsies round their blazing camp-fires; how pleased he was when a *carabinero* in the desolate village of Jaraicejo demanded a second glance at the signature of the "Caballero Balmerson" (Lord Palmerston) on his passport. Gone was the stern evangelist who had frowned on the innocent festivities of Aldea Gallega: in his stead was the swaggering, bearded figure of Don Jorge in battered Andalusian hat and rusty black cloak.

Antonio took leave of Borrow at the foot of the Pass of Mirabete. Now the way led over a spur of the Sierra de Guadelupe, and as he reached the summit he reined in his *burra* with a gasp of sheer joy. Far below him the plain shimmered in the sun like a vast lake. On the one side towered the Sierra de Gredos, on the other the Montes de Toledo. Slowly he descended the rocky, twisting path until he came to the Tagus boiling between high banks. There was no bridge—it had been destroyed during the Peninsular War—but an old man ferried him across to Almarez, where he spent the evening in queer but satisfying company, for round the *posada* fire were clustered several shepherds and their dogs, a hunter, a sick soldier home from the wars, and a vociferous beggar

[1] In March, 1836, the Bible Society gave permission to print St. Luke's Gospel.

who occasionally broke off from chattering to chant his plaint for alms, *"por las siete llagas de Maria Santissima!"*[1]

It was the following morning, close to the granite pillar marking the Castilian boundary, that Borrow fell in with the "Herculean" Jew with the tranquil eyes called Abarbenel, who boasted of his immense riches although he was dressed in coarsest garments. Together they tramped to Talavera, Borrow leading the *burra* by the halter, and next day he actually succeeded in selling that miserable animal to his new friend before taking the coach for Madrid.

V

The Madrid of Borrow's day held within its mud walls a swarming population of about 200,000. It was no cosmopolitan capital, as he soon found out in his wanderings, and while some of its inhabitants were fiercely Carlist and others fiercely National, practically all were Spanish. The aristocracy did not interest Borrow: that "extraordinary man", the ordinary Spaniard, did. . . .

"Hail, ye aguadores of Asturia! who, in your dress of coarse duffel and leathern skull-caps, are seen seated in hundreds by the fountain sides, upon your empty water-casks, or staggering with them filled to the topmost stories of lofty houses. Hail, ye caseseros of Valencia! who, lolling lazily against your vehicles, rasp tobacco for your paper cigars whilst waiting for a fare. Hail to you, beggars of La Mancha! men and women, who, wrapped in coarse blankets, demand charity indifferently at the gate of the palace or the prison. Hail to you, valets from the mountains, major-domos and secretaries from Biscay and Guipuscoa, toreros from Andalusia, riposteros from Galicia, shop-keepers from Catalonia! Hail to ye, Castilians, Estremenians and Aragonese, of whatever calling! And lastly, genuine sons of the capital, rabble of Madrid, ye twenty thousand manolos,

[1] The seven wounds of the Virgin.

whose terrible knives, on the second morning of May, worked such grim havoc amongst the legions of Murat!"

Left to himself, Borrow would doubtless have spent his days amongst these people, and his nights translating the New Testament into *Caló*, or Spanish gypsy; but his conscience bade him remember "the hope of obtaining permission to print the New Testament in the Castilian tongue for circulation in Spain". The Society had not as yet made any resolution regarding such a printing, although they had cast a favourable eye on a Roman Catholic edition by Father Philipe Scio de San Miguel[1] which had been printed at Barcelona in 1820. But the Society, thought Borrow loftily, knew naught of Spain. (He himself had been in the country less than a month!)

Within a day or two of his arrival in Madrid Borrow found lodgings—a huge bare sitting-room and a tiny bedroom—in the *Calle de la Zarza*[2] a narrow, slummy street near the famous *Puerta del Sol*. His landlady was enormously fat, hailed from Vallodolid, and had a rascally son called Baltasar, a tailor of diminutive stature but of "fanfaronading air", whose boast was that if he stood in the *Puerta del Sol* he could rally every National in Madrid to his banner.

Borrow knew absolutely nobody in Madrid. Bowring's letters of introduction had not yet been received. His store of money was dwindling and he had to expend two pounds, fifteen shillings on a new suit. He walked along the *Prado*, head bent against the cruel wind which whistled down from the Guadamara range, cogitating the best method of seeking an interview with Don Juan Alvarez de Mendizabel, that enigmatic Basque who held the precarious position of Prime Minister of Spain. Suddenly he jerked upright and clapped a hand to his forehead. Of course! he must enlist the good offices of the British Minister, Sir George Villiers![3] Without more ado he sped in the direction of the *Calle de Torija*.

Sir George was most sympathetic and helpful. He told

---

[1] *El Nuevo Testamento, Traducido al Espanol de la Vulgata Latina por el Rmo. P. Philipe Scio de S. Miguel.*

[2] "Street of the Brambles", long since pulled down.

[3] George William Frederick Villiers (1800–1870), afterwards fourth Earl of Clarendon.

Borrow to call upon him over any difficulty, gave him an introduction to the Prime Minister, and warned him that since Mendizabel hated all foreign evangelists it was extremely unlikely he would grant an interview. The warning fell on deaf ears: on the morning of 7 February the enthusiastic agent scurried up the steps of the Palace in the *Calle de Alcala*, where he shivered in an icy ante-room for three hours before being ushered into the presence.

"Yours is not the first application I have had," said Mendizabel coldly, "ever since I have held the reins of government I have been pestered in this manner, by English calling themselves Evangelical Christians, who have of late come flocking over into Spain . . . And now you . . . have almost persuaded me to embroil myself yet more with the priesthood as if they did not abhor me enough already. What a strange infatuation is this which drives you over lands and waters with Bibles in your hands. My good sir, it is not Bibles we want, but rather guns and gunpowder, to put the rebels down with, and above all, money, that we may pay the troops; whenever you come with these three things you shall have a hearty welcome, if not, we really can dispense with your visits, however great the honour."

Borrow answered passionately: "There will be no end to the troubles of this afflicted country until the gospels have free circulation"; whereupon Mendizbel said dryly that his thirteen years' residence in England had prepared him for such a reply, and dismissed his visitor with the suggestion he might call again when the war had ended—say, in six months time.

Borrow's credulity never showed more plainly than in his reception of Mendizabel's words. Their irony passed him by, and although any Spaniard could have told him that Cabinets came and went at alarming speed he dashed off a lyrical letter to Mr. Brandram. "The game is now in our hands!" he wrote, going on to tell how he had actually seen the Prime Minister, "whom it is as difficult to get nigh as it is to approach the North Pole." A very few months, he thought, would see all printing negotiations settled; then the Society must employ an agent (obviously himself) "to engage colporteurs and to come to arrangements with booksellers, both in Spain and in the provincial towns of Portugal, but let him not be a hesitater and starter of needless doubts and difficulties; anything may be accomplished with a little shrewdness, a little boldness, and a great trust in God".

Meanwhile, he enquired, did the Society wish him to visit Granada; or should he return to Badajoz and finish his translation of St. Luke with the aid of the gypsies; or would they prefer he went back to Lisbon, as he now held most important letters of introduction (presumably from Dr. Bowring) to people there?

It was perfectly clear that Borrow's own desire was to renew the fascinating acquaintance of Antonio Lopez and his family in Badajoz. Mr. Brandram thought otherwise: "In the matter of (the gypsy) translation," he replied primly, "we say *festina lente.*" He added that while the Committee would prefer their agent to return to Lisbon, they were prepared to leave this to his discretion. "In these wondrous days," he ended piously, "opportunities may open unexpectedly."

Still convinced that Mendizabel would send for him any day Borrow stayed on in Madrid; but on 13 May the Government fell. The new Prime Minister was another Basque, Don Francisco Javier de Isturiz. Thanks to the intervention of Sir George Villiers permission to print 5,000 copies of Scio's Spanish Testament "without note or comment", was given by the Duque de Rivas, the new Minister of the Interior, on 9 June.

Borrow was overjoyed—so was the Committee in London. Arrangements were made with the Government printer, a "Don Carlos Wood", an Englishman who had established his most profitable business in Madrid. For a short time everything seemed settled, and as Borrow strolled along the tree-lined bank of the canal which runs to the west of Madrid through the lush meadows of the Manzanares he felt content with the world.

It was through a canal-side orange-seller with whom he made friends that he met that fantastic character Benedict Mol, the Swiss who had once been a Captain in the Walloon Guard and now, in his old age, peddled soap-balls through Spain because a dying war comrade had told him that in the Church of Saint James at Campostella in Galicia, lay buried a huge copper kettle containing "gold moidores and a packet of huge diamonds from the Brazils".

"When my wife died," Benedict Mol told Borrow, "I left Minorca with a determination to go to St. James, but on reaching Madrid, I fell into the hands of a Basque woman, who persuaded me to live with her, which I have done for several years; she is a great hax[1], and says that if I desert her she will breathe a spell which shall cling to me for ever. *Dem Got sey dank*—she is now in the hospital, and daily expected to die."

Benedict Mol was convinced that once he reached Compostella he could lay hands on this treasure without delay—his trouble was to scrape up enough money for the journey, for, as he said sadly, "I know little more of soap-boiling than I do of tailoring, horse-farriery, or shoe-making, all of which I have practised."

Many readers of the *Bible in Spain* have expressed doubts as to whether this singular man, who keeps reappearing throughout the book, ever existed in real life. That he did is made plain by a letter written to Borrow from his Santiago friend Rey Romero in June 1839:

"The German of the *Treasure* came here last year bearing letters from the Government for the purpose of discovering it. But, a few days after his arrival, they threw him into prison; from thence he wrote me, making himself known as the one you introduced to me; wherefore my son went to see him in the prison. He told my son that you also had been arrested, but I could not credit it.[2] A short time after, they took him off to Corunna; then they brought him back here again, and I do not know what has become of him since."

Whether Benedict Mol really popped up at such opportune moments in Borrow's Spanish travels is, however, open to question. That ardent admirer, Dr. Knapp, cried fervently: "True, every word of it! Remember our artist never created; he painted from models." With due respect to Dr. Knapp

[1] Witch: German *Hexe*.
[2] This information was true.

Borrow had an extraordinary gift for *drawing* from a model, then colouring his drawing so richly that the original was wellnigh obliterated—but oh, so much more vivid and exciting! He had always exaggerated: during his years in the Peninsula his exaggeration became hyperbole. Characters, places, dates, events, were changed as the whim took him. In this way he pointed each slightest incident: to the description of a desolate moor he added a gibbering maniac; to the portrait of an aged, sombrely dressed archbishop he added a huge and dazzling amethyst ring; to the cathedral of Palencio he added stained glass windows by Murillo.

The result entirely justified all these little "touchings up". The *Bible in Spain* was, and has remained, the best book about that country ever written by any foreigner—in truth, *it is Spain*.

But we left Borrow in the meadows near the Manzanares, talking to Benedict Mol. His peaceful mood was not destined to last, for in August the revolution of *La Granja* broke out just as he was about to leave for England, secure in the knowledge that the printing of his Testaments was going ahead.

Cristina, the Queen-Regent, had retired for the summer to *La Granja*, about forty miles from Madrid, and with her had gone her lover, Muños. The army, supposedly on her side in the struggle with Don Carlos, had long been angered by her insistence upon absolute monarchy and her refusal to countenance the Cadiz Constitution of 1812. On the night of 12 August her guards, led by a Sergeant Garcia, forced their way into her apartments and demanded she should sign a document promising constitutional rule. Cristina refused, whereupon they marched her down to a courtyard and pointed at the blindfold Muños, saying he would get four bullets through his brain if she persisted in her Bourbon haughtiness. Only when the wretched Muños was made to kneel by the wall and four soldiers levelled their muskets did she capitulate.

The repercussions in Madrid were swift and noisy. The Cabinet resigned; the Calatrava Ministry was installed[1]; the *Puerta del Sol* resounded with shouts of "*Viva la Constituçion!*"; everybody forgot the real villain of the piece, Espartero, and growled for the blood of Quesada, Captain-General of the city.

[1] The Calatrava Ministry lasted a full year.

Needless to say, George Borrow was a spectator of the scene when the brave Quesada, preceded by his infantry, rode into the square mounted on a superb bay horse, crying: "Long live the absolute Queen!" Time and again he spurred his beast and charged into the dense crowd, his sword flashing bright in the sunlight, until the rabble ran for their lives down the narrow streets. At sight of such courage George Borrow forgot, to his eternal credit, his often reiterated refusal "to be of any politics save Gypsy politics", and leaned from a window yelling: "*Viva Quesada! Viva Quesada!*"

By the evening Madrid was quiet. Isturiz had fled to France; the Duque de Rivas to Gibraltar; Quesada, in the guise of a civilian, had ridden as far as Hortaleza, a village near the city; the revolution had died as suddenly as it had begun. But the following night, as he sipped his coffee in the *Café Nuevo* on the *Calle de Alcala*, Borrow saw the last of the Captain-General. A party of Nationals entered, arm-in-arm and two by two, stamping their feet and singing:

> "Que es lo que abaja
> Por aquel cerro?
> Ta ra ra ra ra.
> Son los huesos de Quesada,
> Que los trae un perro—
> Ta ra ra ra ra!"[1]

"A huge bowl of coffee was then called for, which was placed upon a table, around which were gathered the national soldiers: there was silence for a moment, which was interrupted by a voice roaring out '*el panuelo!*' A blue kerchief was forthwith produced, which appeared to contain a substance of some kind; it was untied, and a gory hand and three or four dissevered fingers made their appearance, and with these the contents of the bowl were stirred up. 'Cups! Cups!' cried the nationals."

By 18 August Borrow left Madrid for Granada and Malaga

Borrow's own translation runs as follows:
> "What down the hill comes hurrying there?—
> With a hey, with a ho, a sword, and a gun!
> Quesada's bones, which a hound doth bear—
> Hurrah, brave brothers!—the work is done."

by coach, since the New Government had made a declaration
that "the Press was now free", and he, credulous as ever,
believed them. No record of his journey remains, and one can
only presume that travel in a *diligence* held little appeal for
one accustomed to Andalusian stallions, bucking mules, and
obstinate donkeys; and that the tatterdemalion crew which
infested the hillsides of Granada in his day and still infest it
in ours, scarcely lived up to his idea of gypsies. That he actually
visited Granada in August is written indelibly in the writer's
mind, because when she visited the Alhambra in 1949 and asked
brightly if she might look over their visitors' book for 1836,
a priest next to her enquired if he might assist in the search.
At his command a dusty volume was produced after much
delay. The priest turned the heavy pages, intoning grandiloquent Spanish names until he felt a clutch at his arm. There it
was, staring from Folio XIII in a fine copperplate hand:
GEORGE BORROW NORVICENSIS, August 30th, 1836.
"Ah-h-h," the priest's breath escaped in a hiss. "A bitter
enemy of my country," he said; and for the remainder of her
stay in Granada regarded her with deepest suspicion.

VI

The beginning of October saw Borrow haranguing the
Committee in Earl Street on the necessity of distributing the
5,000 Testaments now printing throughout Spain. To this they
cordially agreed. (Had not their excellent agent told them
"that the last skirts of the cloud of papal superstition are
vanishing below the horizon of Spain; whoever says the
contrary either knows nothing of the matter or wilfully hides
the truth"?[1]) Furthermore, they urged Mr. Borrow to return
to Madrid as quickly as possible, an instruction he was only
too happy to obey—but first, of course, a visit to Norwich
had to be paid; and Norwich was very near to Oulton Broad.
It was during this month of October 1836 that Mary
Clarke began to realize what manner of man she had called
into being when she had introduced a penniless and passionate

[1] In a letter to Mr. Brandram, 30 May, 1836.

"six foot three" to the Rev. Francis Cunningham. The Borrow who had returned from St. Petersburg a year earlier had delighted her by displaying a blend of new-found assurance and chivalrous deference to her wishes: the Borrow who had come home from the Peninsula seemed strangely altered. Of course, he was just as devoted to her—but in the very middle of her long story about her father's recent death, and the mortgage she held on the estate, and the disconcerting manner in which her sister-in-law, Mrs. Breame Skepper, was behaving, he suddenly burst into a lyrical description of some hazardous journey he had undertaken in the company of a gypsy called Antonio Lopez. Again, when she turned the discussion to a subject which had been dear to both their hearts—that he should take Holy Orders—he said, with a positively wild glint in his eye, that he could not even consider the idea until he had fulfilled his sacred mission and converted every Spaniard to Protestantism.

It was all very disturbing to one who had envisioned her "dear George" safely ensconced in a dog-collar and a nice rural living. Missionary zeal was one thing: this fanatical talk about Spain—a country strangely different from the one she had learnt about in school geography books—quite another. And gypsies?—surely they should be consigned to the limbo wherein childish things were stored?

Mary Clarke's heart performed astonishing antics when she looked at her tall, bronzed lover: her head remained set firmly on her pretty neck. Outwardly she showed no sign of distress when Borrow bade her a hurried good-bye: inwardly she decided to pit herself against Spain, that fiery mistress who threatened her peace.

And George Borrow himself? His heart, so he truly believed, remained at Oulton Broad: his mind was already travelling the highway from Madrid to Corunna. Before leaving London in the S.S. *Manchester* on 4 November, he sent his mother £130 out of the £150 drawn from the Society on account of salary and for the next nine days gave himself up to sheer bodily misery, for the ship was overcrowded with passengers, "most of them poor consumptive individuals, and other invalids fleeing from the cold blasts of England's winter",

By courtesy of Mr. Cherry Kearton

General View of Toledo

Valencia

and they nearly foundered off Cape Finisterre owing to the bad state of the *Manchester's* engines and the inability of her captain, "a person picked up in a hurry", to combat the storm they encountered in the Bay of Biscay.

On 13 November they limped up the Tagus to Lisbon, where they stayed a week for repairs, and Borrow not only discovered that "the minds of the people had been so engrossed with politics, that they found scarcely any time to think of the welfare of their souls"; but that Gomez, the famous Carlist leader, was "ravaging Andalusia", the province he had to pass through on his way from Cadiz to Madrid. Cordova had been sacked; Señor Gomez was lurking in Seville for no other purpose than to apprehend the wicked Mr. Borrow, who had "full confidence that the Lord would open the path" before him.

All hyperbole must be forgiven Borrow when we consider the man's courage in undertaking the desperate journey of over three hundred miles from Seville to the capital. (Under vastly more civilized conditions the writer threw herself, her mule and her *arriero* upon the mercy of the burghers of Cordova and refused even to contemplate the passes through the Sierra Morena, the flat loneliness of the La Mancha plain, the loud-sung charm of Aranjuez.)

But from the moment Borrow stepped on to the quay at Cadiz his gypsy friends demonstrated their welcome, proof of which was given by his fellow-passenger, the Marquez de Santa Coloma,[1] in his description to the Rev. Wentworth Webster of St. Jean de Luz:

"When they stepped on to the quay" (wrote Mr. Webster) "Borrow looked around, saw some Gypsies lounging there, said something that the Marquis could not understand, and immediately 'that man became *une grappe de gitanos*. They hung round his neck, clung to his knees, seized his hands, kissed his feet, so that the Marquis scarcely liked to join his comrade again, after such close embraces by so dirty a company.'"

Cadiz, with its tall white houses, its steep narrow streets,

[1] A Carlist agent who paid several visits to England.

its tangy spray-filled air, was in a state of great confusion. While half the populace argued loudly about the deplorable state of the country and the possible intervention of Britain or France, the other half erected barricades round the city. Everyone was far too busy to take interest in a mad foreigner who preferred talking about the New Testament, a "work not sought after and little known", to discussing the war. Borrow, depressed by the ungodliness of the people and a stomach upset which he felt quite sure was cholera, spent four days dosing himself with oil and brandy before crawling shakily abroad the Spanish steamer *Betis*.

Later, on a summer visit to Seville, he wrote a wonderful description of that fabled city; but as the *Betis* chugged her way up the muddy, weedy Guadalquivir he lay miserably on deck, and even sight of Seville dreaming in the moonlight failed to impress him—though he wrote Mr. Brandram a meticulous account of the cathedral with the La Giralda tower up which Ferdinand VII used to ride his horse; of the Alcazar with its magnificent Moorish halls; of Triana with its hordes of gypsies and of Italica, in the ruined amphitheatre of which he sat on the "time-worn granite benches, from whence myriads of human beings once gazed down on the arena below, where the gladiator shouted, and the lion and leopard yelled".

In truth, it was no time to stroll around appreciating the beauties of Seville. Gomez was reported to be at nearby Ronda; various quarters of the city were continually raided by Carlist bands who made short work of the road blocks and earthworks hurriedly prepared by the frightened inhabitants; the whole of Andalusia lay in the grip of famine; the road to the capital was closed, even the bold *arrieros* refusing to run any risk of meeting the plundering Basque and Aragonese Carlist soldiery who, only a few days earlier, had "intercepted an unfortunate courier, and after scooping out his eyes put him to death with most painful tortures, and mangled his body in a way not to be mentioned".

Borrow did many brave things in Spain; the bravest was his decision to ride to Cordova with no escort save an elderly Genoese who was pathetically anxious to act as colporteur for the Society when the war should be over. On 9 December they rode forth in brilliant weather to face "more perils than beset Christian in his route to the Eternal Kingdom", and by night-fall had reached Carmona, in Moorish times the key to Seville. Next morning they reluctantly left the shelter of the dark battlemented walls which guard the hill-town and rode down into the desolate plain that stretches to the Sierra Morena, the boundary between Andalusia and La Mancha.

In Borrow's day there were only a few scattered settlements on the plain, and these were occupied by Germans who had been lured to Spain in the eighteenth century by the false promises of "some potent lord". The wretched inn at Moncloa was owned by a couple who were grandchildren of these colonists, and as Borrow ordered barley for the horses and a meal for themselves the Genoese whispered: "They are evil people, and this is an evil house; it is a harbouring place for thieves, and murders have been committed here, if all tales be true." Very likely they escaped with their lives owing to Borrow's inordinate curiosity regarding his fellow men, which led him to ask all manner of questions concerning their ancestry, finally disarming them by remarking: "The Germans are the most honest people in the world: being their legitimate descendants you have of course no thieves among you?"

The sun was setting before the travellers reined in their horses on the brow of the *Cuesta del Espinal* (hill of the thorn tree), and gazed down on the gilded outlines of Cordova. They were still several miles from the city; their horses were tired; the poor Genoese confessed tearfully that before their departure from Seville he had not sat in a saddle for thirty years, that he could go no farther, and that bandits abounded in the district they had to traverse. If they did not reach Cordova before nightfall, he quavered, then assuredly they would be foully murdered. Borrow rallied him as best he could; but before half the distance was covered the old man and his horse were spent and the moonless night enshrouded them.

Borrow rose grandly to the occasion. Fastening the bridle of his companion's horse to the crupper of his own, he spared neither spur nor cudgel to force his weary mount into a trot. On through the blackness they went, the terrified Genoese imploring the mad Englishman to stop, until the lights of

Cordova gleamed ahead and they clattered across the Guadalquivir bridge, through the city gate, and up a street running
the entire length of the town to a *posada* which greeted them
with grim iron gratings and deathly silence. Numerous knock-
ings and shoutings brought a porter who said: "Travellers?
Jesus Maria knows we have not so many of them that we need
repulse any!" and ushered them in to a welcome from the
landlord, "a most egregious Carlist", who brandished his
torch before Borrow's face and cried: "Juanito, open not the
gate any more tonight . . . Should the nationals come to
make any disturbance, tell them that the son of Belington
(Wellington) is in the house ready to attack them sword in
hand unless they retire . . .!"

"You recognized me at once for an Englishman," said
Borrow. "Do many of my countrymen visit Cordova?"

"*Toma!*" exclaimed the garrulous landlord, "I have had
Englishmen in this house of all grades, from the son of Belington
to a young medico, who cured my daughter, the chica here, of
the ear-ache. There were two with Gomez, serving as volunteers.
Vaya que gente; what noble horses they rode, and how they
scattered their gold about; they brought with them a Portuguese, who was much of a gentleman but very poor; it was
said that he was one of Dom Miguel's people, and that these
Englishmen supported him for the love they bore to royalty;
he was continually singing:

> "*El Rey chegou—El Rey chegou,*
> *E en Belem desembarcou!*"[1]

He added, with a flourish of his torch, that he had forgotten
to ask Don Jorge what political opinion he favoured; but he
was so obviously a Carlist that it was not surprising he crossed
swords the next morning with the Genoese, who heard him
speaking disrespectfully of the Queen-Regent and her daughter
Isabel. Despite the fact that they were Neapolitan Bourbons
he considered them his countrywomen. "I confess," the old
man told Borrow, "that I lost my temper and returned the
compliment, by saying that Carlos was a knave and the

[1] "The king arrived, the king arrived, and landed at Belem."

Princess of Beira no better than she should be." Having delivered himself of this dangerous pronouncement he had had his breakfast cup of chocolate knocked sky-high by the landlord's wife, who shrieked: "Begone, dog of a negro, you shall taste nothing more in my house; may you be hanged even as a swine is hanged!"

"I forgot to say," added the Genoese piteously, "that the knave of a landlord told me that you had confessed yourself to be of the same politics as himself, or he would not have harboured you."

Borrow's answer was infinitely nearer the truth than his usual assertion that he never talked or concerned himself with any politics save gypsy ones: "My good man," he said, "I am invariably of the politics of the people at whose table I sit, or beneath whose roof I sleep, at least I never say anything which can lead them to suspect the contrary; by pursuing which system I have more than once escaped a bloody pillow, and having the wine I drank spiced with sublimate."

The Genoese was in a fever to be off, preferring the perils of the road to a Carlist knife between his ribs; but Borrow lingered in Cordova, giving the unsafe state of the route to Madrid as an excuse. One suspects, however, that he was fascinated by the conversation of an ancient and seemingly harmless priest who now bred pigeons for the market. Borrow, who had supposed him to indulge in metaphor about his "dovecote", was intrigued by his robust statement: "My birds are very celebrated, and plumper or fatter flesh than theirs I believe cannot be found in the entire kingdom." But he added with a leer: "I suffer no dovecotes but my own within my district. With respect to the souls of my parishioners, I trust I do my duty . . . I always took great pleasure in these spiritual matters, and it was on that account that I attached myself to the Santa Casa of Cordova . . ."

He went on to tell with relish of his years as an Inquisitor, when the holy office exercised its functions upon "sorcery, Judaism, and certain carnal misdemeanors". There was the nun in a Seville convent, who developed the reprehensible habit "of flying through the windows and about the garden over the tops of the orange trees", there was the ecclesiastic suspected of black Judaism, who had hidden beneath his floor "a small shrine of silver, enclosing three books in black hogskin, which, on being opened, were found to be books of Jewish devotion"; there were "certain acts of flagitiousness practised by the clergy in lone and remote palomares (dovecotes) in olive grounds and gardens . . ."

It was a great pity that Borrow allowed himself to listen to this old reprobate who had not only sold his fellow-priest to the Carlists but advocated worship of *Maria Santissima*, because "she stands there, *tan bonita, tan guapita*—so well dressed and so genteel—with such pretty colours, such red and white. . . ." To any other man the encounter would have been something to laugh off and forget; to Borrow it was another indictment against a Church he already, and wrongly, detested. The charm of old Cordova with its winding alley-ways, its view of the silvery olive groves on the slopes of the Sierra Morena, its walks by the banks of a younger but clearer Guadalquivir, went unregarded. True, the cathedral, originally a mosque, won his attention for a brief space; but always he returned to listen, spellbound, to the old man's droning reminiscences of a hideous time long past.

Even his leaving of Cordova savoured of the priest's influence, for he engaged, at the enormous fee of forty dollars, the *contrabandista* brother-in-law of the landlord to see him through the dangerous passage to Madrid; and one can only say that the La Mancha weather—"the Lord breathed forth a frozen blast, the severity of which was almost intolerable; no human beings but ourselves ventured forth"—was a bountiful but undeserved act of providence. On the night of Christmas Day Borrow was fortunate to find lodging in an Englishman's home at Aranjuez. "I swallowed nearly a pint of brandy," he wrote to the surprised Mr. Brandram, "it affected me no more than warm water."

On 26 December he rode into Madrid, which presented a welcome contrast to Andalusia. The Calatrava Ministry was still in power and under its influence the city was tranquil. Borrow took lodgings in the *Calle de Santiago*, a little street between the *Calle Mayor* and the Opera House, his new land-lady being a remarkable woman called Maria Diaz who was to prove the staunchest possible friend and who, when Borrow went to live in Seville in 1839, was to write to him with true Castilian courtesy: "Fare ye well, and command as you please your unprofitable but attached servant—QBSM." (*Quien besa sus manos*—who kisses your hands.)

Whether Borrow found that Don Carlos Wood had failed to set up the type for the Testaments, or whether there was some disagreement between the two was never made clear[1]; but within a very few days of his return to the capital a new contract was drawn up with another printer called Borrego, and this bore also the signature of Don Luis de Usoz y Rio, a scholarly Basque who was of the greatest assistance to Borrow. Borrego started printing on 20 January, and pledged himself to have the 5,000 copies ready for distribution by 1 April.

Now Borrow began to bombard the Society for permission to "ride forth, Testament in hand, and endeavour to circulate the word of God amongst the Spaniards, not only of the towns but of the villages". He proposed to journey first through the plains of Old Castile and then to "traverse the whole of Galicia and the Asturias", an idea which caused much head-shaking in Earl Street and led Mr. Brandram to shrewd comment. "Can the people in these wilds read?" he asked. "Is there no middle sort of course? Can you not establish a depot in some principal place, and thence make excursions of two or three days at a time, instead of devoting yourself wholly to the wild people?"

Borrow replied with a long and dramatic letter in which he demanded: "Does the man deserve the name of a follower of Christ who would shrink from dangers of any kind in the cause of Him whom he calls his Master?" and informed his startled employers that he had bought a second horse (one had already been dearly purchased from the *contrabandista*), "a black Andalusian stallion of great power and strength, and capable of performing a journey of a hundred leagues in a week's time". This animal, he added, was unbroken and savage, but he trusted that he would be thoroughly tamed by the time

---

[1] The Society wrote to Borrow on 28 January, 1837: "What does Mr. Wood say to the change of arrangement, as it respects him? Does he acquiesce without any remonstrance?"

he had climbed the flinty hills of northern Spain with a cargo of Bibles on his back.

As usual, his eloquence won the day. Borrego duly delivered the Testaments on 1 April, and on the 3rd, the Society authorized the proposed tour in rather cautious terms—"for the purpose of circulating the Spanish New Testament in some of the principal cities of Spain". Mr. Brandram added a warning: "I would just call your attention to what I wrote about your journey from Seville to Madrid—'Pray for wisdom to discern between presumptuousness and want of faith'. I shall often commend you to Him who alone can keep you."

In his fever of last-minute preparations it is doubtful if George Borrow paid much attention to these solemn words. He advertised the Testaments in the leading newspapers, dashed round the city browbeating booksellers to take stocks, placed his affairs in the hands of Usoz, and engaged as servant that strangely colourful character who haunts the pages of the *Bible in Spain*, Antonio Buchini, the wandering Greek. Sir George Villiers most kindly dispatched quantities of Testaments to the various British Consuls throughout Spain, with orders to circulate them and to afford Borrow every aid within their power. All was in readiness for departure when, much to his chagrin, he fell ill with a violent chill and cough. In desperation he summoned a "barber-surgeon", who bled him "of sixteen ounces of blood", pocketed a large fee, and assured him merrily that he would be perfectly recovered by the following morning.

Alas, when Antonio brought the horses to the door at noon, Borrow could scarcely crawl downstairs, and when he did manage to stagger forth his Andalusian stallion indulged in such a fit of temperament that Antonio cried: "It is a bad sign, and in my country they would defer the journey till tomorrow!"

Borrow smiled. "Are there whispers in your country?" he asked, caught the horse by its mane and crooned into its ear:

> "The Rommany Chal to his horse did cry,
> As he placed the bit in his horse's jaw;
> Kosko gry! Rommany gry!
> Muk man kistur tute knaw!"

On the instant the animal quietened and he swung himself easily into the saddle. They were off with a clatter of hooves for the gate of San Vicente and the Guadarrama mountains. The date was the fifteenth of May.

VII

Three days later Borrow gazed across the plain of Old Castile to the spires and towers of Salamanca. Then, as now, that ancient town, crowned by the great dome of its cathedral, seemed to rise like a desert mirage from the dusty, chestnut-coloured soil: then, as now, the traveller knew a sense of sick disappointment as he crossed the high bridge over the dried-up Tormes river and watched the mirage resolve itself into a mass of high crumbling buildings, grass-covered courtyards, empty convents, echoing halls: then, as now, all the sorrows of Spain brooded over the University once thronged by eight thousand ardent students, the cloaked and shovel-hatted priests stood in whispering groups in the Piazza, the beggars stalked past holding out arrogant hands for alms.

Borrow and Antonio put up at a *posada* called the Bull, a vast rambling place where wounded soldiers, *arrieros*, small merchants, and pedlars shared quarters with their horses, mules or donkeys. In the year 1949 the writer put up at the same *posada* and came to the conclusion that time had stood still in Salamanca for a hundred and twelve years. Four ex-soldiers insisted upon divesting themselves of their shirts and rolling up their trouser-legs to show her the scars won in the civil war—"Four years we fought, Señora, and for what we do not know." A group of railway officials gave a graphic description of an accident *"à la frontera"* in which an entire train had slid from the embankment and turned turtle. A merry little commercial traveller told of the impossibility of existing on his earnings—they amounted to fifteen pesetas a day. There was no food to be bought except Marie biscuits; no drink except yellow water from the Tormes or fiery *domecq* brandy. The heat was appalling and the landlord delivered a long lecture about Wellington's magnificent strategy at the conquest of Salamanca—one couldn't help wondering why he had ever bothered to conquer such a place.

Borrow, however, was in militant mood during his stay at the Bull. He discovered a bookseller called Blanco, "a man of great wealth and respectability", who not only agreed to become agent for the Testaments, but printed posters bearing a typically Borrovian advertisement of the "only guide to salvation" and plastered these all over the town. The Irish priests at the college were also canvassed, and on 10 June Borrow took the road to Medina del Campo well satisfied with his work.

The writer also took that road in company of which Borrow would certainly have disapproved. There were two charming American nuns who were touring Spanish convents, a scowling Catalan priest who kept up a harsh monologue on his missionary work in Waco, Texas, a depressed French-Canadian professor who had been invited by the Salamanca University authorities to lecture on—of all subjects!—metallurgy, and had been most upset to find an audience of three students, and an exceedingly voluble Portuguese gentleman who was an orchestra conductor and had masses of scores in a couple of enormous hat-boxes.

The landscape was the same that Borrow knew; the endless plains where men and women toiled over the sparse crops, the stony defiles, the occasional gaunt pine standing sentinel, the faint jagged line of sierras on the horizon. Five miles out of Salamanca the entire company, including their mules, were coated in chestnut-coloured dust. At Pitiegua a halt was called, the gallant nuns spread extra robes on the ground, the Catalan priest helped himself to the only shady patch, and the writer made herself highly unpopular by reading from the *Bible in Spain* Borrow's description of the bacon and eggs, honey and Hollands Gin he had enjoyed at the house of the village *curé*. The Catalan priest swore violently that no member of his faith had ever treated an infidel so lavishly. To assuage him some very tired ham sandwiches—purchased a week earlier in Lisbon—were produced, but since they were also offered to the *arrieros* he grew angrier than ever and said the English were not only heathen but mad to boot.

The truly grateful members of the party were the *arrieros*, "with their long trains of mules hung with monotonous tinkling bells. Behold them with their brown faces, brown dresses, and broad slouched hats—the *arrieros*, the true lords of the roads of Spain, and to whom more respect is paid in these dusty ways than to dukes and condes—the *arrieros*, sullen, proud, and rarely courteous, whose deep voices may be sometimes heard at the distance of a mile, either cheering the sluggish animals, or shortening the dreary way with savage and dissonant songs." They accepted the sandwiches with the ineffable dignity of their race; then—since hospitality had to be returned—they sat in solemn conclave, each fishing in his pockets for a coin which he tossed into an upturned sombrero set between them. Much anxious counting ensued before one strolled to a nearby *venda* and returned with a large bottle, which he presented with a courtly bow. The contents were fizzy, colourless, and tasted of prussic acid—it was the thought behind the gift that mattered.

Borrow found Medina del Campo "a place of immense ruins . . . attesting the former grandeur of this 'city of the plain'", and crammed with voluble and savage Catalans who had gathered for the annual fair in its huge dark marketplace. In 1949 Medina's streets of towering black houses were deserted, and the whole life of the town centred in its railway station, where not only Catalans but people from all over Spain babbled and clamoured about trains which should or might run under its derelict vaulted girders. Police guards in grey denim, with black boots, leggings, and peaked hats with no brims at the back, were omnipresent. Throughout the long night only one train halted at Medina, the Irun–Madrid express, which stayed just long enough to decant a billowing mass on to the platform and give everybody a glimpse of the *Compagnie Internationale Wagon-Lits* attendants winking horridly from a window.

A honeymoon couple from San Sebastian, who had omitted to apply for a police pass for their journey, wept bitterly. At least five hundred passengers clutched the nearest person in sight and cried "Salamanca!" (Extraordinary the fascination that dreariest of cities seemed to hold for all Spaniards.) At least another five hundred pounced on their waiting comrades and began a brisk black-market trade, any garment the user possessed being willingly exchanged for a seat at the next bullfight. A party of foreign hikers bowed under mammoth knapsacks bleated requests for food and the quickest route to Fuentes de Oñõro, cursed RENFE,[1] and said they had been fleeced by a gentleman called Alfonso at Irun station. Since there wasn't a member of the writer's party who hadn't suffered from Alfonso at Irun and who wasn't sighing for the gargantuan repasts provided in the Vilar Formosa[2] buffet, they received merely a jerk of the thumb and a surly "*a la frontera!*" True, the Catalan priest rose to his country's defence and recommended a wonderful *posada* at Cuidad Rodrigo, but even he soon relapsed into silence and stared longingly at a broken-down coach in a siding which bore the magic legend, "*Grands Expresses Européen*".

It was a funny night altogether. Inspection of the only available rooms in Medina had decided the company to spend the hours until dawn on their baggage in the station. They were, therefore, a fair target for the omnipresent police, who demanded to see all currency, letters of credit, and dutiable articles, adding in a whisper that any contraband might be exchanged for rail-tickets, seats for the *toros*, Spanish shawls, cigars, cigarettes, picture postcards—anything except food or cash, two items no Spaniard could spare.

The company obediently displayed their money and other belongings. Since the three women and the French-Canadian had already traded their superfluous property with various peasants for bullring tickets they would never use, the result was a cascade of paper that maybe Medina had never seen since Borrow's day. The Catalan howled when a sheaf of receipts (perhaps destined to impress his parishioners in Waco, Texas?) revealed his high living in Seville, Madrid, and Lisbon. The Portuguese conductor, despite protestations that he was a "mere man travelling for pleasure", had to submit to a thorough search of his music scores. The writer, well aware that the Spanish law insists upon all foreign passports being

---

[1] *Red Nacional de los Ferrocarriles Españoles.*
[2] The Portuguese frontier station beyond Fuentes de Oñoro.

surrendered each night to the authorities, proffered hers to
the largest policeman. To her astonishment it was refused on
the grounds that he was too busy to bother with such trifles;
but five minutes later he sidled back, an incongruously coy
smile creasing his leathery face. "For a consideration," he
murmured, "I will take the little books of *all* the Señoras."
(Six hours later, after prolonged searching, he was discovered
so sound asleep behind the newspaper kiosk that shouts,
shakes and hand-clappings failed to rouse him. Since his
head was pillowed on the passports it was a simple matter to
retrieve them.)

The road to Valladolid was just as hot and dusty as the
road from Salamanca to Medina. It was pleasant to rest by
the wooded banks of the Duero river, where Borrow had seen
the mad woman crouching by the pool in which her child
had been drowned; but memory of that unhappy mother
haunted the long descent into the town where she had lived
out her life in the *Casa de los Locos*, accentuated the vaguely
sinister atmosphere which hung about the massive granite
cathedral, the magnificent churches, convents, and colleges,
the streets where the buildings were so high that the passer-by
skulked in the wall shadow, terrified lest the top stories should
topple over.

In reality, of course, the physical position of Valladolid
was responsible for the sense of oppression which rested upon
her visitors. In some far century volcanic eruptions had made
this rift in the Old Castilian plain and thrown up around it
rocky, queerly-shaped hills. Through the rift flowed the
Escurva river, and since water was the most precious thing in
Spain man built a city around it; but when the sky was an
inverted bowl of brass, and the river had sunk to the merest
trickle, and the machines from Valladolid's many factories
thrummed through the hot air, one thought irresistibly of some
ancient giant god scooping a great hole in the earth and
flinging into it, pell-mell, everything he happened to dislike.

It was in Valladolid that the writer parted from her companions, who were taking the train to Burgos. Farewells were
sad, even the Catalan priest seeming sensible of the fact that
days of rough travel shared by six vastly different people

induced a feeling of friendship faintly analogous to the comradeship of war. Yet it was with a guilty feeling of relief that the writer, the *Bible in Spain* under one arm, and the first volume of Dr. Knapp's copious biography under the other, set out to view Valladolid.

Dr. Knapp yielded an excellent, time-table route of the journeys to be followed by anybody wishful of tracing Borrow's footsteps,[1] and two terse pronouncements:

"So explicit is the description of this journey in the *Bible in Spain*, that we must pass it over, except so far as to record the mere itinerary." "How much permanent good the journey had achieved it is not for us to estimate. We may only be allowed to remark, from an intimate knowledge of all the towns and provinces visited, that Borrow certainly chose, for his five months' tour, the most unpropitious parts of the country in selecting Old Castile, Leon and Galicia—the Bœotia of Spain. The terrible ride from Ferrol to Rivadeo was utterly useless, there being no towns of importance on the way, while the direct route by Mondoñedo would have had at least one worthy object, namely, that old Episcopal See."

It seemed strange that Dr. Knapp, who championed Borrow's character and works through so many fierce controversies, and who knew Spain well, should have regarded any portion of his hero's immortal journey as useless. Perhaps he did not sell so many Bibles as he anticipated, but nobody in old Castile, Leon, Galicia, the Asturias, or the Basque provinces who saw that picturesque figure or heard him thundering his militant Protestant faith ever forgot him.

A descendant of Julian Pastor, the kindly store-keeper of Valladolid who sold books as a side-line and helped Borrow immensely, showed the writer a letter in a familiar, angular hand. It was dated Madrid, June, 1838, and it expressed whole-hearted thanks for Señor Pastor's "grand courage" in disposing of so many Testaments.

Today Valladolid is one of the busiest factory towns in

---

[1] Borrow's route is given at the end of this book.

Spain; when Borrow stayed there commerce was chiefly in the hands of the Catalan colony, against whom the venerable religious and academic institutions were fighting a desperate rearguard action. Beyond the monstrous hills lurked the Carlists—they had seized possession before Borrow's return in October—and in the English and Scots colleges and the Philippine Mission sat those "pale smiling half-foreign priests" before the paintings of their predecessors who had, according to Borrow, "eventually suffered martyrdom in England, in the exercise of their vocation in the angry times of the Sixth Edward and fierce Elizabeth. . . ."

Valladolid had provided the teaching for the men who, "like stealthy grimalkins, traversed green England in all directions; crept into old halls beneath umbrageous rookeries, fanning the dying embers of Popery, with no other hope nor perhaps wish than to perish disembowelled by the bloody hands of the executioner; amongst the yells of a rabble as bigoted as themselves. . . ."

That was Borrow at his most fanatical; also at his most stupid, for no priest of Holy Rome ever wooed martyrdom with such zeal as he did—yet in the deserted courtyards of Valladolid one saw not only the shades of the priests but the ghost of a vivid personality who moved, as Richard Ford said five years afterwards, like an old Spanish ballad, "going from incident to incident, bang, bang, bang!"

From Valladolid Borrow rode to Leon, that most delightful Spanish town with its sparkling streams and lush meadows; but no sooner had he negotiated with a bookseller for sale of his Testaments and personally supervised the plastering up of his posters, than he was "seized with a fever". In the light of present-day knowledge this was probably malarial; but Borrow wrote dramatically to Mr. Brandram that "the heats of summer-time raise noxious exhalations from the waters, which generate all kinds of disorders, especially fevers and tertian agues. It is the Feversham of Spain".

But Leon was a Bishop's See, and while Borrow shivered and sweated on his bed in the *posada*, the Leon clergy tore down his posters, banned the reading of "these accursed books", summoned the bookseller to appear before an ecclesiastical court, and sent a posse of ex-Carlist soldiers to enquire about this heretic who was attempting the seduction of the innocent Spaniards. Antonio was so alarmed that he dragged Borrow, weak as he was, from his couch, and at three o'clock one morning they galloped off to Astorga through a terrific thunderstorm.

Borrow was still wretchedly ill. The only accommodation in Astorga was a vermin-infested shed next a stable. The town had no bookseller and its inhabitants, the Maragatos (Moorish Goths), were a fierce brawling crowd who said plainly that the Englishman and his servant were a couple of vagabonds. Borrow crawled feebly round, trying to interest the Maragatos in religion, but found "their hearts gross, and their ears dull of hearing, and their eyes closed". One might say indeed, that Astargo was the only place he visited which utterly defeated him, and after three days he was thankful to ride on northwards towards Galicia.

He and Antonio now travelled through wild mountainous country and many adventures befell them before they limped into Villafranca at dead of night to be greeted by a "horrid squalling of cats" and a furious female voice issuing from an upper window of the only *posada*:

"I cannot be disturbed. . . . They will be wanting supper, and there is nothing in the house; they must go elsewhere."

Borrow cried they merely needed a resting-place as they were almost dead from fatigue, whereupon the voice changed miraculously: "Surely that is the voice of Gil, the German clock-maker from Pontevedra. Welcome, old companion; you are come at the right time!"

The lady was not too pleased to discover one Englishman and one Greek when she opened the door, but she did give them house-room, which was all Borrow wanted. Despite his pronounced dislike of Gallegans and their ways he knew a consuming desire to reach Galicia unshared by Antonio, who said he had "already lost two or three excellent situations in Madrid, solely owing to Gallegan chambermaids", and produced a series of arguments against so much as entering that savage province.

Borrow waved aside his protests. Early the following

By courtesy of Mr. Cherry Kearton

View of Seville from Cathedral

By courtesy of Mr. Cherry Kearton

The Cathedral, Seville

morning they began to climb the pass of Fuencebadon, of which Borrow wrote:

"Everything here is wild, strange, and beautiful: the hill up which winds the path towers above on the right, whilst on the farther side of a profound ravine rises an immense mountain, to whose extreme altitudes the eye is scarcely able to attain; but the most singular feature of this pass are the hanging fields or meadows which cover its sides. In these, as I passed, the grass was growing luxuriantly, and in many the mowers were plying their scythes, though it seemed scarcely possible that their feet could find support on ground so precipitous: above and below were driftways, so small as to seem threads along the mountain side. A car, drawn by oxen, is creeping round yon airy eminence; the nearer wheel is actually hanging over the horrid descent; giddiness seizes the brain, and the eye is rapidly withdrawn . . ."

By nightfall they were in Nogales, where they were fortunate enough to fall in with the grand post from Madrid to Corunna; and since this was escorted by soldiers as guard against the pillaging bands of Carlists who were very busy on the Lugo road, Borrow decided to travel under their protection. He had driven himself hard since leaving Leon and had not thrown off the effects of his fever, also his eyes were troubling him, and he jogged along in a sort of nightmare while the soldiers sang:

> "Don Carlos is a hoary churl,
> Of cruel heart and cold;
> But Isabel's a harmless girl,
> Of only six years old . . ."

Lugo provided solace for both mind and body. A rich bookseller eagerly snapped up the last thirty Testaments Borrow carried and clamoured for more: the baths near the Minho, which were fed by a hot mineral spring, drew the aches and pains from his bones. The moment he felt better he decided, much to Antonio's consternation, to press on to Corunna

o

ahead of the post, being irked by the slowness of their progress. Besides, five hundred Testaments awaited him there, and he was anxious to distribute these all over Galicia and Biscay. The journey was rough, the Andalusian stallion was poisoned by bad water and only saved by his master's prompt action in bleeding him, but at last Borrow's tired eyes were cheered by sight of an English squadron anchored in Corunna bay.

The town was clean and prosperous; the people cheerful and intelligent; one of the shopkeepers proved to be a Milanese called Luigi Piozzi, who had once kept a stall in Norwich market during Borrow's boyhood. Everything about Corunna was pleasing, from the streets that shone jewel-bright owing to the frequent and violent deluges which swept them, to the marble tomb erected by the French in honour of a gallant enemy, Sir John Moore.

"Yes" (wrote Borrow), "there lies the hero, almost within sight of the glorious hill where he turned upon his pursuers like a lion at bay and terminated his career. Many acquire immortality without seeking it, and die before its first ray has gilded their name; of these was Moore. The harassed general, flying through Castile with his dispirited troops before a fierce and terrible enemy, little dreamed that he was on the point of attaining that for which many a better, greater, though certainly not braver man, had sighed in vain . . . There is scarcely a Spaniard but has heard of this tomb, and speaks of it with a strange kind of awe. . . ."

Corunna awakened a nostalgia for England in Borrow. It was also an excellent centre for his Testament selling and many people (including Dr. Knapp) have wondered why he did not linger there instead of pressing on with his perilous journey to Finisterre. Some say his sense of duty to the Society drove him forth: others that his evangelical fervour bade him mortify his flesh. The writer's view—and it may be entirely wrong—is that Borrow was the perfect traveller, that rare being who simply has to follow some particular road to its end and is so exhilarated that at the time he hardly notices the hardships involved.

On 1 August Borrow left Corunna. After making the acquaintance of the good Rey Romero at Santiago and encountering Benedict Mol—who had somehow managed to reach Compostella and was full of wild plans for recovering the *schatz*—he rode on through Padron and Pontevedra enjoying the "hum of insects, the cheerful bark of dogs, the rude songs of Galicia", and about the middle of the month he clattered through the gate of Vigo, that town which clings, limpet-wise, to the rocky hill beside the bay. No wonder Borrow wrote of Vigo:

"Well may the people of Pontevedra envy the natives of Vigo their bay, with which, in many respects, none other in the word can compare. . . . The waters are dark, still, and deep, without quicksands or shallows, so that the proudest man-of-war might lie within a stone's throw of the town ramparts without any fear of injuring her keel . . . It was here that the bulky dragons of the grand armada were mustered, and it was from hence that, fraught with the pomp, power, and terror of old Spain, the monster fleet, spreading its enormous sails to the wind, and bent on the ruin of the Lutheran isle, proudly steered;—that fleet, to build and man which half the forests of Galicia had been felled, and all the mariners impressed from the thousand bays and creeks of the stern Cantabrian shore. It was here that the united flags of Holland and England triumphed over the pride of Spain and France; when the burning timbers of exploded warships soared above the tops of the Gallegan hills, and blazing galleons sank with their treasure chests whilst drifting in the direction of Sampayo. It was on the shores of this bay that the English guards first emptied Spanish bodegas, whilst the bombs of Cobham were crushing the roofs of the castle of Castro, and the vecinos of Pontevedra buried their doubloons in cellars, and flying posts were conveying to Lugo and Orensee the news of the heretic invasion and the disaster of Vigo . . ."

When Borrow left Vigo he had only one copy of the Testament with him. He said himself that it was "difficult to assign any plausible reason" for his decision to return to Padron, leave Antonio there with the horses, and hire a guide and ponies to take him, Bible in hand, to Finisterre. Certainly he qualified this remark by adding that "ever since the Lord revealed himself to man, it has seemed good to him to accomplish the greatest ends by apparently the most insufficient means", but somehow one feels this piece of sententiousness was intended for the folk at Earl Street and not for the general reader.

With a desperado of a guide and two villainous ponies Borrow set forth over rocky moorlands above which the dreaded *Estadea* (a thick mist that bore with it the spirits of the dead carrying candles in their hands) hovered continually. Tired, bewildered, soaked through, his sole companion a half-mad Gallegan, Borrow floundered his way to Cape Finisterre, sleeping in rude huts and subsisting on what poor food was obtainable—yet when he stood at last on a bluff and gazed down on the ocean he knew his tribulations had not been in vain.

> "There is an air of stern and savage grandeur in everything around which strongly captivates the imagination. This savage coast is the first glimpse of Spain which the voyager from the north catches, or he who has ploughed his way across the wide Atlantic; and well does it seem to realise all his visions of this strange land. Yes" (he exclaims), "this is indeed Spain—stern, flinty Spain—land emblematic of those spirits to which she has given birth. From what land but that before me could have proceeded those portentious beings who astounded the Old World and filled the New with horror and blood—Alba and Philip, Cortez and Pizarro—stern colossal spectres looming through the gloom of bygone years, like yonder granite mountains through the haze, upon the eye of the mariner . . . ?"

But his odyssey was not yet complete. Down the cliff he zigzagged to Corcuvion and soon reached an immense bay, on the northwest side of which the Cape of Finisterre stretched out to sea:

> "Along the beach of dazzling white sand we advanced towards . . . the bourne of our journey. The sun was shining

brightly, and every object was illumined by his beams. The sea lay before us like a vast mirror, and the waves which broke upon the shore were so tiny as scarcely to produce a murmur . . . Strange recollections began to throng upon my mind. It was upon this beach that, according to the tradition of all ancient Christendom, St. James, the patron saint of Spain, preached the gospel to the heathen Spaniards. Upon this beach had once stood an immense commercial city, the proudest in all Spain. This now desolate bay had once resounded with the voices of myriads, when the keel and commerce of all the then known world were wafted to Duyo.

" 'What is the name of this village?' said I to a woman, as we passed by five or six ruinous houses at the bend of the bay, ere we entered upon the peninsula of Finisterra.

" 'This is no village,' said the Gallegan—'this is no village, Sir Cavalier; this is a city—this is Duyo.' "

" 'So much for the glory of the world!' (cried Borrow). 'These huts were all that the roaring sea and the tooth of time had left of Duyo, the great city! Onward now to Finisterra!' "

VIII

The golden leaves lay in heaps along the *alameda* in the Manzanares meadows and the wind whistled shrilly down the *Calle de Santiago* before Don Jorge returned from his wanderings to be greeted with shouts of joy from the faithful Maria Diaz and her household.[1] *Vaya!* What a man he was to be sure, and what wondrous stories he had to tell! Borrow was a big man, but one imagines he appeared more than life-size as he crouched by the stove and, with a wealth of gesture, recounted his amazing adventures. Not only had he been to "the end of the world" (Finisterre), but he had been taken for a Catalan in one village and for Don Carlos himself in another! In Corcuvion he had met an *alcade* whose favourite author was Jeremy Bentham; in Pontevedra a "prodigy of learning" with the glorious name of Don Claudio Gonzalez y Zuñiga. Scores

---

[1] Borrow reached Madrid about the end of October, 1837.

of times he had been within an ace of arrest, abduction, violent death—and the songs he had learned! The room resounded to the Basque verse:

> "Ichasoa urac aundi,
> Estu ondoric agueri—
> Pasaco ninsaqueni andic
> Maitea icustea gatic . . ."

("The waters of the sea are vast, and their bottom cannot be seen; but over them I will pass, that I may behold my love.")[1]

It mattered little to his listeners that Borrow put into the mouth of Martin, his guide from Rivadeo to Gijon, the port for Oviedo, an *English* riddle-song:

> "A headless man had a letter to write;
> 'Twas read by one who lost his sight;
> The Dumb repeated it word for word,
> And he was Deaf who listened and heard."[2]

In the eyes of the household at 16 *Calle de Santiago*, Don Jorge could do no wrong.

Unfortunately he could, and did, do wrong in the eyes of a great many more important people. Probably because of those early years when he was compared odiously with his brother John, Borrow was always extraordinarily susceptible to admiration—and this he found waiting for him in full measure on his return to Madrid. Sir George Villiers congratulated him; Usoz and many other Spanish friends lauded him; the stack of waiting letters from the Society commended his bravery in warmest terms. Unable to resist such adulation and forgetful of the sad necessity to read all correspondence thoroughly, Borrow determined to become his own publisher and bookseller and on 20 November took over the lease of a shop in the *Calle del Principe*. The manager bore the unprepossessing name of Jose Calzado, but Borrow (even in his letters to Brandram and Jowett!) alluded to him fondly as Pepe. The rent was considerable, since the shop was in the centre of Madrid.

From the business point of view Borrow had absolutely no

---

[1] Borrow's version and translation from *The Bible in Spain*.
[2] *Book of Riddles*, mentioned by Laneham, 1575.

right to open such a shop, for since he had distributed his Spanish Testaments far and wide—including that copy he had carried to "the extreme point of the old world" and left in the "hands of Antonio de Trava, an ancient mariner of Finisterre" —he had only a stock of a few hundred left. From the political point of view he was simply courting disaster, for the liberal Calatrava Government had fallen and been succeeded by the Bardaji-Espartero Cabinet, which was rapidly weakening under pressure of the Moderado opposition led by the Count de Ofalia.

Unfortunately, at this moment Borrow was not the prudent agent of the Bible Society: he was the mighty Don Jorge, the militant missionary, the renowned traveller who had braved untold perils to spread the Gospel among the savage hordes of Galicia and Biscay. He was certainly not going to be defeated by lack of stock and the machinations of politicians. He forthwith decided to print his Gospel of St. Luke in Spanish-Gypsy together with another little volume dear to his heart, a bilingual Vocabulary, or Word-Book[1]; and he began to plan an advertisement campaign such as Madrid had never seen. In a mood of terrific enthusiasm he tore around the city cajoling printers, designing posters, interviewing sandwich-men, hectoring authority.

The very day the shop opened trouble began. The Society's letters were full of complaint concerning Mr. Borrow's expenditure, his dilatoriness in rendering accounts, his over-optimism, his lack of interest in their other agents in the Peninsula. Mr. Borrow might go ahead with the printing of 250 copies of St. Luke "in the Rommanee Dialect",[2] as passed by their

[1] The *Lavo-Lil* of its day.

[2] In the original edition was the inscription: "This Gospel was turned into Spanish-Gypsy by George Borrow, a servant of the Bible Society, in the City of Badajoz, on the frontier of Portugal, in the winter of the Year of Our Lord, 1836." In the London Edition, published thirty-six years later, Borrow adds: "And he gave it to the world for the first time, in Madrid, the Royal City of Spaniards, in the year 1837, and now he sets it forth for the second time, with many corrections and improvements, in London, the Royal City of Britain, an island of the sea, in the year of Christ 1872."

The German philologist, Pott, made good use of Borrow's translation in his *Gypsies in Europe and Asia* (*Die Zigeuner in Europa und Asian. Ethnographisch-linguistische Untersuchung, vornehmlich ihrer Herkunft und Sprache, nach gedruckten und ungeddruckten Quellen von Dr. A. F. Pott. Halle*, 1844–45, 2 vols. I *Grammatik: II Worterbuch u. Sprachproben.*

Resolution of 13 March, 1837, but under no circumstances must he proceed with the Word-Book. The newly-formed Ofalia Government, fearful of losing the support of the Church, cast an unfavourable eye on the doings of the troublesome Englishman.

Borrow, furious at the Society's cold attitude to his Word-Book, sent them several impassioned letters—and the long overdue accounts—explaining how impossible it was for a unique agent to keep abreast of all the puerile requests made by individuals who clearly had no knowledge of Spain. He received his just reward—or thought he did—in a letter written by Mr. Brandram on 16 January, 1838:

"Your letter of December 25th, was read Monday. Its contents afforded us no little merriment. The idea of your placards and your placard-bearers in Madrid is indeed a novel one. It cannot but be effectual in giving publicity. I sincerely hope it may not be prejudicial. Pray do let us hear from you again shortly."

Before that letter was ever written Borrow's advertisement campaign was doomed—one might go farther and say his whole mission in Spain was doomed. Towards the end of December Madrid had awakened to find flaring posters on the walls of its public buildings and a procession of sandwich-men bearing highly-coloured placards marching through the streets. The clergy, now thoroughly roused, demanded action. On 14 January an order was issued by the Civil Governor, Don Francisco de Gamboa, banning the sale of Testaments from the shop in the *Calle del Principe*.

Borrow loved a fight and entered into this one with characteristic zest; bombarding the authorities, from the Count de Ofalia downwards, with long, dramatic pleas for justice which began, *"Excelentisimo Señor!"*; harrying the amiable Sir George Villiers—who warned him plainly that his methods were likely to hinder rather than help his cause; dashing off involved explanations to the Society; beseeching the printer to hurry with the Gospel of St. Luke.

Now if Borrow had only studied carefully all the Society's

communications which had been waiting for him on his return to Madrid, he might have realized sooner exactly what he was up against. But before Borrow had ever landed in the Peninsula he had been told by the Earl Street Committee that a very charming retired Naval officer, Lieutenant Graydon, was acting as their unofficial and unpaid agent at Barcelona, where he printed Bibles in Spanish and Catalan and distributed them down the Mediterranean coast as far as Malaga. He was greatly interested in evangelical matters and, since he was retired on half-pay, was pleasantly averse to accepting money for his excellent services. Borrow had no use for meddling amateurs and immediately conceived a violent dislike for the unknown Lieutenant Graydon, of whom he complained bitterly, sometimes justly but often unjustly, in his letters to the Society. In fact, the last thing he wished was to be reminded of Graydon's existence, so when he met his name in papers from Earl Street he promptly skipped a page.

Consequently he had missed the all-important news that Graydon had incurred the wrath of the authorities by issuing little tracts at Valencia, Murcia, and Malaga which called attention to the wickedness of the Spanish Government and the malevolent influence of the Spanish clergy. In large print was added the information that he worked for the Bible Society and was co-agent for them with Mr. George Borrow. Copies of these tracts, which were undoubtedly of highly political flavour, were forwarded by Malaga to the Central Government at Madrid, and reached there just before Borrow's advertisement campaign. Not surprisingly, the Government decided that the menace of these foreign evangelists must be stamped out once and for all and began the struggle which ended in the complete suppression of any sort of Bible distribution in Spain for the next thirty years.

It must be admitted that Graydon behaved in an extremely stupid manner; that he had no right to link his name with that of a man who had won respect and popularity simply because he refrained from political mud-slinging; that his friendship with the energetic Mr. Rule, a Wesleyan missionary stationed at Cadiz who shared his desire to dabble in things controversial, was calculated to make trouble; and that the Society should have ceased dealings with him months earlier. It must also be admitted that Borrow's own behaviour was childish. If he had not taken such an irrational dislike to a man he had never met, then he would have read his letters properly, kept an eye on Graydon and Rule's activities, conducted his Testament distribution in Madrid along different lines, and thus avoided the disaster of the Government ban.

There is, however, proof that Borrow knew in November 1837 that Graydon was giving away free copies of a Spanish Bible printed in London[1] to the poor of Valencia, a gesture which inspired the Bishop of that city to write a virulent letter on the evils of the Bible Society to the newspaper, *El Español*. Borrow not only wrote sternly to Mr. Brandram on the subject but induced the editor to print a fiery answer which no Holy Catholic could possibly condone. There is further proof that in the spring of 1838 Borrow was visited by Mr. Rule, "of whose zeal, piety, and discretion" he formed a high opinion, and that the information provided by this gentleman caused him to demand Graydon's dismissal. He was, therefore, fully cognizant of all the facts by the end of March—and yet he persisted in bringing out St. Luke's Gospel in Spanish-Gypsy and in Basque!

The result was a foregone conclusion. On 30 April, an *alguacil* (constable) arrived at Borrow's lodgings with a warrant to seize the "Gypsy books"; whereupon the loyal Maria Diaz flew into a fit of hysterics and announced that a trap had been set for Don Jorge! Thanks to this temperamental warning Borrow sensibly shifted his quarters to a French inn, from which he could easily reach the British Legation in the *Calle de Torija*. This move, however, availed him nothing. The very next day, as he was hurrying back to his tavern from the Legation, he was arrested in the name of the Queen-Regent and hustled ignominiously across the *Puerta del Sol* to the Governor's office, where he was locked in the police department along with the ordinary criminals awaiting examination.

[1] Borrow wrote Mr. Brandram that the sending of these Bibles to Spain was a "most ill-advised" gesture; yet it had been printed from the Felipe Scio edition which was used in the Madrid printing. Whatever amendments Borrow had made, it was certainly a "most ill-advised" gesture to write to the Society as he did.

Borrow's Basque servant Francisco—who had succeeded the temperamental Antonio—rushed to Sir George Villiers, who immediately sent Mr. Henry Southern, his Secretary, to argue with the Governor, now the haughty Don Diego de Entrena. George Borrow, he was told, was charged with insulting an officer in the performance of his duty and with introducing into Spain a forbidden book printed in Gibraltar. (The book turned out to be the St. Luke Gospel, on the title page of which Borrow had omitted to put the words "printed in Madrid".)

Meantime, Borrow had been taken to the *Carcel de Corte*, or Metropolitan Prison, where he stayed for eleven days while Villiers gallantly fought for his release. Since he was a "paying" prisoner, and since Maria Diaz brought him food, blankets, and furniture, one cannot wholly agree with the description of his incarceration given in the *Bible in Spain*. True, everybody he met in the exercise yard was verminous, but he had clean sheets every day, his meals were brought in, and Sir George sent his butler to wait upon him! In truth, Borrow was an intolerable nuisance to His Majesty's Government, the Spanish Government, the Bible Society and everybody else during the few days of his imprisonment; but one cannot but admire the arrogance with which he stalked through the gates the morning that Ofalia (of whom Borrow had long said scornfully that in a previous incarnation he must have been a mouse) signed the order for his release.

A Royal Order of 25 May prohibited the sale of all Bibles throughout Spain. The Society, who had doubtless received a sharp rebuke from the Foreign Office and in any case were horror-struck at the mere thought of their agent's rashness in getting himself arrested, forwarded a series of Resolutions which were distressingly vague. They were recalling Lieutenant Graydon "for reasons of health". They could not authorize any further travel on the part of their Mr. Borrow. They might, or might not, find it necessary to recall him—not for health reasons.

Borrow was furious. Refusing even to contemplate the idea that his work in the Peninsula was finished he set off, with the remainder of his Testaments and the Gypsy and

Basque versions of St. Luke, on a tour of nearby provinces. That his release had been obtained only because Ofalia had no wish to cause a "diplomatic incident" with Britain over such a minor matter as a heretic pedlar, and that he was deliberately disobeying the edict of 25 May, worried him not one whit. To begin with he considered that no man-made laws should be permitted to interfere in his "holy duty": to end with he blamed the Spanish Government for the death from typhus of his servant Francisco, who had caught that dread disease while looking after him in gaol.

First he rode to Toledo, where he actually had an interview with its Archbishop, the Primate of Spain; then he journeyed on across La Sagra, the fertile plain lying north of the Tagus. In Vargas, Villa Seca, Mocejon, Cobeja, Villaluenga, and Yuncos he spread the word of salvation before turning back towards La Mancha. Here he met with a set-back, for not far from Aranjuez he met a Jew who told him:

". . . The corregidor of Toledo, on whom may all evil light, in order to give pleasure to the priests of Maria, in whose face I spit, has ordered all the alcaldes of these parts, and the escribanos and the corchetes to lay hands on you wherever they may find you, and to send you, and your books, and all that pertains to you to Toledo. Your servant was seized this morning in the town above, as he was selling the writings in the streets, and they are now awaiting you in the posada; but I knew you from the accounts of my brethren, and I have been waiting here four hours to give you warning in order that your horse may turn his tail to your enemies, and neigh in derision of them . . ."

Borrow took the hint, wheeled about, and started on the long climb over the Navacerrada Pass to Segovia, whence he followed the westbound high road in the direction of Valladolid. His visits to various villages, Abades, Labajos, Arevalo, and Celayos are described wonderfully in the *Bible in Spain*, but in reality those summer wanderings of 1838 were melancholy affairs. The Primate at Toledo may have granted him an interview: that same Primate issued orders to arrest the colporteur at Ocaña on the borders of La Manchu and to catch his villainous master should opportunity arise. The Central Government kept a vigilant eye on his progress; the local authorities put every difficulty in his way; the correspondence between the Society and himself grew ever more acrimonious. The old Don Jorge flashed out in a letter he sent from Labajos on 23 August to Lord William Hervey, Deputy-Minister at Madrid in the absence of Sir George Villiers, when one of his sub-agents, Juan Lopez, was thrown into prison at Velayos for selling Testaments:

". . . It had been hinted to Lopez" (wrote Borrow) "that as the factious[1] were expected, it was intended on their arrival to denounce him to them as a liberal, and to cause him to be sacrificed. Taking these circumstances into consideration, I deemed it my duty as a Christian and a gentleman, to rescue my unfortunate servant from such lawless hands, and in consequence, defying opposition, I bore him off, though entirely unarmed, through a crowd of at least one hundred peasants. On leaving the place I shouted, '*Viva Isabel Segunda*'."

With supreme effrontery he added that he believed the local *curé* to be "capable of any infamy", and besought Lord William to forward a copy of his letter to the Count de Ofalia.

But the Borrow who rode slowly back to Madrid a day or two later was a tired, despondent man who looked twenty years older than his real age of thirty-five. The three diseases he had contracted during his Spanish travels, fever, dysentery, and ophthalmia, took advantage of his lowered vitality to attack him with renewed vigour. And at his lodgings he found a letter from Mr. Brandram containing the ominous notice:

"RESOLVED, that it be recommended to the General Committee to recall Mr. Borrow from Madrid without delay. (Read and confirmed at a Meeting of the General Committee held in London August 6th, 1838—the Rt. Hon. Lord Bexley, Prest., in the Chair.)"

[1] Followers of the Carlist chieftain, Balmaseda.

The Borrow of 1836 would have taken the next coach south to Cadiz and the first available ship to England in a fine rage. The Borrow of 1838 wound up his affairs grimly and purposefully, journeyed slowly through the Pyrenees, spent a fortnight in Paris, and crossed the Channel by the Boulogne–Folkestone route; and all the way he nursed his smouldering resentment like any Corsican, only allowing it to burst into flames when he stood on the very doorstep of the Earl Street office. Then, for the last time, the passionate Don Jorge faced his detractors.

IX

On 23 December George Borrow sailed from Falmouth in the *Thames*, reaching Lisbon on the 29th, and Cadiz on the 31st. He left behind him in England a dazed and shaken Committee—who kept asking each other exactly what they had promised their Mr. Borrow and why they had promised it at all—and an ecstatic Mrs. Clarke. At last her dear George, wrung by her account of the deplorable quarrel between her and her now widowed sister-in-law over the Oulton estate, had suggested that she and her daughter Henrietta should come out to Seville in the summer, when the long-expected marriage would take place.

But the man who leaned on the deck-rail as the *Thames* edged her way into Cadiz harbour did not bear the look of one who had lately vanquished his critics and was soon to wed the woman he loved. In the light of the setting sun the tall houses glowed rose and amber, the steep narrow streets became vivid purple streaks, the waters of the bay shimmered silver and gold; yet he seemed not to notice the fairy-like beauty of the scene. Hunched in his old cloak of rusty black he stared gloomily at the shining sea, the colourful city, only aware of his own melancholy. For some reason, he knew not how or why, the glory had departed.

Borrow had been sent back to Spain at his own insistence and against the Society's better judgment to try to dispose of the remaining stock of Testaments and Gospels. His first action, however, when he stepped ashore at Cadiz, was to arrange his passage to Seville, where he sent for a courier called Juan Antonio Bailly to collect any gypsy books or papers he could find in that part of Andalusia. Only when this business was concluded did he visit the bookseller with whom he had left one hundred Testaments. Upon being told that the Ecclesiastical Governor had seized the seventy-six unsold copies several months earlier he flew into a fury and stalked off to beard that dignitary at his private residence. "He brought powerfully to my recollection," wrote Borrow scornfully, "the grim old inquisitor who persuaded Philip the Second to slay his own son as an enemy to the Church."

The interview was stormy and unprofitable, but it had the merit of temporarily restoring Borrow's confidence, and he took the coach for Madrid in fighting vein. Alas, conditions in the capital were even more unfavourable than before. Ofalia had resigned and been succeeded first by the Duque de Frias and then by Perez de Castro. Sir George Villiers, now Earl of Clarendon, was on the point of leaving. The Spanish authorities, while they had wisely given up all idea of putting Don Jorge behind bars, had taken the far more effective step of placing a complete embargo on any distribution of any Scriptures. Whether Borrow fully realized the extent of this ban or whether he deliberately ignored it is not clear, but from the end of January until the third week in April he, Lopez, and a few trusted colporteurs travelled La Sagra and La Mancha selling Testaments, or rather trying to, for at every turn they met trouble.

On 24 April Borrow arrived in Seville, having ridden there by way of Manzanares on Sidi Habismilk, the famous horse he later brought to England. He put up at the *Posada de la Reyna*, bitterly conscious that every door had been successfully closed against him and that his work for the Society in Spain was virtually at an end. This knowledge festered within him, and each letter from Earl Street rubbed salt in the wound. Mr. Borrow must not write such extraordinary letters about "luck" and "superstitions". Mr. Borrow must not report conversations with a "mad prophetess at Manzanares". Mr. Borrow must understand that the Society could no longer pour out money on a campaign which had proved both costly and disastrous. *Mr. Borrow must not linger in Spain.*

Unfortunately, that last was just what Mr. Borrow was determined to do. He considered, rightly, that he had done a grand work in Spain: he considered, wrongly, that the Bible Society had treated him in the shabbiest possible fashion. He would stay in Seville just as long as it suited him—and Earl Street could pay.

A queer change had crept over Borrow since his journey to Finisterre—what had really happened was that the evangelist had given place to the creative writer. So in his room at the *Posada de la Reyna* he sat at his desk surrounded by gypsy writings and planning a title-page:

CANCIONCITAS DE LOS GITANOS

SONGS

OF THE SPANISH GYPSIES

Translated from the Spanish Dialect of
The Romanee

by

GEORGE BORROW
(with the Originals).

The Society's urgent communications lay neglected in a corner, and on his journeyings abroad Borrow spent all his time with those "people out of Egypt" with whom he knew true affinity.

In May he rented a house in the *Plazuela de la Pila Seca* and furnished it, saying vaguely that it was for the use of a lady and her daughter who were old friends. Probably it was about this time he wrote his wonderful description of Seville:

"Oh how pleasant it is, especially in springtide, to stray along the shores of the Guadalquivir! Not far from the city, down the river, lies a grove called Las Delicias, or the Delights . . . This grove is the favourite promenade of the Sevillians, and there one occasionally sees assembled whatever the town produces of beauty or gallantry. There wander the black-eyed Andalusian dames and damsels, clad in their graceful silken mantillas; and there gallops the Andalusian cavalier on his long-tailed, thick-maned steed of Moorish ancestry. As the sun is descending, it is enchanting to glance back from this place in the direction of the city; the prospect is inexpressibly beautiful. Yonder in the distance, high and enormous, stands the Golden Tower, now used as a tollhouse, but the principal bulwark of the city in the time of the Moors. It stands on the shore of the river, like a giant keeping watch, and is the first edifice which attracts the eye of the voyager as he moves up the stream to Seville. On the other side, opposite the tower, stands the noble Augustine Convent, the ornament of the faubourg of Triana; whilst between the two edifices rolls the broad Gualadquivir, bearing on its bosom a flotilla of barks from Catalonia and Valencia. Farther up is seen the bridge of boats which traverses the water. The principal object of this prospect, however, is the Golden Tower, where the beams of the setting sun seem to be concentrated as in the focus, so that it appears built of pure gold . . . Cold, cold must the heart be which can remain insensible to the beauties of this magic scene . . . Often have I shed tears of rapture whilst I beheld it, and listened to the thrush and the nightingale piping forth their melodious songs in the woods, and inhaled the breeze laden with the perfume of the thousand orange gardens of Seville.

" '*Kennst du das land wo die citronen bluhen?*' "

That spring, too, Borrow met Lieutenant-Colonel Elers Napier, who alluded to him as the "Unknown", and described him as of fair complexion, but with brilliant dark eyes, adding: "Though apparently in the flower of manhood, his hair was so deeply tinged with the winter of either age or sorrow, as to be nearly snow-white." Napier was tremendously impressed by Borrow's gift of tongues, friendship with the gypsies and

P

knowledge of Indian affairs, saying that he "entered freely and with depth and acuteness on (discussion of) the affairs of the East, most of which part of the world he had visited". Napier was, in his own phrase, "dying with curiosity" as to the identity of his companion, who told him he was thirty years old (he was almost thirty-six) but vouchsafed no further information except vague references to gypsies who had saved his life, and time spent in Moultan. "But in his dark and searching eye," wrote Napier, "there is an almost supernatural penetration and lustre, which, were I inclined to superstition, might induce me to set down its possessor as a second Melmoth."[1]

Now Colonel Napier had lived in the East for many years, and his interest in the "Unknown" was so acute that we may be sure he quizzed him pretty thoroughly; yet he remained convinced that his Seville acquaintance had really known Moultan—which says a very great deal for George Borrow's dramatic abilities and quite a lot for the linguistic gifts so derided by several philologists.

Colonel Napier would have been shocked to know that the "Unknown" who displayed such frightening power over the savage gypsies living in the ruins of Italica employed his evenings writing such essentially domestic epistles as this:

"Houses in Spain are let by the day: and in a palace here you will find less furniture than in your cottage at Oulton. Were you to furnish a Spanish house in the style of cold, wintry England, you would be unable to breathe. A few chairs, tables, and mattresses are all that is required, with of course a good stock of bed-linen . . .

"Bring with you, therefore, your clothes, plenty of bed-linen, etc., half-a-dozen blankets, two dozen knives and forks, a mirror or two, twelve silver table-spoons, and a large one for soup, tea things and urn (for the Spaniards never drink tea), a few books, but not many—and you will have occasion for nothing more, or, if you have, you can purchase it here as cheap as in England."[2]

[1] *Excursions along the Shores of the Mediterranean*, Elers Napier, 2 vols., London, 1842.
[2] Letter from Borrow to Mrs. Clarke.

He might have been even more shocked had he read the following wail from Mr. Brandram: ". . . I scarcely know what to say. You are in a very peculiar country; you are doubtless a man of very peculiar temperament . . . What, *e.g.*, shall we say to your confession of extreme superstitiousness?"

He could not, however, have been more shocked than was Mary Clarke when, after a harassing voyage, she arrived on 17 June, to be greeted by a very shaggy "dear George" (despite the heat he was still wearing his *zamarra*, a sheepskin jacket with the wool outside), who informed her jovially that everything was ready for her in the "Little Square of the Empty Trough". As if the appalling name were not enough, everything about the place dismayed her—the heat, the flies, the proximity of Sidi Habismilk stamping in his stall, the wild-looking servants, the dusty books piled on rickety chairs, the smells . . . One imagines that Mary Clarke registered a vow there and then to remove her dear George from such deplorable surroundings as quickly as possible.

Never before, however, had she recognized Borrow's chameleon-like quality. (After all, she had only seen him at Oulton Broad.) In Seville there was no vestige of the ardent, humble young missionary: in his stead was a stranger who spoke, dressed and walked like an Andalusian. Fortunately, the stranger had also adopted the Andalusian's gallant manner towards women, and this did much to assuage his lady's feelings while it quite captivated her daughter Henrietta, now a young woman of twenty-one. Soothed by her lover's chivalrous attentions Mary Clarke decided to put on a brave face and endure Seville for a little while.

It was, indeed, advisable that she should remain abroad at least a month or two. On the death of her brother Breame in May 1837, it had been found that he had appointed two trustees to sell the whole of the Oulton estate for the benefit of his widow and six children. Mary Clarke bitterly opposed the trustees and flourished her mortgage in their faces. With the aid of her solicitor, Mr. Pilgrim of Norwich, it was eventually agreed to sell to a Mr. Webb for £10,000, Mrs. Clarke to receive a certain sum out of this and to retain possession of Oulton Cottage. But the trustees delayed the sale in the hope that the estate would increase in value, and Mr. Webb filed a Bill in Chancery to force them to conclude the deal. At this point the astute Mr. Pilgrim advised his client to prolong her Spanish trip until the affair was settled.

It must have been a curious *ménage à trois* in the *Plazuela de la Pila Seca*, with Mrs. Clarke bustling around trying to bring order out of chaos, and Borrow wrestling with his Spanish Gypsy book, and Henrietta peering delightedly through the lattice at some flashing-eyed cavalier strolling through the square beneath. To the Sevillians it appeared a highly irregular one, for though Borrow gravely introduced the pair as his wife and daughter his friends regarded this statement as a correct but palpable lie and chuckled at the thought that their Don Jorge, despite his earlier protestations of celibacy, was as human as themselves. Being Spaniards, they gossiped pleasantly about the matter and before long the authorities and the foreign missionaries found another lever with which to prise the English heretic from his new home—he was living in sin!

It seems unlikely that he was. Mrs. Clarke's aim was marriage, and she had been extremely upset when told by the Consul in Cadiz that Protestants were barred from marrying in Spain. Borrow, until the very day of his wedding in 1840, preserved a queerly lackadaisical attitude towards his bride— only a month before his marriage he wrote to Mr. Brandram that he wished "very much to spend the remaining years of my life in the northern parts of China"—and it is probable that the household in Seville was conducted in the most proper manner.

In intervals of writing about Spanish Gypsies, Borrow, with Mrs. Clarke and Henrietta, went round from house to house distributing Testaments. These excursions so enraged the Canons of Seville Cathedral that on 18 July the *Alcalde del Barrio* (Chief Constable) raided the house and seized all the Testaments and Gospels they could find. Borrow decided therefore to visit San Lucar—the only place bar Madrid where he had a hidden stock—and smuggle his Holy Books across to the Barbary Coast. Deaf to the pleadings of Mrs. Clarke he left Seville at the end of July, picked up the chest of Testaments and St. Luke Gospels, bribed officials to give him a pass for

Typical view of Seville from the Giralda

Street in Seville

them to Cadiz, and reached Gibraltar in safety. On 8 August he crossed to Tangier, where the Consul-General, Mr. Drummond Hay, cautioned him against any attempt at Bible distribution. Undeterred, Borrow engaged a young Jew, Hayim Ben Attar, and peddled his Testaments with much success for five solid weeks.

On his return to Seville he found, to his wrath, that Lord Palmerston had sent a circular to all British Consuls in Spain forbidding them "to afford the slightest countenance to religious agents". Ignoring both his own part in bringing about this ban and the frosty relations existing between himself and the Society, Borrow wrote with all his old arrogance to Mr. Brandram demanding an explanation and ending his epistle with the unfortunate remark: "When dead flies fall into the ointment of the apothecary they cause it to send forth an unpleasant savour."

Not unnaturally this letter led to definite hostility on Mr. Brandram's part. He upbraided Borrow roundly and hinted again that it was high time he stopped his gallivanting and came home. Borrow retaliated with a stinging letter saying he had gathered enough material for several books on Spain, and immediately sent to Maria Diaz for the Testaments he had stored with her. Mr. Brandram wrote again—this time with the backing of the Committee—and ordered him home to England: Borrow stormed around Andalusia peddling his Testaments as usual, and on 24 November had the audacity to apply to the *Alcalde* for his passport "as he wished to go to Cordova and La Mancha".

The *Alcalde* failed to send the passport, so Borrow went to see the *Alcalde*. A terrific scene ensued in the street, Barrow yelling: *"Viva Inglaterra y viva la Constituçion!"* and the *Alcalde* yelling back: *"Yo te hare abajar la cabeza!"*[1] The crowd were overjoyed and Borrow was hauled off to prison, where he was locked up for some thirty hours until Mr. Williams, the Consul at Seville, obtained his release.

Needless to say, Borrow kicked up a terrific shindy over this ignominious incarceration. All over again, the harassed British officials from the Minister in Madrid downwards had to

[1] Roughly: "I will make you lower your head!"

write innumerable memorandums, soothe the angry Spaniards, placate the angrier Borrow, send long explanatory letters home to the Foreign Office. Borrow himself journeyed to Madrid, found the Minister was away, and told the *Chargé* dramatically: "I have been fighting with wild beasts!"

Somehow the fuss died down and he returned in the sulks to Seville, where he shut himself up with his gypsy book. Letters tumbled in from the now thoroughly alarmed Society but he simply pushed them aside. The sands were running out and he knew it—but he wanted to leave Spain in his own time, as the great Don Jorge, with drums beating and flags flying.

"Where," wrote the Society piteously to their few acquaintances in Spain, *"is* Mr. George Borrow?" Not until they received a letter from the Consul at Cadiz in March did they know that he and his companions proposed to sail from that port on 3 April, 1840.

Poor Borrow! He had made such plans for a magnificent exit—a journey to Saragossa on Sidi Habismilk with Hayim Ben Attar in attendance; a last glorious distribution of Testaments before galloping to freedom through the passes of the Pyrenees. But he was no longer a Romany Rye: he was an ordinary Gorgio who, as he wrote to his friend Usoz, had changed his opinion about it being "better to suffer the halter than the yoke". Mrs. Clarke's home affairs were settled and she was all the more determined to return to England because she had heard the most distressing rumours concerning what was being said about the house in the *Plazuela de la Pila Seca*. Tamely, laden with ladies' parasols and travelling rugs, George Borrow trailed aboard the little craft which was to take them round to Cadiz. He said staunchly that he was glad to leave Spain where "the Spaniard has no conception that other springs of action exist than interest or villainy", and where he had met "only *three* who were not scoundrels, thieves, or assassins".[1] But one wonders if he did not turn his head for one last glance at Seville's gleaming Golden Tower; if he did not repeat softly to himself:

"Kennst du das land wo die citronen bluhen?"

[1] Andres Borrego, Maria Diaz, and Don Luis de Usoz y Rio, to whom he made the remark.

CHAPTER SIX

"I SHALL TELL THE WORLD!"
(From a letter to Mr. John Murray, 1843)

(1840–1854)

I

ON Thursday, 16 April, the crowd of idlers hanging about the
Spread Eagle in Gracechurch Street, were rewarded by sight
of a very large man in a sheepskin jacket and a sombrero hat
mounted on a great snorting black horse, followed by an
extraordinary coffee-coloured figure dressed in robes and a
fez—George Borrow, with his servant Hayim Ben Attar and
his steed Sidi Habismilk, were home from Spain! Exactly
where servant and horse were lodged is not mentioned, but
"Mr. Borrow, Mrs. Clarke, and Daughter" booked rooms at
the Spread Eagle. A week later, at St. Peter's, Cornhill, a curate
married "George Henry Borrow—of full age—bachelor—
gentleman—of the City of Norwich—son of Thomas Borrow—
Captain in the Army", and "Mary Clarke—of full age—widow
—of Spread Eagle Inn, Gracechurch Street—daughter of
Edmund Skepper, Esquire"; the two witnesses being Mr.
Pilgrim, the solicitor, and Henrietta Clarke.

Towards the end of the first week in May the party
journeyed to the new Mrs. Borrow's home at Oulton Cottage
near Lowestoft, calling first on old Mrs. Borrow at Norwich,
who was delighted to welcome them, for she had long decided
that Mary was the wife for George and had written to Seville
when she heard of their engagement:

"I am not surprised, my dear Mrs. Clarke, at what you
tell me . . . It put me in mind of the Revd. Flethers; you
know they took time to consider. So far all is well. I shall
now resign him to your care, and may you love and cherish
him as much as I have done. I hope and trust that each will
try to make the other happy. You will always have my
prayers and best wishes. Give my kind love to dear George

and tell him he is never out of my thoughts. I have much to say, but I cannot write. I shall be glad to see you all safe and well, Give my love to Henrietta; tell her *I* can sing *'Gaily the Troubadour'*; I only want the guitar. God bless you all.

ANN BORROW."

In his own words Borrow was now "in tolerably easy circumstances, and willing to take some rest after a life of labour". His dispute with the Society had been more or less patched up—although it was made fully clear that any future appointment under their auspices was out of the question. Borrow received his salary up to June 1840, and a handsome if empty tribute was paid him in a Resolution passed at the Annual General Meeting.

Mrs. Borrow owned the Cottage, with its pretty garden, its lawn running down to Oulton Broad, and its large, stoutly-built summer-house. She also had an income of some £450 from the estate, thanks to Mr. Pilgrim's handling of her affairs and, we suspect, her own business acumen. She promptly decided that the summer-house would make an ideal "library" for dear George, so fitted it up with chairs, table and couch. To these Borrow added the piles of books and papers he had brought from Spain and—incongruous touch—his dead father's faded regimental coat and sword.

There was now absolutely nothing to stop him from sitting down to write all the wonderful books which seethed through his head. He was by no means entirely dependent on his wife's money, for he had saved a considerable amount during his years in Spain and his wants were few. The early summer weather was delightful. The one-storied Cottage was charmingly furnished and its situation surely one that any author might envy, for as Richard Ford said, it hung "over a lonely lake covered with wild fowl, and girt with dark firs, through which the wind sighed sadly. A regular Patmos, an *ultima Thule*; placed in an angle of the most unvisited, out-of-the-way portion of England".[1]

---

[1] *The Letters of Richard Ford* (1797–1858), Ed. R. E. Prothero, London, 1905.

And yet—so many things interrupted Borrow's wooing of his Muse. To begin with there were the inhabitants of Oulton village and the various small-holders scattered round the neighbourhood. These cautious folk were scared out of their wits by Hayim Ben Attar and Sidi Habismilk. True, they possessed ghosts of their own, a huntsman, hounds, and a lady in white carrying a poisoned cup, who issued on wild nights from the "High House on the hill"; but these were familiars— not a gibbering dark man in a sort of night-gown and a champing black horse that gnashed its teeth at you. The new master too, he was a queer one and no mistake, with his black cloak and white hair, and his outlandish questions about foreign words to fellows who were only using ordinary speech. Why, he even came into the bar of the inn at night—a thing no gentleman would do—and sang songs as he drank his beer; while our Mary, she from Mutford Bridge who was the maid-servant at the Cottage, did say that when she handed him a dish at dinner he roared at her, "Bring me a piece of flesh!"

Then there were all the friends who trooped over to Oulton to congratulate the newly-married pair. Borrow was hospitable by nature and dearly liked to entertain guests to a good meal and a bottle of rare wine: but also liked to be the centre of attraction and did not suffer fools gladly. If anyone interrupted his long discourses he was sharply rebuked; and he had a disconcerting habit of suddenly seizing a book, setting it before a guest, and barking, "Read it!" If the wretched visitor protested he did not know the language his host roared: "You ought; it's your own—Saxon!" Again, he would break into a Romany song, shaking his fist and tossing his mane of white hair until the women at table almost relapsed into the vapours; while if any guest dared to introduce a French, Italian or German word into the conversation he would shout: "What's that, trying to come over me with strange languages?" On the whole, it was not surprising that the visitors, no less than the villagers, spread tales about Borrow's eccentric manners.

These worried Borrow more than he cared to admit. Often, when supposed to be writing, he brooded over what he mis-takenly and persistently called the "hostility" of others towards him. He was a gregarious man—he said in the *Bible in*

Spain, "Curiosity is the leading feature of my character"—and an abnormally sensitive one in many ways; he simply could not understand when people resented his cross-examination, and the least suggestion of a snub sent him into a state of despondency.

Borrow had returned from Cadiz a sick man. Fever and dysentery had sapped his strength, and when they arrived at Oulton his wife made the building up of his health her first duty. For a time he found it pleasant enough to be run after with glasses of milk, hot possets, dainty sandwiches and anxious enquiries as to his well-being; but presently these attentions began to irk him. During his years of wandering he had been accustomed to going without food for long periods and then stuffing himself with a gargantuan, highly seasoned repast: at Oulton he was given meals at regular hours, and in between them somebody was always popping into the summer-house with a tray. If its contents were left untouched, or if he preferred to drink a gallon of cold water instead of eating bacon and eggs for breakfast, there were wails of despair from Mrs. Borrow and ominous repetitions of the word "decline".

That word haunted Borrow until he really believed that the "strength of an elephant" of which he had been so proud had vanished for good. In an effort to regain it he did the most stupid things. If he could not sleep he got up and tramped the twenty-five miles to Norwich, and after a rest at his mother's house tramped home again. If his work did not go right he saddled Sidi Habismilk and rode round the country-side like a madman until the horse was white with lather. If there were visitors who irritated him he would walk half across Norfolk, only returning when he thought they had gone. Naturally, since his constitution was still weakened, he suffered for these escapades.

But it was not only Borrow's physical health which worried him—indeed, his fits of nervous exhaustion, his attacks of indigestion, his insomnia, were principally due to his state of mind. The ill-treatment he had received at the hands of the Spanish authorities and the knowledge that he had not fought against their persecution to the bitter end rankled within him. For all his vainglorious words to Mr. Brandram it was gall

and wormwood to realize that never again would he voyage
to a far country with a Testament in his hand. The comfort
and loving care with which he was surrounded at Oulton made
him feel as though he were being smothered in a bed of cotton-
wool. But in Borrow's day the effect of mental worries upon
a sick body was not considered. If a man had a pain in his
stomach, couldn't sleep, and sometimes could scarcely walk,
then he was physically ill and that was that.

To do her justice Mrs. Borrow did everything in her power
to help him, and it was hardly her fault if her treatment turned
him into a hypochondriac. She had been sadly disappointed
when her dear George had not immediately taken on the
colour of Oulton; his temperamental outbursts alarmed her;
she could not understand why, when he had that nice quiet
summer-house, he couldn't use it as other men used their
offices and write there with effortless ease from nine till one
and two till six. George was ill, she decided, *very* ill; so she
collected remedies, consulted doctors, and used that terrible
word "decline" far too frequently.

Her perpetual fussing had one good effect; it exasperated
Borrow so much that he did retreat to the summer-house and
take refuge among the gypsies of Spain.

It would be incorrect to say that the book which eventually
appeared under the title of *The Zincali; or, An Account of the
Gypsies of Spain. With an original Collection of their Songs and
Poetry, and a copious Dictionary of their Language,*[1] was written
at Oulton. It had been begun at Badajoz, added to at various
intervals during his Spanish travels, and virtually finished—
with the aid of Juan Antonio Bailly—at Seville. All that
remained to be done was to collect, arrange and transcribe the
material: but this did not prevent Borrow providing a vivid
description of how he worked on it in the summer-house on
stormy nights when

"sickness was in the land, and the face of nature was over-
cast—heavy rain-clouds swam in the heavens—the blast
howled amid the pines which nearly surround the lonely
dwelling, and the waters of the lake which lies before it, so

[1] Published April, 1841, John Murray; later entitled *The Gypsies of Spain.*

quiet in general and tranquil, were fearfully agitated. . . .
'Bring light hither, O Hayim Ben Attar, son of the miracle!'
And the Jew of Fez brought in the lights . . ."[1]

Despite his general malaise the book grew to completion
and was transcribed by Mrs. Borrow. "In November, 1840,"
so Samuel Smiles tells us, "a tall athletic gentleman in black
called upon Mr. Murray, offering a manuscript for perusal and
publication."[2]

What a moment it must have been for Borrow when Mr.
Murray[3] granted him an interview, for had he not, fifteen years
earlier, leaned hopelessly against the railings of 5 Albemarle
Street waiting for the chance to show "Glorious John" his
translations? And now, here he was sitting in the great man's
office and being treated with the utmost courtesy!

Mr. Murray was impressed both by his visitor's appearance
and his accounts of his work for the Bible Society; and though
he said frankly that he doubted whether the book would sell,
he promised to have it read by an authority on Spain.
Borrow was in strangely humble mood—perhaps owing to an
attack of ear-ache, for which Mr. Murray kindly suggested a
remedy—for he presented his manuscript with diffidence, saying he agreed it might not appeal to the public and adding that
he would remain in London to await Mr. Murray's verdict.

From rooms at 58 Jermyn Street Borrow wrote to the
publisher:

"MY DEAR SIR,—I return you my best thanks for the
remedy, from which I have already derived considerable
benefit. When poured into the ear, I found that, besides
removing the pain to a great degree, it produces delicious
slumber. Don't you think that it might be administered to
horses having the influenza? This complaint is becoming
quite alarming. Mrs. B. writes to me this morning that all
the carriage horses in the neighbourhood are afflicted by it,
and she is anxious for her own.

"About the manuscript. I wish to observe that it was

[1] From *The Gypsies of Spain*.
[2] *A Publisher and his Friends*, Samuel Smiles.
[3] John Murray II.

By courtesy of Mr. Cherry Kearton

View from the Alhambra, Granada, overlooking the caves of Tirana

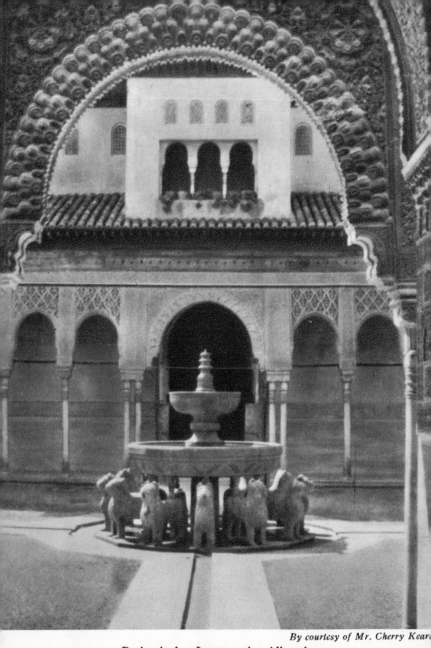

Patio de los Leones, the Alhambra

written (out) by a country amanuensis and probably contains many ridiculous errata—such things will happen. . . ."

This artless epistle probably amused Mr. Murray; but one cannot think it would have amused Mrs. Borrow, who was the "country amanuensis" in question.

The "authority" on Spain was none other than Richard Ford, who had himself spent three years riding all over the Peninsula gathering material for his famous *Hand-Book for Travellers in Spain and Readers at Home*,[1] before returning to his home at Heavitree, near Exeter, where he shut himself in his library to study the hundreds of Spanish local histories he had collected. He was actually writing the first volume of his Hand-Book when Borrow's manuscript arrived, and he wrote an enthusiastic report on which Murray acted at once, drawing up an agreement to print 750 copies of *The Gypsies of Spain* and share the profit equally with Borrow.

Busy though Ford was, he took immense pains to advise Borrow and help him in every possible way. "I have made acquaintance," he wrote to a friend in January 1841, "with an extraordinary fellow, *George Borrow*, who went out to Spain to convert the *gypsies*. He is about to publish his failure, and a curious book it will be. It was submitted to my perusal by the hesitating Murray."[2] From this time onwards the generous Ford—who had apparently talked with Borrow in London—did his utmost to bring out the very best in his new-found friend. It was not an easy task, for Borrow was hypersensitive to criticism, but Ford tackled it supremely well—so well that he literally drummed the idea and the composition of the *Bible in Spain* into its author's head.

II

The Gypsies in Spain, dedicated to the Earl of Clarendon, G.C.B. (Sir George Villiers), "in remembrance of the many obligations under which your Lordship has placed me by your

[1] Published 1845, John Murray.
[2] *The Letters of Richard Ford*, Ed. R. E. Prothero, 1905.

energetic and effectual interference in time of need", was published on 17 April, 1841; but although Ford wrote to Murray, "The book has created a great sensation far and wide", sales were poor and reviewers dilatory. The *Athenæum*, the *Literary Gazette*, the *Monthly*, and the *Westminster* gave favourable notices, but other journals ignored the book; while several eminent scholars condemned its casual philology and hinted that its writer owed too much to study of Richard Bright's works. The public, who knew nothing of gypsies except as back-door pests who sold clothes-pegs and stole chickens, showed a marked reluctance to read two whole volumes about such unpleasant people.

Oddly enough, Borrow did not sink into his usual depression when Murray wrote him in June: "Your book is doing fairly, though not quite three hundred copies have yet taken their departure, in spite of the favourable notices . . ." Probably the reason that the book's comparative failure did not wound him was that he had really written it out of gratitude to one man whom he knew would appreciate it—Jasper Petulengro. When he wrote he could not remember the time "when the very name of Gypsy did not awaken within me feelings hard to be described", he was clearly referring to that friend who coloured his childhood. He knew perfectly well that most gypsies—including Jasper—were liars, cut purses and rogues; but he also knew that if they pledged their word they never broke it, that if they made a gorgio a blood-brother he remained one for life. He was Jasper's blood-brother and *The Gypsies in Spain* was his way of showing Jasper the strength of the bond between them. Other people might dislike the book; they did not count because they had never known the call of vagabondage, poor, timid creatures.

So a positively jaunty Borrow strode over the field by Oulton Broad, his mind already busy with a travel-book on Spain. Time and again he paused and dragged a well-thumbed letter from Ford out of his pocket:

"How I wish you had given us more about yourself, instead of the extracts from those blunder-headed old Spaniards, who know nothing about Gypsies! I shall give you a *rap* on that, and a hint to publish your whole adventures for the last twenty years. . . . I am glad to see that you are accustomed to a little bantering on the company you have kept and the small spiritual success. I have been much entertained with your book, and hope to make a review like it—that is, entertaining and instructive. How much better you might have made it, if you had thrown all those twaddling Spaniards and their books into the *Brijindope*! I intend to administer the rack to Messrs. Quinones, Fajardo and Co., and possibly to give you a twist, if only a *pellizco de monja, como señal de mi cariño*."[1]

There had been other wonderful letters from Ford, and as Borrow tramped on phrases from them sang in his head:

". . . My advice again and again is to avoid all fine writing . . . Poetry is utterly to be avoided. If Apollo were to come down from heaven, John Murray would not take his best manuscript as a gift. Stick to yourself, to what you have seen, and the people you have mixed with. The more you give us of odd Jewish people the better . . . Give us adventure, wild adventure, journals, thirty language books, sorcery, Jews, Gentiles, rambles, and the *interior* of Spanish prisons—the way you got in, and the way you got out. No author has yet given us a Spanish prison. Enter into the iniquities, the fees, the slang, etc."

Just the advice to appeal to Don Jorge! Besides, Borrow had already asked the Society for the return of his letters to them, and after some hesitation (poor Mr. Brandram was loath to part with the letters about Graydon and demanded an assurance that Mr. Borrow would exercise all prudence in their use) these had been sent from Earl Street. Together with the countless notes he had made while in the Peninsula they would form a book which would need but slight alteration.

The putting together of the final manuscript did not prove quite so easy as Borrow imagined. While he toiled in the summer-house Mrs. Borrow transcribed in the parlour. Both

[1] "A nun's pinch, as a mark of my esteem."

suffered excruciatingly from writer's cramp and there was "scarcely a gleam of sunshine" throughout the summer. Work, close confinement and appalling weather combined to upset Borrow's digestion and temper, and he knew—as is shown in his letters to Hasfeld and Ford—an aching nostalgia for the sun and for freedom. By July he was contemplating going to live and study in Berlin, in August he thought of Africa, by the autumn he was undecided as to the rival merits of Constantinople and the Barbary Coast. As winter approached a note of whining self-pity crept into his letters and he was extremely annoyed when neither of his friends gave him much sympathy. Surely they realized that he was a very sick man? What right had Ford to quip about Africa as "the land from which few travellers return", or Hasfeld to remind him pompously that he had wandered enough and must now settle down! "I have not," he wrote gloomily to Mr. Murray, "the least idea of what is going on save in my own immediate neighbourhood. I still scribble occasionally for want of something better to do, and hope, by the middle of November to have completed my *Bible in Spain.*"

It was not, however, until January 1842 that the manuscript was received at Albemarle Street, whence it was despatched immediately to Ford. Mrs. Borrow heaved a sigh of relief as she returned from Lowestoft Post Office. Now, surely, dear George would prove a little more amenable to suggestion. She had not renounced any of her ideas about her husband's future; once more she led the conversation carefully round to the subject of a nice country living. Borrow was furious, saying he had long ago lost interest in the taking of Holy Orders. Besides—here Mrs. Borrow's eternal fussing about his health came back at her like a boomerang—he felt far too ill to worry about anything.

For a week he moped about the house in the daytime, complaining about his various ailments, dosing himself with physic, snapping at his wife, Henrietta and the maid, cursing the wind, the rain, the cawing of the rooks in the tree-tops. In the evenings he shut himself in the summer-house and sang strange songs at the top of his powerful voice until stray passers-by shivered, turned up their coat-collars, and bolted

Courtyard in the Alhambra

yours affectionately

John Murray

By courtesy of Sir John Murray, K.C.V.O., D.S

John Murray the Second

for their homes. There was no doubt that Mary Clarke had picked a devilish awkward husband—but she was still a very clever woman. While George raged or sang she sat placidly with her sewing, only the tight line of her mouth betraying her displeasure.

Then a bulky letter came from Mr. Murray, stating that he was prepared to publish the *Bible in Spain*, but pointing out that the manuscript was in a very unfinished condition. He enclosed a long report from his reader, advising that the breaks between March 1836 to June 1837, and November 1837 to July 1839, should be filled in, that the "air of mystery" should be abandoned, a biographical note and map included, the actual letters to the Society cut out, and the abrupt ending softened. The report went on: "The Dialogues are amongst the best parts of the book, but in several of them the tone of the speakers, of those especially who are in humble life, is too correct and elevated, and therefore out of character."

Borrow was delighted by Murray's acceptance, but his hackles rose at the criticisms offered, although these were excellent. For some inexplicable reason he never imagined these had been made by Ford, and the following day he wrote to Mr. Murray:

"I have received the MS. and likewise your kind letter . . . Pray thank the Gentleman who perused the MS. in my name for his suggestions, which I will attend to. I find that the MS. was full of trifling mistakes, the fault of my amanuensis; but I am going through it, and within three days shall have made all the necessary corrections . . . The lower classes in Spain are generally elevated in their style and scarcely ever descend to vulgarity."

Most authors have wildly optimistic ideas as to the speed at which they will be able to finish or alter their books, but Borrow beat his colleagues hollow in that direction. Nine days later he again wrote—this time a letter which might well have caused a less considerate publisher to break off negotiations:

"We are losing time; I have corrected seven hundred

Q

consecutive pages of MS., and the remaining two hundred will be ready in a fortnight."

He then explained (the effrontery of it!) that

"during the last week I have been chiefly engaged in horse-breaking. A most magnificent animal has found its way to this neighbourhood—a half-bred Arabian—he is at present in the hands of a low horse-dealer; he can be bought for eight pounds, but no person will have him; it is said that he kills everybody who mounts him. I have been *charming* him, and have so succeeded that at present he does not fling me more than once in five minutes. *What a contemptible trade is the Author's compared to that of the jockey."*

By the end of February the first volume was in Mr. Murray's hands, but since there were two more volumes to complete and since Borrow had finally consented to fill in the breaks which occurred in them, there was still a tremendous amount of revision to be done. This time the work was interrupted by a most unseemly dispute with the Oulton vicar, the Rev. E. P. Denniss, over a series of dog-fights. Borrow's dog and the vicar's dog were sworn enemies and every time they met—which was frequently as they were close neighbours—they had a fight. Naturally each master stuck up for his own pet, but nobody except Borrow would have sent a note stating that he was about to complain to the Bishop and that the vicar had better have his dog shot before he did so!

Within half an hour a messenger from the vicarage delivered this letter at Oulton Cottage:

"Mr. Denniss begs to acknowledge Mr. Borrow's note, and is sorry to hear that his dog and Mr. Borrow's have again fallen out. Mr. Denniss learns from his servant that Mr. D's dog was no more in fault than Mr. B's, which latter is of a very quarrelsome and savage disposition, as Mr. Denniss can himself testify, as well as many other people. Mr. Denniss regrets that these two animals cannot agree when they meet, but he must decline acceding to Mr.

Borrow's somewhat arbitrary demand, conceiving he has as much right to retain a favourite, and in reality very harmless animal, as Mr. Borrow has to keep a dog which has once bitten Mr. Denniss himself, and oftentimes attacked him and his family. Mr. Borrow is at perfect liberty to take any measure he may deem advisable, either before the magistrates or the Bishop of the Diocese, as Mr. Denniss is quite prepared to meet them."

Borrow's reply was unforgivable:

"Mr. Borrow has received Mr. Denniss's answer to his note. With respect to Mr. Denniss's recrimination on the quarrelsome disposition of his harmless house-dog, Mr. Borrow declines to say anything further. No one knows better than Mr. Denniss the value of his own assertions . . . Circumstances over which Mr. Borrow has at present no control will occasionally bring him and his family under the same roof with Mr. Denniss; that roof, however, is the roof of the House of God, and the prayers of the Church of England are wholesome from whatever mouth they may proceed."

No wonder the *Bible in Spain* was not published in May, as Mr. Murray had intended! Yet late as Borrow had been in sending it in by July he was writing:

"What are your intentions with respect to the *Bible in Spain?* I am a frank man, and frankness never offends me. Has anybody put you out of conceit with the book? . . . Or would the appearance of the *Bible* on the first of October interfere with the avatar, first or second, of some very wonderful lion or Divinity, to whom George Borrow, who is *neither*, must of course give place? Be frank with me, my dear Sir, and I will drink your health in Romany and Madeira. . . . Allow me to assure you that I am quite willing to release you from your share of the agreement into which we entered . . . Unless you go on with it I shall remit to Woodfall (the printer) the necessary money for the

purchase of paper, and when it is ready offer it to the
world . . ."

The House of Murray must have been sorely tempted to
tell their unruly author to take his book where he pleased;
but they truly believed in Borrow's genius and they had Ford's
private and glowing advice beside them:

". . . A rum, very rum, mixture of gypsyism, Judaism, and
missionary adventure. . . . Depend upon it that the book
will sell . . . Borrow is such a *trump* . . . as full of meat as
an egg, and a fresh-laid one. Borrow will lay you golden
eggs, and hatch them after the ways of Egypt; put salt
on his tail and secure him in your coop, and beware how
any poacher coaxes him with 'raisins' or reasons out of
the Albemarle preserve."[1]

III

The *Bible in Spain* was eventually published on 10 December,
1842. Its success was instantaneous; but its author was so busy
preparing for the entertainment of his friend Jasper Petulengro
on 26 December, when that gentleman arrived "dressed in
true regal fashion. He sang me Rommany songs and drank me
two quarts of *levina*",[2] that he scarcely realized this until the
New Year, when laudatory notices, letters of congratulation,
and requests for autographs fell like a snowstorm upon Oulton
Cottage. The great Mr. J. G. Lockhart himself praised the book
in his *Quarterly Review*, adding a handsome apology for his
failure to notice *The Gypsies of Spain*; every other critic in
the country hailed it as a work of genius; Mr. Murray wrote
that a second edition was printing; Ford said Borrow's name
would "fill the trump of fame"; Hasfeld that he "ached in
every joint with the vividness of his descriptions"; and the
only vicious attack was the *Dublin Review's* statement that

[1] *The Letters of Richard Ford.*
[2] A full account of this visit was first published in the 2nd. edition of
The Gypsies of Spain, Murray, 1843.

"Borrow was a missionary sent out by a gang of conspirators against Christianity", to which Borrow replied characteristically, "It is easier to call names and misquote passages in a dirty Review than to write the *Bible in Spain*."

This was no flash in the pan success. Borrow's name was on everybody's lips and by March 1843 a third edition was published; while in the House of Commons Sir Robert Peel made his famous allusion to the author:

> "Difficulties! Were they to be deterred from proceeding on that account? Let them look at Mr. Borrow; why, if he had suffered himself to be prevented from circulating the Bible in Spain by the difficulties he met with, he could never have spread such enlightenment and information through that country."

As early as February Borrow wrote to Murray, "I have begun my *Life*. D.V. it shall beat anything I have yet accomplished." This is the first direct reference to the writing of *Lavengro* and *The Romany Rye*, and shows that Borrow intended these volumes to be a complete autobiography; but it was a work destined to take many years and suffer many vicissitudes before it was ever published. In any case, the literary lion of the moment was far too busy writing to his admirers and accepting the invitations of the great to bother much with writing. All the world and his wife were anxious to meet the man of whom the *Quarterly* said:

> "We are frequently reminded of *Gil Blas* in the narratives of this pious, single-hearted man. As a book of adventures it seems to us about the most extraordinary which has appeared in our own or any other language for a long time past."

The nineteenth-century *Gil Blas*—backed by his gratified wife—was only too delighted to attend receptions where he met "Princes and Members of Parliament", to dine with the Prussian Minister and Mme Bunsen, to lunch with Bishops and Barons, to be fêted, petted, listened to, admired; and it was at this point that Mrs. Borrow really came into her own. She had worked very hard and waited a long time for her dear George's worldly success; now that her aim had been achieved she wished to see it consolidated. On the plea (probably justified) that he was over generous in money matters, she took over the entire management of his affairs; and since she had no liking for London festivities herself, preferring to bask in her husband's reflected glory among her East Anglian friends, she festooned him about with chest protectors, bottles of medicine, and boxes of dyspepsia tablets, and packed him off to the Jermyn Street rooms where he had stayed before.

Alas, her hopes of social stardom for her dear George were not fulfilled. There was far too much of the vagabond in Borrow for high society. At parties he was restless, ill at ease, taciturn, and though he liked women they, oddly enough, found his personality repellent. He hated what he called "the extreme gentility" of the upper-classes; he twisted innocent remarks into snubs; he was altogether too gloomy a lion to be popular and, when he sensed hostility in the atmosphere, he took refuge in rudeness.

Stories of his insolence are legion. When a lady gushed, "Oh, Mr. Borrow, I have read your books with so much pleasure!" he drew himself to his full height and said icily, "Pray, what books do you mean, madam? My account books?" When Miss Agnes Strickland asked if she might send him a copy of her *Queens of England* he growled, "For God's sake don't, madam, I should not know where to put them or what to do with them," adding in an audible aside, "What a damned fool that woman is!" When Thackeray, who had struggled to start a conversation with him, said in desperation, "Have you seen my *Snob Papers* in *Punch*?" he received the answer, "In *Punch*? It is a periodical I never look at." Indeed, the only person who succeeded in placating him was Wyndham Richard Phillips, to whom he sat for his portrait. Unable to make anything of a sitter who persisted in scowling and twitching his mouth, the painter asked if Persian were really a beautiful language, whereupon Borrow's whole countenance lightened and, with flashing eyes, he began declaiming Persian poetry.

Borrow had been unhappy at Oulton: he was even more unhappy in London. He had, although he would never admit it, a strong streak of snobbishness in his nature which made him resent the growing evidence of his unpopularity—not for a moment did he realize that the fault lay in his own stars, not other peoples'. "Who *are* the Ethnological Society?" he wrote arrogantly to Mr. Murray upon receiving an invitation to join that august body. "At present I am in great demand. A Bishop has just requested me to visit him. The worst of these Bishops is that they are all skinflints, saving for their families; their *cuisine* is bad and their Port-Wine execrable, and as for their cigars . . . !"

Strange words from a militant Churchman; but they serve to show Borrow's reaction to what he considered "patronage" on the part of those better born or better blessed with influence than himself.

But the pathetic part of that inglorious London season was Borrow's sudden realization of his utter dependence upon his wife. Without her he was lost. He had no money unless he wrote home, whereupon he received a five-pound note with a lecture on the necessity of economy. He suffered from pains in his eyes, ears, nose, throat and stomach—that ominous word "decline" had done its work well and truly—and had no least idea of what to do to cure them. He had failed to obtain a "situation" with something nice and respectable like the Consular Service, and he had received strict injunctions to do so. In a letter to Mrs. Borrow his complete reliance on her is made abundantly clear:

"London, May 29th, 1843.

"MY DEAREST CARRETA,—

"I have not been particularly well since I wrote last; indeed, the weather has been so horrible that it is enough to depress anybody's spirits, and, of course, mine. I did very wrong not to bring you when I came, for without you I cannot get on at all. Left to myself a gloom comes upon me which I cannot describe. I will endeavour to be home on Thursday, as I wish so much to be with you, without whom there is no joy for me nor rest. You tell me to ask for *situations*, etc. I am not at all suited for them. My place seems to be in our own dear cottage, where, with your help, I hope to prepare for a better world . . . I dare say I shall be home on Thursday, perhaps earlier, if I am unwell; for the poor bird when in trouble has no one to fly to but his mate. . . ."

Ludicrously enough "Carreta", the name by which Borrow always addressed his wife, is the Spanish for "dray-cart" (a fact which greatly worried Dr. Knapp), but one assumes this was some playful family joke that probably had its origin in Mrs. Borrow's ignorance of the Spanish language when she visited Seville.

Mr. Arthur Dalrymple, a Norwich solicitor who had no great affection for the Borrow family, gave two strangely different views on the relationship between husband and wife. Writing of the Seville episode he said: "At this time the widow of a merchant living at Mutford or Oulton near Lowestoft in Suffolk, found him out, having travelled half over Europe in search of him, and took possession of him, and upon her income of £300 or £400 per annum, with what his writings have produced,[1] he has lived ever since." Yet further on he wrote that he had often seen Mr. and Mrs. Borrow out walking, "he stalking along with a huge cloak wrapped around him in all weathers, and she trudging behind him like an Indian squaw, with a carpet bag, or bundle, or small portmanteau in her arms, and endeavouring under difficulty to keep up with his enormous strides".[2]

One cannot place much credence upon Mr. Dalrymple's judgment. Obviously he did not know the couple well: equally obviously he had at some period crossed swords with Borrow; but the idea of Mrs. Borrow ever acting the part of "Indian squaw" is laughable. From 1843 onwards—and in July of that year Borrow reached his fortieth birthday—his attitude towards his wife was one of devoted subservience; while her attitude towards him was a combination of that of a fond

---

[1] Altogether Borrow received from the Murrays £3,437 10s., most of it earned by the *Bible in Spain*.
[2] Autobiographical MS., written *circa* 1860.

mother to a spoilt child and a proud mistress to a performing dog. Most certainly she had "taken possession" of Borrow and remoulded him nearer to her heart's desire, and in the process the world had lost Don Jorge and gained Lavengro.

IV

Borrow's return to Oulton did not cure his uneasy restlessness, although he galloped for a fortnight through Norfolk, exhausting himself and almost killing poor Sidi Habismilk. His mood varied from despair, as when he learnt that 30,000 copies of the *Bible in Spain* had been sold in America from a "pirated" edition,[1] to supreme arrogance, as when he wrote to Mr. Murray, "Would it be as well to write a preface to this *fourth* edition with a tirade or two against the Pope, and allusions to the Great North Road?"[2] The growing number of his detractors—for people whom he had offended lost no time in branding him an insufferable impostor—disturbed him although he said vaingloriously, "Let them call me a nonentity if they will. I believe that some of those, who say I am a phantom, would alter their tone provided they were to ask me to a good dinner; bottles emptied and fowls devoured are not exactly the feats of a phantom. No! I partake more of the nature of a Brownie or Robin Goodfellow, goblins, 'tis true, but full of merriment and fun, and fond of good eating and drinking." The death of Mr. John Murray II on 23 June upset him greatly, but did not prevent him from harassing his son, John Murray III, about business details which could well have waited and adding: "Pray keep up your spirits, and that you may be able to do so, take long walks and drink plenty of Scotch ale with your dinner. Stick to business and publish nothing save what is sure to sell, viz., the works of Norfolk authors."

The *Bible in Spain* went into six editions before the end of the year, but Borrow seemed to have lost interest in its success.

[1] At that date there were no copyright laws governing American sales.
[2] Mr. Murray wisely replied: "With due submission to you as author, I would suggest that you should not abuse the Pope in your new preface."

Mrs. Borrow was far from well and kept pleading with him to find a good job—apparently she had realized that the lot of an author's wife was not all she had imagined it to be. Egged on by his Carreta, Borrow had written to Lord Clarendon two years earlier asking for a Consulship, but had been told he had no chance; now he did his best to be sent to Ireland to deal with Daniel O'Connell, whom he called "that cowardly, bawling vagabond". "I wish the Government would give me some command," he wrote to Murray grandly. "I wish I were acquainted with Sir Robert Peel. I could give him many a useful hint with respect to Ireland and the Irish . . . Whenever there's a row I intend to go over with Sidi Habismilk and put myself at the head of a body of volunteers."

The sad part was that nobody wanted George Borrow in Ireland or anywhere else. He was forced to remain at Oulton annoying the neighbours, making desultory notes for *Lavengro*, puttering about the house and garden, writing quarrelsome letters. Occasionally he went over to Norwich to stay a few days with his mother, and it was here that Caroline Fox met him and described him as "a tall, ungainly, uncouth man, with great physical strength, a quick penetrating eye, a confident manner, and a disagreeable tone and pronunciation. He was sitting on one side of the fire, and his old mother on the other. His spirits always sink in wet weather, and to-day was very rainy, but he was courteous and not displeased to be a little lionised, for his delicacy is not of the most susceptible".[1]

So the year which had begun so brilliantly drew to its melancholy close with Borrow fretting about the way "Popery is springing up in every direction", about his continual nervous disorders—he had lately suffered a renewal of the "horrors"—about the slowness of the autobiography's progress. In the January of 1844 a visit from Ford cheered him temporarily, but when his gay and delightful visitor had departed his depression was intensified. He would not, could not, languish any longer in Oulton—and at last summoned courage to tell his wife so.

Mrs. Borrow's body was racked by bronchitis but her brain was as astute as ever. Certainly her dear George must go right

[1] 23 October, 1843. *Memories of Old Friends*, London, 1882.

away by himself, take a trip abroad to soothe his nerves. Now suppose he retired to the summer-house and finished the first volume of his autobiography while she looked up ships and coaches and made all arrangements for his little holiday? Poor Borrow, who had hitherto always travelled where the fancy took him without the least fuss or preparation, quite perked up and scribbled so furiously that by mid-March his manuscript was ready for transcription and he was off to London, where he spent some six weeks before departing for Paris. Elizabeth Rigby (afterwards Lady Eastlake) met him at some party on 20 March, and, like her stern fellow-critics, Harriet Martineau, Frances Power Cobbe, and Agnes Strickland, heartily disliked him. "Borrow came in the evening; now a fine man, but a most disagreeable one; a kind of character that would be most dangerous in rebellious times—one that would suffer or persecute to the utmost. His face is expressive of strong-headed determination."[1]

As Borrow crossed the English Channel his spirits rose. He was free once more, off on one of those wild, romantic expeditions that so gladdened his heart! Yet somehow, by the time he reached Vienna he knew the savour had gone out of travel. There were all the tickets, itineraries, time-schedules and maps with which his dear Carreta had buttressed him about; all the worries over letters of credit—for the careful Mrs. Borrow had seen to it that the necessary cash should be doled out in driblets at different ports of call; all the grand people who wished to shake hands with the famous author of the *Bible in Spain*. True, he had met M. Vidocq, whom he had so long admired, in Paris; but that gentleman had been so anxious to obtain a copy of his book and so "extraordinarily civil" that Borrow suspected he really wished to pirate a French translation of it. True, when he reached Buda-Pesth, which reminded him of Edinburgh, he was wined and dined by many hospitable people; but the whole affair lacked the wide, swaggering freedom to which his earlier journeys had accustomed him.

From Buda-Pesth he travelled across the great Danubian plain to Rumania. During this part of his trip he felt more

[1] *Journals and Correspondence of Lady Eastlake*, John Murray, 1895.

at home, for here he was among gypsies, with whom he could yarn interminably and about whom he could make copious notes. But all too soon he was in Bucharest, which he said had "much grandeur and much filth", and where he was welcomed by the British Consul, Mr. Colquhoun. Mid-September found him in Constantinople being presented to the Sultan, Abdul Medjid, and from there he visited Salonika, Thessaly, and the Albanian coast before taking ship from Corfu to Venice and Rome.

Meantime, Mrs. Borrow, who archly confessed she was allowed the rare privilege of opening her husband's letters, kept Mr. Murray informed of his movements. "The accounts from him are, I am thankful to say, very satisfactory. It is extraordinary with what marks of kindness even Catholics of distinction treat him when they know who he is, but it is clearly his gift of tongues which causes him to meet with so many adventures, several of which he has recorded of a most singular nature." And again: "Thus far, thank God, he has prospered in his journey. Many and wonderful are the adventures he has met with, which I hope at no distant period may be related to his friends."

Borrow's letters to his wife reveal no adventures worth the recording. Apart from one or two good descriptive passages they are filled with irrelevant detail—confessions of drawing extra money and promises not to spend it all; accounts of his various aches and pains; lists of the well-known people who want to entertain him; reiterations of how sadly he misses his dear Carreta.

All that really came out of his seven months' journey were the manuscripts: *Vocabulary of the Gypsy Language as spoken in Hungary and Transylvania*, and a *Bohemian Grammar*[1]; a few odd passages which were introduced into the 1846 edition of *The Gypsies of Spain*; the Hungarian's story in the *Romany Rye*; and the bitter knowledge that his travelling days were done.

To give Borrow his due he determined, on reaching Oulton in November, to press on with the other volumes of his autobiography. "Take pen in hand," Ford wrote to him, "and strike

[1] MSS. purchased by The British Museum, 1892.

on the anvil while the iron is hot and the impressions vivid; knock off a thousand fiery thoughts, daughters of new excitement . . . but first let us lift up a corner of the curtain over *those seven years*."

Borrow must sometimes have wished from the bottom of his heart that he had not told his publisher and a host of friends that he had undertaken mysterious and dangerous travels between the years 1826 and 1833—yet what else could he have done, after his many allusions to Moultan, Timbuctou and heaven knew where else in the *Bible in Spain*? Now he was hoist with his own petard, and one feels that his long delay in finishing *Lavengro* was partly due to his repeated and unsuccessful efforts to surmount the obstacle of the "veiled period".

There were, of course, other reasons as well. Early in 1845 Mr. Samuel Morton Peto (afterwards Sir Morton Peto) decided to enlarge and rebuild Lowestoft harbour. He then had the progressive idea of constructing a railway to Reedham, half-way to Norwich, which was to run right between Oulton Hall and Oulton Cottage, and very wisely obtained the right to do this by Act of Parliament. To say that Borrow was angry would be grossly to understate the violent fury that seized him when he found out that he would have to cross a railway bridge each time he wanted to go to church or reach the highroad. He immediately started a campaign to stop this outrage and wrote condemnations of Peto to all his friends. Ford advised, "Sell and be off!" while Mr. Murray wrote, "I hope you will make the railway pay dear for its whistle"; but Borrow was determined not to be driven out of his home and was in no mood to consider the great material benefit compensation would bring. He felt even more outraged when he heard gossip that Peto was boasting the gravel he had lifted from the Oulton estate had more than repaid the price he gave for the land; and afterwards, when Peto bought Somerleyton Hall and asked Borrow jokingly why he had not called upon him, he received the reply, "I call on you! Do you think I don't read my Shakespeare? Do you think I don't know all about those highwaymen Bardolph and Peto?" Borrow then strode back to the summer-house and immortalized his enemy as that evil man "Mr. Flamson, flaming in his coach with a million", who appeared in the *Romany Rye*.

The railway was not completed until 1847, but Borrow fumed and fretted over the prospect of it all through the spring of 1845. By May he was in a hopeless state of nerves, and just then he received a copy of Ford's *Hand-Book*—a work which had cost its author fourteen years of labour—with the reminder that he had long promised to review it in the *Quarterly Review*. On 2 June Mrs. Borrow sent Mr. Murray a bulky article of thirty-seven folio pages with a letter explaining that her husband was "very unwell . . . Shivering fits have been succeeded by burning fever . . . and he at present remains in a low and weak state, and what is worse, we are by no means sure that the disease is subdued". She wished it understood that the review was not so able as it would have been if Mr. Borrow had been well, but that he had "considered his promise to Mr. Ford sacred".

The trouble was that the article was not a review of Ford's book at all. The first half of it was a scathing indictment of the Spanish Government and several leading figures in it: the second half gave Borrow's own views on Spain and its people. J. G. Lockhart immediately asked him if he objected to alterations and apparently received a broadside by way of reply, because he wrote to Mr. Murray that he was sorry he could not use it, adding perfectly reasonably:

"Mr. Borrow would not have liked that, when his *Bible in Spain* came out, we should have printed a brilliant essay by Ford on some point of Spanish interest, but including hardly anything calculated to make the public feel that a new author of high consequence had made his appearance among us—one bearing the name, not of Richard Ford, but of George Borrow."

Ford, who was genuinely distressed, made bad worse by dashing off a note to *El Gitano*, as he called Borrow, saying he had recommended the article to *Blackwood's*. Borrow took this as a direct insult, promptly forgot all Ford's kindness and help, and sent a surly answer. From that day one of the most valuable friendships he ever formed began to deteriorate, and though Ford still wrote him occasionally his letters lacked their usual warmth.

The year 1845 passed and most of 1846, but there was still no sign of the autobiography. Mr. Murray wrote tactfully in the autumn, pointing out that this was the most favourable season for publications: Borrow replied insolently: "My work will be ready next year, and about Christmas I shall be thinking of advertising it"; but Christmas came and went and nothing happened, while by January 1847 Borrow was again off at another tangent. This time he wished to become—of all things —a magistrate! The idea had first occurred to him soon after his arrival at Oulton, because the woods and coppices surrounding his cottage were, so he averred, full of poachers and thieves. "A horrible neighbourhood this," he complained, "not a magistrate that dares do his duty", and thereafter he bided his time until one of the existing magistrates died in the autumn of 1843, when he wrote to the long-suffering Mr. Murray: "Present my compliments to Mr. Gladstone and tell him that the *Bible in Spain* would have no objection to become one of the *Great Unpaid.*"

Mr. Gladstone's sole connection with Borrow was that he had told Mr. Murray how greatly he admired the *Bible in Spain*, and had asked if the author would alter an offensive sentence in his description of the Tangier Mosque which ran: "I looked around for the abominable thing, and found it not; no scarlet strumpet with a crown of false gold sat nursing an ugly changeling in a niche." With an ill-grace Borrow changed the sentence to "the besetting sin of the pseudo-Christian Church did not stare me in the face in every corner", a revision scarcely likely to appeal to Mr. Gladstone or to make him regard Borrow as a suitable candidate for the local Bench. Mr. Murray evidently turned the request down, for Borrow then appealed to J. G. Lockhart, who very sensibly said that as a Scot he was not conversant with the methods of approach to the Lord-Lieutenant of Suffolk, then the aged Duke of Grafton. There the matter rested; but Borrow had not forgotten his ambition and nearly four years later he returned to the attack in a letter to Lord Clarendon, begging him to influence the Lord Chancellor in his favour.

It was an amazing epistle, for it stated grandly that the writer was a "large land-owner" in the district—Mrs. Borrow had succeeded in buying back the estate the year before—that the neighbourhood swarmed with vile characters, and that there was no magistrate to attend to it. Lord Clarendon hedged politely, and while promising to speak to the Lord Chancellor, explained that the proper thing to do was to apply direct to the Lord-Lieutenant, now the Earl of Stradbroke, giving his name as a reference.

Borrow dashed off to Norwich, rounded up his friends, got an introduction to the Hon. William Rufus Rous, Lord Stradbroke's brother, and blandished that gentlemen into putting forward his claim. For the next two months the household at Oulton lived in a state of twitter while Borrow anathematized the slow ways of the English and bombarded the wretched Mr. Rous for a quick answer.

Naturally Lord Stradbroke made enquiries, as a result of which the whole horrid history of Borrow's iniquities was revealed. He was deplorably inquisitive, always poking his nose into other people's business. His habits were not those of an English gentleman—he drank ale in public-houses, sang "foreign" songs in a loud voice at dead of night, galloped round the countryside on a snorting black horse. Worse still, he not only allowed the gypsies to camp on his land but sat with them round their fire singing in some outlandish tongue until the gypsy men started fighting each other, and the gypsy women kicked tins cans about, and everybody in the neighbourhood shook with fear. Worst of all, he himself was much too fond of "the fancy" (fighting), and if he heard there was an innocent tramp about he would track the fellow down, take off his coat, and challenge him to decide there and then who was the better man.

There was no evidence that any tramp ever accepted the challenge; all the same it was a damning dossier and Mr. Borrow was clearly unsuitable as a candidate for magistracy. On 16 March Lord Stradbroke wrote carefully to Lord Clarendon saying that he was perfectly satisfied with his present magistrates and with their attention to duty. If at some future date he felt their strength should be increased he

John Murray the Third

By courtesy of British Railways

Llangollen, Fifteenth-Century Bridge over River

would call on the "assistance of those gentlemen living in the neighbourhood, who, living on terms of intimacy with them, will be able to maintain that union of good feeling which, I am happy to say, exists in all our benches of the Petty Sessions, and if Mr. Borrow should be recommended to me by them, I shall have much pleasure in placing his name on the list for the approval of the Lord Chancellor".

Nicely wrapped up though it was, this letter contained the snub direct—and Borrow knew it. In a white heat of rage he denounced the Lord-Lieutenant, the local gentry, the tittle-tattling yokels, and trumpeted to all and sundry that he was not the man to be insulted with impunity. Perhaps fortunately for the peace of Suffolk he then hared off in pursuit of another red-herring in the shape of his old friend, Dr. Bowring.

The coolness which had developed between these two after Borrow's impudent request for Portuguese and Spanish introductions had given place to genial warmth. Dr. Bowring had been elected Member of Parliament for Bolton in 1841 and had, so people said, the ear of Lord Palmerston. Borrow, who embraced every rumour as absolute truth, wrote to him and asked if he would recommend him for the Consulship at Canton: Bowring answered most courteously and said he would do all in his power to help. Then came the début of the literary lion and consequent meetings at parties when Borrow seized upon "my old, indeed, my only friend", and Bowring, being like most successful men a bit of an opportunist, was quite glad to be hailed as the faithful comrade of the famous author. Thereafter the two saw each other frequently and at some period Bowring asked for the loan of Borrow's eight-volume New Testament in Manchu.

In April 1847 Bowring wrote from the House of Commons: "We have a Committee investigating our Commercial Relations with China. We want information as to the Russian route through Kiakhta. Can you put us in the way of getting it?"

On reception of this note Borrow's mercurial spirits soared—the name Kiakhta evidently still retained its old magic. Immediately his vivid imagination pictured himself advising Her Majesty's Government on their conduct of Far Eastern affairs, being sent to China as Ambassador, covering himself

R

with glory through his brave handling of tricky Oriental situations. He pushed *Lavengro* aside and spent days composing a lengthy and garbled account of the fabled land of the Tatars, which he sent to Bowring.

For the next week Oulton Cottage resounded with Romany songs, scraps of Russian verse, and requests to Henrietta Clarke to play the *Redowa* polka because it was such a gay, delicious tune. Don Jorge was himself again! The "horrors" were forgotten, the aches and pains vanished like snow before the sun, there was much strenuous rowing on the lake, little parties were given, astonished local children were given pennies and pats on the head.

At the end of April the blow fell. Bowring wrote:

"MY DEAR BORROW,—The existence of the Treaty of 1728 is well known, but on mentioning the matter to Sir George Staunton, Mr. Matheson, and other gentlemen who have been long resident in China, they doubt whether effect is practically given to any article by which 'two hundred merchants are allowed to visit Pekin every three years'. Are you certain this is in practice now? *Have you ever been to Kiakhta?* As, if summoned, your expenses must be paid by the public,[1] I should like to know what are the facts to which you would give evidence on your personal knowledge. Krusenstern's voyage was performed long ago. Do you know Timkowski's book?"[2]

"Have you ever been to Kiakhta?" The terrible question danced before Borrow's eyes. Those six brief words smashed all his golden hopes into smithereens, for they meant that Bowring *knew* he had lied, knew he had never walked among the Tatar hordes in that dusty border town. What awful, monstrous thing had Bowring done? What was the reason behind the doing of it?

Crouched over the letter in his summer-house Borrow lashed his mind to fury, sent his memory chasing back across the years to hunt up evidence against this wicked man who had dared to destroy a mighty legend. Bowring had always

[1] Borrow had suggested he should give evidence.
[2] *Travels of the Russian Mission through Mongolia to China, and Residence in Pekin*, 1820 *and* 1821, London, 2 vols., 1826.

picked his brains, Bowring had kept his Scandinavian translations for thirteen years, during which time he had doubtless used them for his own ends. Bowring had borrowed the Manchu New Testament—ah, that was it! For what purpose had he been so anxious to obtain a copy? Why, to appropriate the translation of it to himself, to flaunt his claims to being the greatest polylinguist of his time before the stupid, dull members of the House of Commons Committee. Bah! the thing was as plain as a pikestaff—and to think that his friend, his old, indeed, his only friend, had played such a dastardly trick.

Dr. Knapp was a firm believer in Borrow's story of Bowring's duplicity, but apart from Borrow's indictment in the appendix to the *Romany Rye* there is no shadow of evidence to support his accusations. They are, quite simply, the revenge of a man against the one person who ever taxed him directly with not telling the truth about his Eastern wanderings. If further proof is needed, it lies in the fact that Borrow did not reply to Bowring's letter—and if he had had even the ghost of a leg to stand on we may rest assured that he would have launched out on a terrific spate of correspondence.

The Oulton household exchanged merriment for gloom as its master wandered from room to room brooding on his lost dreams. He had been so sure, so very sure, of that glittering vision of a tall, commanding figure, breast ablaze with Orders, bowing over the hand of the last of the Manchu Empresses in the Summer Palace at Pekin. Now it was gone, never to return. There was "no peace in the world" and every man's hand was against him. And pacing to and fro those six words burned and seared themselves into his brain, *"Have you ever been to Kiakhta?"*

V

By the summer of 1848 Mr. Murray was growing seriously disturbed about the non-delivery of Borrow's completed manuscript. He knew too well the danger of a gap of years between an author's first success and his next book, and a man less kindly might long since have gone down to beard the surly lion of Oulton in his den. Borrow was indeed fortunate in his publisher, for Mr. Murray's rare reminders were always couched in the gentlest terms: the trouble was that Borrow considered the publisher fortunate in his author and took no pains to conceal the fact, either writing haughtily that *he* hoped to be able to print on such-and-such a date—which was never kept to—or ignoring Mr. Murray's notes altogether. An announcement of the book appeared in the firm's Autumn List for 1848:

MR. MURRAY'S LIST OF
NEW WORKS IN PREPARATION

LAVENGRO: AN AUTOBIOGRAPHY
By George Borrow, Author of the
"Bible in Spain", etc.
3 vols. Post 8vo.

On 7 October Mr. Murray pointed out how necessary it was for the book's circulation that he should be able to announce to his salesmen at their annual dinner in December that the manuscript had gone to press; and Borrow must have answered with some more emphatic promise than usual, for the first volume—which had been held since 1844—was sent to Woodfall, the printer, the same month. At Borrow's request the title was changed to *Life, a Drama*, and Mr. Murray advertised the book in the *Athenæum* and the *Quarterly Review*, being unaware that further cyclones had hit Oulton Broad.

For Borrow was suffering an attack of the "horrors" which surpassed all earlier ones. This was due to two causes; the lesser a guarded hint from the Trustees of the British Museum that they were interested in sending a mission to the Middle East in quest of a valuable Codex, an original fourth-century copy of the Greek New Testament presented to the Convent of St. Catherine on Mount Sinai by the Emperor Justinian which "still existed in the Convent, and, if acquired, would render the British Museum the admiration of the world".[1]

---

[1] In 1844 Tischendorf stole forty-three leaves of the *Codex Sinaiticus*, publishing these in 1846 under the misleading title, *Codex Friderico-Augustanus*. In 1859 he again visited the Sinai Peninsula, then under the protection of Russia, and prevailed upon the monks to give the remainder of the *Codex* as a present to Tsar Alexander II, who published a magnificent edition in 1862, and retained the manuscript until it was placed in the Imperial Public Library, St. Petersburg. Its later history is well known.

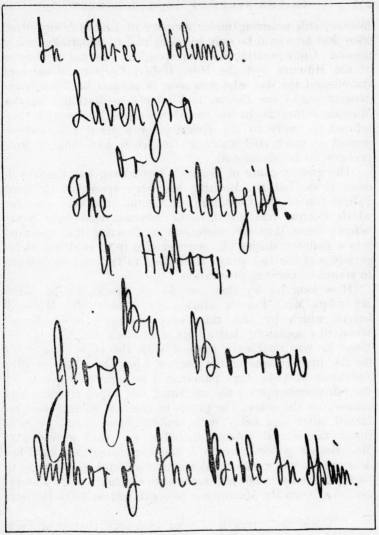

In Three Volumes.

Lavengro

or

The Philologist.

A History.

By

George Borrow

Author of The Bible In Spain.

The Original Title Draft of *Lavengro*, sent by George Borrow to John Murray II, June 23, 1848

Borrow, still smarting under memory of Kiakhta, replied at once that he would be only too delighted to undertake such a mission. Unfortunately his correspondent was not a Trustee of the Museum, but the Hon. Robert Curzon, an eminent traveller of the day who was soon to publish his *Visit to the Monasteries of the Levant*, and after consultation with the Museum authorities he was forced to write to Borrow that they refused to apply to the Treasury for a grant and, indeed, poured so much cold water on the whole idea that it had, perforce, to be abandoned.

The greater cause of Borrow's breakdown was the unwelcome news that Dr. Bowring had been appointed by Lord Palmerston to the Consulship at Canton, the very post for which Borrow had asked to be recommended eight years before! Since Borrow's suspicions of Bowring had mounted into a delusion during the summer this fresh evidence of his perfidy was the last straw. He retired to bed and succumbed to complete nervous prostration.

How long he lay there we do not know; but in January 1849 Mrs. Borrow started to answer Mr. Murray's letters, which by this time were becoming more abrupt. Woodfall complained that all his other work was held up because he was unable to proceed with the type already set for the first volume of the Borrow *Life*. The whole of 1849 and most of 1850 were punctuated by anxious requests for the full manuscript on the one hand, and vague promises and excuses on the other. The proofs of the first volume were returned, after long delay, with multitudinous scrawled corrections; the second volume drifted in by small instalments; Mrs. Borrow wrote dramatic letters explaining how hard her dear George was working and how unreasonable people were to expect miracles in the mid-nineteenth century. On 11 December, 1849, even Mr. Murray lost patience and wrote to Borrow:

"Upon the strength of your assurance that your book would be finished in February, I offered it to the Booksellers at my sale last week, and I have disposed of more than one thousand copies. Now I entreat you not to slacken in your labours, or I shall be in bad plight, and your book will

most certainly suffer if its publication be further delayed . . .
I beg you to answer by return of post, whether you would
like the book reviewed in the next *Quarterly*. If you are
willing, I will give the sheets to Lockhart."

Probably the mere mention of Lockhart and the *Quarterly*
was enough to drive the lion of Oulton—now shut securely
in the summer-house by his loving wife—into a frenzy. Anyway, Mrs. Borrow sent an abrupt answer which showed how
little either she or her dear George knew of publishing,
authorship, or the ever fickle public:

"In compliance with your request, I write a line *by
return of post* to say, that my husband does not wish his
book reviewed in the next *Quarterly*. He is, I assure you,
doing all he can, as regards the completion of his book."

The despairing Mr. Murray took a last gamble and put a
large advertisement in the *Quarterly Review* (after all he
owned the paper). It read:

JANUARY 1850—MR. MURRAY'S LIST OF BOOKS—
NEARLY READY FOR PUBLICATION—

LAVENGRO, AN AUTOBIOGRAPHY

By GEORGE BORROW, Esq.

3 vols. Post 8vo.

If this was intended as an appeal to Borrow it fell on stony
ground. Mr. Woodfall hastened down to Suffolk in December,
was greeted hospitably—for Borrow could always play the
grand seigneur to a guest—and returned to London in high
feather. Yet on 4 March, 1850, he had a lugubrious epistle from
Mrs. Borrow: "I begged my husband to allow me to write and
tell you that he has of late been complaining. At one time he
probably overworked himself, having written one hundred and
thirty pages since you were here." She added briskly that
perhaps "one of your kind encouraging notes shortly, will do
Mr. Borrow good", which was small comfort to a man who

had types locked up to the detriment of his business; but Woodfall really saw red when he received a letter from Mrs. Borrow in the middle of April which informed him that they had been to Yarmouth for a change of air and that her dear George had had "many plunges into the briny Ocean, which seemed to do him good".

Any man who could enjoy bathing in the North Sea in the month of April was clearly entitled to no consideration whatsoever; yet Mrs. Borrow's siren song was so compelling that at the end of August the thoroughly bewildered Woodfall wooed Borrow with soft words:

"I do not, God knows! wish you to over-task yourself; but after what you last said, I thought I might fully calculate on your taking up, without further delay, the fragmentary portions of your 1st and 2nd volumes and let us get them out of hand . . ."

As usual Mrs. Borrow sprang to her husband's defence, but for the first time a note of supplication crept into her letter:

"I beg to assure you that my husband has been doing something since you were here; indeed, all he is able to do. It strikes me that if he is taken off the proof sheets, it will stop the rest from going on. You can scarcely judge of him from seeing him, as you did, for two or three days, with spirits cheered by the company and conversation of a friend. I feel quite sure he will do all he can; but when once he feels himself hurried, it puts a stop to his getting on. I hope in time your patience may be rewarded."

Nobody except the Borrows could have accused a publisher who had waited six years for a manuscript of "hurrying" an author!

At last, on a murky November day, Mrs. Borrow arrived at Albemarle Street with a bulky parcel containing the remainder of the second and third volumes; but even after these had been sent down to an ecstatic Woodfall there were arguments, displays of temperament, last-minute alterations. Mr. Murray decided to have an engraving of Phillips's portrait for a frontispiece, and this affronted Borrow so much that Murray had to resort to strategy and tell Mrs. Borrow that he wished *her* assent. "I do not ask Mr. Borrow's leave, remember . . . I beg and entreat that the proofs may be quickly returned. My sale is fixed for December 12th, and if I cannot show the book then—I must throw up." Mrs. Borrow answered majestically that *she* liked the engraving and had reminded her husband that *"his* leave was not asked"; but there were further muddles over the title-page as Borrow announced he no longer wished the words "Autobiography" or "Life" to be used and wanted the book to be called *LAVENGRO: The Scholar—The Gypsy—The Priest.* Then there was the question of the preface which Borrow insisted upon providing, and this caused another delay as Mrs. Borrow calmly wrote: "My husband had no idea that Mr. W. was stopped in the printing for want of them (corrected proof sheets and the preface). We were unavoidably idle at Christmas for a few days." When the preface did reach Mr. Murray he was seriously perturbed by its attack on "what is called Papal aggression" and advised that the reiterated expression "Damnation cry" should be omitted, which led to renewed argument; but on 7 February, 1851, 3,000 copies of *Lavengro* appeared, with the announcement that Mr. Murray would shortly publish "in one vol. Price 10s., *THE ROMANY RYE*, being the fourth volume of *LAVENGRO*".

The finished preface to *Lavengro* opened with the words: "In the following pages I have endeavoured to describe a dream, partly of study, partly of adventure, in which will be found copious notices of books, and many descriptions of life and manners, some in a very unusual form." The third volume ended abruptly with the postilion's story as supposedly told to Borrow in the year 1825. These significant passages give the clue to the long delay in completing that book which was to have been an autobiography and to the reason behind the many changes which had been made to Borrow's original conception of the work. There is no doubt that he intended the book to be his life history—that is proved by his letters to Mr. Murray and to Ford, as well as by many recorded conversations with friends; there is ample proof that he stuck

to his intention until the year 1847—and then what happened?
Dr. Bowring found him out and the whole glorious idea of
recording the magnificent adventures of Mr. George Borrow
in foreign parts was blown sky-high. True, he had had many
real adventures both in Spain and in Russia; but the Spanish
ones had been fully described in the *Bible in Spain*, and as for
the Russian ones—well, how could he give those to the world
without bridging that most uncomfortable chasm between the
years 1816 and 1833, and how could he bridge it without
calling the attention of his ever-watchful enemy to certain
gross inaccuracies of which he was certain to make the most
evil use?[1]

The only thing to do was to cover himself by opening with
the allusion to a dream and finishing the book in the year
1825, well before his first meeting with Bowring; but this meant
rewriting the bulk of the second and third volumes, and while
he rewrote Borrow's hatred of Bowring flamed afresh until,
as with a forest fire, the sparks flew far and wide to alight on
various objects loathed in a lesser way—Lord-Lieutenants, publishers, editors, reviewers, the power of the Holy Roman Church.

The principal victim of Borrow's pyromania was, of course,
John Bowring. He was the "old Radical", the man in whose
service the postilion had learned such shocking details of the
private lives of the great. Murtagh was employed as the agent
for descriptions of travels in 1826–1827 which had been attributed to the author in the original version. The Hungarian
was introduced in order to show that the author really had
been in Debreczen and Koloszvar.[2] But such was Borrow's
obsession about Dr. Bowring's machinations that the public
were lost in a fog through which they groped in such ill-temper
that they decided unaminously they were sadly disappointed
in this sequel to the *Bible in Spain*.

The reviewers were equally whole-hearted in their condemnation. Their criticisms streamed forth—the *Athenæum*:

"Few books have excited warmer expectations than this
long-talked-of autobiography; and great is the disappoint-

[1] Borrow's early dealings with Dr. Bowring were in the years 1829–1839
followed by letters over 1830–1833.
[2] Borrow's journeys of 1844.

ment which it will leave in the minds of those who expected anything beyond a collection of bold picaresque sketches. It is not an autobiography, even with the licence of fiction. . . . It can scarcely be called a book at all . . . Mr. Borrow is never thoroughly at his ease except when among gypsies."

Fraser's Magazine:

"He knows all languages; he dives into all secrets. . . . Let the public sit and wink in humble submission, while the great Wizard of the East fires off in its face his never-failing artillery of dashes, dots and asterisks . . . A few more observations and we wash our hands of the Tinkers. The story of *Lavengro* will content no one. It is for ever hovering between Romance and Reality, and the whole tone of the narrative inspires a profound distrust. Nay, more, it will make us disbelieve the tales in the *Zincali* and the *Bible in Spain*."[1]

Blackwood's:

"We have read the book, and we are disappointed . . . We are sick of the Petulengros and their jargon, and Mr. Borrow ought now to be aware that he has thoroughly exhausted that quarry . . . We strongly suspect that, in the course of the composition of this book, which, unless our memory strangely deceives us, was announced more than two years ago, considerable changes have taken place in its plan and disposition . . ."

There were many other reviews, all in the same strain, but the *Quarterly* and the *Edinburgh* maintained an ominous silence which Borrow, of course, attributed to Lockhart and Bowring respectively. It was left to two of his friends, Dr. Thomas Gordon Hake and Mr. William Bodham Dunne, to attempt to stem the flood of abuse. W. Harrison Ainsworth, who had already published an uncomplimentary notice of *Lavengro* in the March issue of his *New Monthly* magazine, kindly allowed

[1] The writer was Sir William Stirling Maxwell, to whom Borrow alluded scornfully as "a rich Scotch dandy—a writer of bulky volumes on Spanish pictures".

Dr. Hake space in which to state his view, which was that "*Lavengro's* roots will strike deep into the soil of English letters", a remarkably true prophecy marred by an interminable discourse on Borrow's gifts that ranged from William Taylor's letter to Southey to extracts from the *Targum*. Mr. Donne, in the columns of *Tait's Edinburgh Magazine*, wisely pointed out that the repeated announcements of the book's imminent publication had made the public "half inclined to quarrel with the publisher or the author for its tardiness in forthcoming", and went on to give a fair if uninspired criticism which contained, however, the truest thing ever said by a critic of the day about *Lavengro*. "The public looked for a second Marco Polo and were presented instead with a nineteenth-century Defoe."

That, indeed, was the crux of the matter. Readers of the *Bible in Spain* had looked forward eagerly to another book of adventurous travel and were sadly disappointed with this long, *farouche* story about a nasty little boy who developed an inferiority complex[1] and grew up into a ne'er-do-well owing to his deplorable fondness for "the fancy", gypsies, common folk, and *ale*. It was, indeed, the stress laid upon the drinking propensities of *Lavengro* that was the principal cause of public hostility to the book.

> "Oh, genial and gladdening is the power of good ale, the true and proper drink of Englishmen. He is not deserving of the name of Englishman who speaketh against ale, that is good ale, like that which has just made merry the hearts of this poor family; and yet there are beings, who call themselves Englishmen, who say that it is a sin to drink a cup of ale . . ."

Such passages, and there were all too many of them, literally stank in Victorian nostrils. An Englishman's roistering in foreign (and inferior) countries could be vastly amusing: the same Englishman's visits to his own village public-house were positively nauseating.

---

[1] The writer knows perfectly well that "inferiority complexes" were unheard of in 1851; but she submits that the expression conveys the reaction of the day to the child *Lavengro*.

Many an author has laboured in obscurity his life long and been acclaimed by future generations: few have won in their lifetime such stupendous fame as did George Borrow with his *Bible in Spain* only to descend to being a target for abuse with their next book, as he did with *Lavengro*. The truth was, as the late Mr. Herbert Jenkins said in his *The Life of George Borrow*,[1] that:

"Borrow was estranged from his generation. The years that intervened between the success of the *Bible in Spain* and the publication of *Lavengro* had been spent by him in war; he had come to hate his contemporaries with a wholesome, vigorous hatred. He would give them his book; but they should have it as a stray cur has a bone—thrown at them. Above all, they should not for a moment be allowed to think that it contained an intimate account of the life of the supreme hater who had written it. When there had been sympathy between them, Borrow was prepared to allow his public to peer into the sacred recesses of his early life. Now that there was none, he denied that *Lavengro* was more than 'a dream', forgetting that he had so often written of it as an autobiography, had even seen it advertised as such, and insisted that it was fiction."

It was but natural that Borrow should throw the entire blame for *Lavengro's* failure upon the critics and the public. He was, at the age of forty-eight, a thoroughly unhappy man and one so unbalanced by his unhappiness that he simply could not realize his own limitations. If he, the great Don Jorge, chose to inveigh against the Church of Rome, the builders of railways, the "gentility" of his foolish compatriots, the appalling behaviour of his enemies, then what right had lesser men to say him nay? To his tortured mind there was only one possible answer to calumny, and that was to seek revenge against his detractors in the pages of *The Romany Rye*.

[1] Published by John Murray, 1912.

VI

At some period in the late eighteen-forties the Borrows had moved from Oulton Cottage to Oulton Hall, the original home of Mrs. Borrow, and in the midst of his struggles with *Lavengro* Borrow had dissipated a deal of nervous energy he could not spare upon his mother's affairs. There had been some trouble over structural defects in the King's Court house and he was so certain that the roof would suddenly collapse on the old lady that he began a frantic campaign to bring her to Oulton, building rooms for her on to the Hall, engaging the daughter of a neighbouring farmer to be her attendant, and working his mother into such a state of agitation that she wrote to her daughter-in-law just before her move in September 1849:

"My Dear Mary,—I am sorry to hear you have got a bad cold. What shall I do if you are laid up, for I am as helpless as a child . . . ? I hope you will be able to come here on Monday the 24th, at latest, and then the things may be sent soon after. Glad I shall be when the bustle is over. I wish my dear George would not have such fancies about the old house; it is a mercy it has not fallen on my head before this. And now that my poor woman cannot come to do anything for me, it is not safe to be shut up here alone; do you tell him so. There is a low noisy set close by me. I shall not die one day sooner, nor live one day longer. If I stop here and die on a sudden, half the things might be lost or stolen; therefore it seems as if the Lord would provide me with a safer home. I have made up my mind to the change and only pray I may be able to get through the trouble. The poor Bishop is gone, and not so old as I am by seven years[1] . . . Do come so soon as you can, as I wish to clear the house before the 29th; then the old man (King, the landlord) cannot say I prevented him letting it. Lucy[2] is home and desire her love to all. Give my best love to my dear child—Oh, if he was more composed! I take no rest in the night and God only knows with myself . . ." (The remainder of the letter is torn.)

[1] Bishop Stanley, who died in his seventieth year.
[2] Cecilia Lucy Brightwell, author of *The Life of Mrs. Opie*, 1854.

Oulton Lowestoft
Nov 11th 1852

Dear Murray

I was very glad to receive your
letter, and to hear that you and
yours were well. I think you were
quite right to get out to Wimbledon,
which is one of the most healthy
localities in the neighbourhood of
London. In answer to your enquiries
about the fourth volume of Lavengro
I beg leave to say that I am
occasionally occupied upon it;

Fascimile of letter from George Borrow at Oulton to John Murray II,
Nov. 11, 1852

I shall probably add some notes.
What a state must English criticism
be reduced to when such paltry
cavillings are employed as those
you mention. Perhaps however
the general tone of English literature
is in fault. It appears to me
that people have been so long
accustomed to the veriest common
place that originality of character
and independence of thought are
not in the slightest degree appreciated.
It is probable that I shall be in
London in the Spring. I have had

two letters from Phillips. poor fellow,
I am afraid that his constitution
has received a very severe shock. I
hope he has good medical advice.
With kind remembrances to Mrs Murray
in which my wife joins

I remain,
Dear Murray,
Ever sincerely yours
George Borrow

John Murray Esqr

Facsimile of letter from George Borrow at Oulton to John Murray II,
Nov. 11, 1852

It seems doubtful whether the poor lady found any peace beside her temperamental George. For the first eighteen months of her stay at Oulton he was in the throes of bringing forth *Lavengro*, and for the next two years he was engaged in vilifying his critics and in conducting an acrimonious correspondence—through the medium of Mrs. Borrow for the most part—with Mr. Murray about *The Romany Rye*. Even the faithful Ford had written to Borrow after the publication of *Lavengro*, "I frankly own that I was somewhat disappointed with the very *little* you told us about *yourself*"; and a host of other readers had said much the same, but in stronger terms, to Mr. Murray. "People say of a chapter or of a character: 'This is very wonderful, *if true*; but if fiction, it is pointless'.— Will your new volumes explain this and dissolve the mystery? I hope you have employed the summer in giving them the finishing touches." Needless to say his question brought a volley of abuse from the author. Borrow was already deep in the embroidering of *The Romany Rye*—each stitch was stabbed in with venom—but he would give the world his masterpiece when he thought fit and he would brook no interference from anybody. He was also—as ever—engaged in various pettifogging feuds with his neighbours, the black smoke and piercing whistles of Mr. Peto's railway engines were driving him demented, he was beset by every ailment known to man and some of his own invention into the bargain.

About the year 1847 the Borrows had become very friendly with Dr. Thomas Gordon Hake and his wife, of Bury St. Edmunds, where they also knew two rich and charming sisters, Elizabeth and Susan Harvey, with whom Henrietta Clarke often stayed for months at a time—one imagines the poor girl must have welcomed these respites from her stepfather's whims and fancies. Mrs. Borrow, worn out by her self-appointed role as guide, mentor, amanuensis, and nurse to her dear George, found a sympathetic medical adviser in Dr. Hake, and just before that gentleman went to America with his family in the early summer of 1853 he ordered that she should be "absent from Oulton for the ensuing winter and spring, and thus renew the lease of life". Now the tables were turned with a vengeance!

Instead of Mrs. Borrow dancing attendance upon her hypo-chrondriacal husband, he fussed around her in a terrific state of agitation lest his "dearest Carreta" fall into the "decline" which he firmly believed he himself had fallen into several years earlier. Why wait until the autumn? he demanded. Heaven knew what disaster might come upon them before October. No, no, they must leave Oulton forthwith and move to Great Yarmouth, where the sea-breezes would bring back the colour to Carreta's cheeks and where he would no longer be offended by the sight, smell and sound of Mr. Peto's railway.

Whether Hayim Ben Attar and Sidi Habismilk had been called to their fathers or disposed of in some other way is not told, but there is no mention of either in the grand removal which took place in August. With old Mrs. Borrow, tin trunks crammed with papers, boxes galore, dogs and cats, the family descended upon 169 King Street, Great Yarmouth, where they were to remain for two years before moving on to two further sets of lodgings in the same town. All told, they stayed for almost seven years in Yarmouth, and highly uncomfortable ones they must have been, for while Borrow had proved himself the perfect traveller in Russia and the Peninsula he was not the man to tolerate life at close quarters with his nearest and dearest in an English seaside resort.

It is to Dr. Hake that we are indebted for the most vivid portrait of Borrow at the age of fifty:

"George Borrow was one of those whose mental powers are strong and whose bodily frame is yet stronger. His temper was good and bad; his pride was humility; his humility was pride; his vanity, in being negative, was of the most positive kind. He was reticent and candid, measured in speech, with an emphasis that made trifles significant.

"Borrow was essentially hypochrondriacal. Society he loved and hated alike: He loved it that he might be pointed out and talked of; he hated it because he was not the prince that he felt himself in its midst. His figure was tall and his bearing very noble. He had a finely moulded head, and thick white hair—white from his youth; his brown eyes were soft, yet piercing; his nose somewhat of the Semitic type, which gave his face the cast of the young Memnon. His mouth had a generous curve; and his features, for beauty and true power, were such as can have no parallel in our portrait gallery . . ."[1]

Dr. Hake's delineation of Borrow's character has been called to account for its "laboured paradoxes"—but why? Borrow was one long collection of paradoxes, and if one of them were missed out then any picture of the man entirely lacked reality. One can just imagine him, still wrapped up like the advertisement for Sandeman's Port, striding through Yarmouth and alternately delighting and outraging its inhabitants, fishermen, and holiday-makers.

The "plunges into the briny" which had so annoyed Mr. Woodfall were renewed during that summer of 1853. Borrow had always been a fine swimmer and considered it a "noble exercise, but it certainly does not tend to mortify either the flesh or the spirit". Once, while river-bathing with Mr. Cooke, Mr. Murray's partner, he dived in and stayed under water so long that his companion was seriously alarmed, fearing he had struck his head on a stone or got entangled in the weeds. Suddenly Borrow's head popped up under the far bank a good distance down stream. "What do you think of that?" he cried. "There, if that had been written in one of my books, they would have said it was a lie, wouldn't they?"[2][3]

On 8 September, as we already know, Borrow dashed into a stormy sea and rescued a man from drowning, with the result that his Cornish cousins wrote inviting him to visit them. Bravery apart, the incident proved that for a man of his age George Borrow was remarkably fit physically—an interesting confirmation of his hypochrondiacal state.

According to Dr. Knapp, Borrow spent his autumn "inaugurating a series of Anglo-Celtic philologico-peripatetic excursions, over Cornwall, Wales, the Isle of Man, East Anglia,

---

[1] *Memoirs of Eighty Years*, Dr. T. G. Hake, 1892.
[2] *Good Words: Mr. John Murray.*
[3] In the *Eastern Daily Press*, October, 1892.

Scotland and Ireland",[1] but perhaps this grand description is scarcely justified. Borrow was still extremely sore with the world over *Lavengro*. He shunned society, was out of love with the friends brought him by the *Bible in Spain*, thought himself a grossly ill-treated man. When he received an admiring, warm-hearted letter from his Cornish kinsfolk his quicksilver nature responded immediately. As he had said in *Lavengro*, "to the generality of mankind there is no period like youth", and here were good folk who surely could help him to recapture the *feeling* of youth. Maybe his Christmas stay in Cornwall whetted his appetite for "philologico-peripatetic excursions"; but Borrow never ordered his life far ahead and it is far more likely that his Cornish trip simply gave back to him the vagabond instinct which had been stifled all too long.

Mrs. Borrow had by this time had fourteen years of coping with her dear George—indeed, it was almost fourteen and a half years since she had arrived in "the Little Square of the Empty Trough" at Seville. Heaven knew she had done her best for George, but he really was an unconscionable sort of man. Although he had been so worried about her, so anxious they should move without delay to Yarmouth so that she might benefit from the sea-air, he had suffered one of his queer changes since diving off the jetty in order to save one of those stupid men who had upset their boat—with all his clothes on too, and a good suit ruined! He barged through the tiny sitting-room for all the world like a bull in a china-shop and he never even noticed how ill she looked, lying languidly on her sofa. Mama had certainly chosen the better part when she had packed her traps after a month or two of Yarmouth and returned to her wing at Oulton and the ministrations of her little maid; but she had no such solace. Dear Dr. Hake had said most emphatically that Yarmouth air would arrest her "decline"; therefore at Yarmouth she must remain. Meantime, if dear George wanted to visit these Cornish relatives —and nasty common people they sounded to be sure, just what you might expect from connections of Captain Thomas Borrow, who by all accounts had started life as a private in

[1] *Life, Writings, and Correspondence of George Borrow*, W. I. Knapp, Ph.D., LL.D., Murray, 1899, Vol. 2.

the Army—then he could go, and the sooner the better. Perhaps—here Mrs. Borrow dried her tears, sent Henrietta to enquire about train and coach fares, and fished her petty-cash book from under her pillow—he would return in a more tractable frame of mind. . . . Now, if she got his return tickets in advance and allowed him a five-pound note for expenses . . .?

So George Borrow went to Cornwall—and it is pretty sure that he took little with him save that five-pound note. The wonderful meeting with Henry Borrow of Looe Down, Robert Taylor and his wife Anne Borrow of Penquite, William and Elizabeth Borrow of Trethinnick, Thomas Borrow of Lamellion, Nicholas Borrow of Tremellick, James Jago and Bernard Anstis of Liskeard, obliterated memory of Carreta, Mr. Peto's railway, the little, overcrowded rooms in King Street, Yarmouth. With his umbrella as a staff—that "damning thing . . . gigantic and green"—he tramped happily through the Duchy quizzing his relations, delving into folklore, shouting Celtic songs, enjoying to the full the "return of the native".

Dr. Knapp assures us that Borrow left two volumes of notes on his Cornish travels, written in pencil, which required "several weeks with a powerful glass and a good supply of topographical treatises" before that indefatigable biographer managed to decipher them; but what one wishes to know about that happy six weeks' stay is found in a few hasty notes and letters he wrote and in the observations of his kinsfolk and the Rev. J. R. P. Berkeley, the merry but shrewd Irish vicar of St. Cleer; and the important fact is that for a handful of days Borrow was once more the eager vagabond of 1825.

He entered Penquite, that "house of stone and slate on the side of a hill", on Christmas Eve, and the welcome he received from Anne Taylor and her daughter—also Anne—strengthened the knowledge that he had indeed come home. With the younger Anne, "as gallant a girl as ever rode", he cantered round the countryside on horseback, eyes ever alert for the landmarks his father knew as a boy. With his cousin Elizabeth he sat of an evening before the great log-fire in Trethinnick kitchen listening enraptured to her story of a Cornish pisky:

"Some one had a child, I cannot say who it was. They could not give it enough to eat, do what they would. They made their complaint about the matter to a wise neighbour, and she thought it was a pisky. She recommended that they should put a large quantity of old shoes upon a spit and make the child turn the spit, threatening to beat it unless it did. The child lamented for some time at the hard task which was imposed upon it, but when it found that it was obliged, it began to turn the spit. After it had turned for some time, it said:

> "I am four score years and more,
> But never saw such a roast as this before."

"So then they knew that it was a pisky. Shortly after the pisky-child disappeared and her own child was restored to its mother."[1]

While Borrow was scribbling down this and similar stories, his cousin Anne Taylor was writing to a friend:

"I must tell you a bit about our distinguished visitor. (He is) a fine tall man of about six feet three, well-proportioned and not stout; able to walk five miles an hour successively; rather florid face without any hirsute appendages; hair white and soft; eyes and eyebrows dark; good nose and very nice mouth; well-shaped hands—altogether a person you would notice in a crowd. His character is not so easy to portray. The more I see of him the less I know of him. He is very enthusiastic and eccentric, very proud and unyielding. He says very little of himself . . . He is a marvel in himself. There is no one here to draw him out. He has an astonishing memory as to dates when great events have taken place, no matter in what part of the world. He seems to know everything." (The writer added wistfully) "He has lived years in Russia and Moldavia and Wallachia, and has been in Turkey, Greece and Egypt, all over Germany and Italy, and I cannot tell where. To Spain, of course, he took his wife . . ."

[1] Borrow's note reads: "Written from the dictation of my cousin Elizabeth at Tredinnock (sic), the 5th of January, 1854."

Dear Carreta might languish forgotten in the Yarmouth lodgings: her stamp, together with that which was the prerogative of a famous author, remained indelibly printed on Borrow's mind. Even in the midst of Cornish delight their effect would suddenly colour his behaviour. When dining with the ex-Mayor of Liskeard he deliberately wiped his hands with the greasy rag used for cleaning his gun instead of with the napkin provided; when he met a couple called Hambly he drew back ostentatiously and said in a loud aside to Mr. Berkeley, "Never was one of the name good '; when a card-party given by some local big-wig proved boring he wandered off to a low public-house in Liskeard and regaled an audience of toughs with a record of his adventures; when the conversation at a party given in his honour wearied him he vanished from the table and walked upstairs to the nursery, giving as an excuse the explanation that the children were far more intelligent than their elders and betters; when local folk pleaded for his autograph he waved them aside and walked rapidly away.

But from under the snobbery, the rudeness, the grand references to Moldavia, Wallachia and Egypt, the old Don Jorge flashed out. He thought nothing of striding up to his waist in water through an icy moorland pool to retrieve a bird he had just shot. When the family gathered round the fireside of an evening he sang Celtic Ballads of his own translation, beating time with a carving-knife the while. If Mrs. Berkeley played Irish or Scots folksongs on the piano he danced madly round the room, clapping his hands and chanting the words, pausing only to tell her that her music reminded him of David's harp. The Berkeley's small son, aged ten, entranced him by staring at him round-eyed for several minutes and then crying, "Well, mother, that *is* a man!" He was particularly delighted by the way everybody drew attention to his beautiful, slim-fingered hands—he always insisted these were a legacy from his mother's Huguenot ancestors. On visiting Trethinnick for a gathering of the clans "his feelings were much excited", according to Mr. Berkeley. "He was thinking of the time when his father's footsteps and his father's voice re-echoed in the room in which we were sitting. His eyes wandered from point to point, and at times, if I was not mistaken a tear could be seen trembling in them. At length he could no longer control his feelings. He left the hall suddenly, and in a few minutes, but for God's providential care, the career of George Borrow would have been ended. There was within a few feet of the house a low wall with a drop of some feet into a paved yard. He walked rapidly out, and, it being nearly dark, he stepped one side of the gate, and fell over the wall."

This accident resulted in severe bruises, but the Cornish Borrows were greatly impressed by their kinsman's fortitude, for he never mentioned his injuries and thanked them warmly for allowing him to share the "old-fashioned hospitality of old-fashioned people in an old-fashioned house". They were also pleased with his advice to their children, "Learn to box, and keep a civil tongue in your head," and his caustic answer to a young man who said he had left the Army as it "was no place for a gentleman". "You mean," retorted Borrow sharply, "that it is no place for a man who is *not* a gentleman, therefore you did well to leave it."

But much as Borrow enjoyed the society of his kith and kin the desire to tramp across the Duchy lured him on. He wanted to see those places with names that caressed the tongue like wine—Truro, Penzance, Mousehole, Pentire, Tintagel—and Land's End—ah, he who had been to Finisterre *must* see Land's End! Before he left Penquite on a walking-tour he wrote to his wife: "My relations are most excellent people, but I could not understand more than half they said." He added, with a regrettable touch of Victorian snobbism, that it was beyond his comprehension that Cousin William Borrow of Trethinnick, who was accredited with a fortune of some £70,000, should live in a house "which had not a single open grate—nothing but open chimneys".

On 9 January, 1854, Borrow set out by way of Lostwithiel and St. Austell for Truro, his mind busy with odd bits of knowledge collected from his relatives—how the piskies planned to drain the bottomless pool of Drosmary "with a limpet-shell with a hole in it"; how you must draw a cross with your foot in the dust if you saw magpies, those birds of ill-omen—

> "One for sorrow; two for mirth;
> Three for a wedding; four for death."

How foxes possessed a "wonderful connubial affection"; how the piskies mounted horses' necks at night, using the manes as stirrups, and galloped across the fields, wreaking vengeance on the crops of their enemies and breathing good spells above the grain of their friends.

The weather was abominable but Borrow was completely happy, yarning to the country folk he met on the road, poking his nose into Celtic barrows, waxing wrathful over a cross which "seemed to have been raised by some Puseyite. The base contained a nonsensical inscription to the effect that it had been erected on a place which had been devoted to 'Druidic Idolatry'. "The Druids were no idolators, though the Papists are".

His rough diary is illuminating.

"Saw a nice little Inn called the Dolphin (near Grampound). Looked wistfully at it. Truro was distant yet eight miles. Withstood temptation; strode manfully forward, singing *Look out, look out, Svend Vonved!*' Rain came on heavily; put up my umbrella. In about an hour reached a place called Probus on the slope of a hill; in another hour a place called Tresilian. Passed a bridge under which a rivulet was rushing furiously. Drank out of a quadrangular stone basin into which two or three gushes of water fell. Strode forward. River looking wildly beautiful in the moonshine on my left. High bluffs on the farther side. Valley on the right in which water was sounding. Thought I heard bells from a great distance. Imagined them to be those of Truro. Felt cheered. Rain which had ceased again came on. Strode forward. . . ."

From Truro he walked to Redruth and climbed Carn Brae, where the cairn itself reminded him of "huge rhinoceroses piled upon one another".

"On the top of the Carn there are two little basins about seven feet from each other; three mysterious little holes about the diameter of a penny seem to have connected them. . . . In the principal basin—the horrid place of sacrifice—there are outlets for the blood to stream down."

Above Rosewarne he spied a caravan and some tents, and in spite of torrential rain Borrow could not resist paying the gypsies a visit.

"Dark woman addressed me. Asked her her name in Rommany. She pretended at first not to understand; then answered me. Presently her husband, a remarkably knavish-looking personage, put out his head and began to discourse with me. Told me their names were Bosvile. Heard the sound of fiddles in the tents in a field over a low stone wall. The woman asked me into the caravan. Told them I was *mokado*,[1] gave them a fourpenny piece and departed."

Mousehole brought a delicious meeting with the Coastguard, Mr. Burney—whose "amiable wife" was a distant cousin of Borrow's. After a gigantic dinner of spare rib of beef Burney and his guest repaired to the Inn, where they drank quantities of ale and Borrow listened enthralled to the ex-sailor's gruesome stories of the slave trade on the West African coast. He also saw "a large cannon-ball said to have been shot by the Spaniards in old times (1595) against the church of St. Paul—where he 'sat in a pew under a black suit of armour belonging to the Godolphin family, with two swords' "; was delighted with the resemblance of Mr. Burney's home to a "Spanish Galician house"; and held a fascinating conversation with an eighty-year-old fisherman who, as a lad, had known the famous Dolly Pentreath of Mousehole, the last person to speak the Cornish language, and had so bewitched a man called Cancrin that he frequently refused to go out fishing, saying that "it was no use, as he had heard old Doll Pentreath swear like a devil . . ."

Mr. Burney and Mr. Cleland—from whom Borrow learnt much regarding the Cornish mines—rowed him across to St. Michael's Mount,

"a castellated high house seated upon a lofty hill rising from the sea on the North East side of Penzance Bay,

[1] Literally "wet through", therefore "dirty". From the Spanish *"mojado"*.

accessible also by a narrow causeway overflowed at flood-tide, opposite to Marazion or Market Jew. Ascended by a flight of steps to a small town or village; then mounted a hill by a rugged path, till we came to a sort of bastion partially demolished. Oliver's men, in the time of the Civil Wars, are said to have entered by this bastion. Ascended the hill to the principal entrance. Arms of the St. Aubyn family over it. . . . Candles brought to show the vault. There is in this Castle a stone vault below the Chapel about six and a half feet high in which a skeleton was found . . . The Guard room contains ancient armour. I put on a skull-cap weighing at least fourteen pounds. Shown over castle by an exceedingly civil young woman. Descended to Marazion or Market Jew. Tolerably large place. Curious little church with singular market house. Returned on foot to Mousehole."

By 18 January Borrow was striding towards the Logan Rock with a Cornish guide by the name of Cronan:

"The daughter of the king of Norroway—Finding of Finn in Veintry Bay—His being fostered by a giant—His entering into service with Dermod David Odeen—His cooking the salmon—The blister on the skin—His sucking his thumb and so becoming acquainted with all witchcraft—His killing Odeen by shaking hands with him and pulling off his arm."

These disjointed entries in Borrow's diary have a peculiar interest. For one thing they provide an excellent example of the day-to-day happenings from which he built up his books; for another they show how little he thought of lifting some episode which appealed to him out of the place of its origin and depositing it carelessly in another county, another country, even another continent. A clear case of this habit is found in the telegraphic notes upon Finn, which became translated, through some mysterious process known only to Borrow himself, into the adventurous tale of the Irish Finn-ma-Coul as told by Murtagh in *The Romany Rye*.

By 29 January he was back at Penquite, where he drank in Nicholas Borrow's tales of the "tremendous big fellows up in

St. Minver; it is the beer that makes them so big", and saw William Borrow's eighty blood-red Devonshire bullocks with "long noble white horns". He asked Henry Borrow of Looe Down if he believed in piskies—but Robert Taylor of Penquite hastily protested that such belief was ridiculous, an opinion scorned by George, who automatically touched any tree he happened to pass and, curiously, questioned that sturdy farmer Henry, who confessed he "scarcely knew what to say about the pisgies (piskies); he had never seen them, but he supposed there might be such things, as he had himself heard the 'durdy dogs'. When a boy he was sent to Liskeard for salt and other articles; as he was riding back to Trethinnick at night, passing by Treworgy he heard over his head in the air the most beautiful cry of hounds that he had ever heard in his life. It was the cry of the 'durdy dogs'".

Borrow, having given his verdict upon Harriet Beecher Stowe's *Uncle Tom's Cabin*—which everybody was reading with avidity—as "A lot of Uncle Toms and Tom fools", swept off on a tour of North Cornwall, during which he visited Pentire Point and Tintagel, and was convinced that the name "Jennifer" in some Parish Registry was really the signature of Queen Guinevere. But in February as he rumbled London-wards by rail—he always hated railway travel, saying it reminded him of Mr. Peto—his mind was full of Druids and piskies, those dear but dire little folk who, as Betty Wedmouth, had told him all in the same breath with the information that she was a spinster because her mistress "never allowed her any time for courtin'", were queer creatures:

"She said that at St. Ive there was a house in the hollow of a hill, and that near it was a large hollow tree and the *pisgies* were in the habit of dancing around it. One night the women of the house, getting out of bed and looking out of the window, heard the pigsies dancing violently with much laughter, and the next morning there was a circle of peculiar colour on the grass around the tree."[1]

Cornwall had rejuvenated George Borrow; the pity of it was that rejuvenation did not last.

[1] Lavengro.

CHAPTER SEVEN

"FEAR GOD AND TAKE YOUR OWN PART"
(Isopel Berners, *The Romany Rye*).

(1854–1869)

I

REFRESHED in mind and body George Borrow stayed in London for several days in order to do some research at the British Museum. He lodged with a Mrs. Webster at 53A Pall Mall from 10 February to 25th, visited Mr. Murray and Mr. Cooke, and collected a lot of data for the Appendix to *The Romany Rye*; but his peace was marred by several letters from his wife, who felt he had been away from home too long. Judging from his answers Mrs. Borrow had remonstrated with him severely for spending too much money, for on three occasions he wrote rather peevishly on financial matters:

Feb. 13th. "I am at present at Mrs. Webster's, but not in the three guinea lodgings. I am in rooms above, for which I pay thirty shillings a week. I live as economically as I can; but when I am in London I am obliged to be at a certain expense. I must be civil to certain friends who invite me out and show me every kindness. Please to send me a five pound note by return of post."

Feb. 17th. "I write again today on account of the letter which I received from you this morning. It was hardly worth while making me more melancholy than I am. 'Come home, come home!' is the cry. And what are my prospects when I get home? though it is true they are not much brighter here. I have nothing to look forward to. Honourable employments are being given to this and that trumpery fellow; while I, who am an honourable man, must be excluded from everything. With respect to literature, I am tired of it and believe there is little to be got by it, unless by writing

humbug, which I can't and will not do. My spirits are very
low and your letters make them worse. I shall probably
return by the end of next week; but I shall want some more
money. I am sorry to spend money, for it is our only friend,
and God knows I use as little as possible, but I can't travel
without it."

Feb. 21st. "I propose coming home on Saturday. You had
better inform me at what hour the train will start that I
ought to come by. The dinner went off beautifully, but it
was expensive; however, the people I invited were, I believe,
my friends. The money arrived safely, but whether it will
be sufficient is a question. Perhaps you had better send
another note, and I will bring it home unchanged, if I do
not want any part of it. I have lived very economically, as
far as I am concerned personally; I have bought nothing,
and have been working hard at the Museum. Our money is
our best friend."

So short a while had Cornish exhilaration lasted! From this
time on the picture grows more and more dismal, with Borrow
tramping downhill into the shadows which were so soon to
engulf him.

Certainly on his return to Yarmouth he worked hard on
The Romany Rye, but the book itself had ceased to interest
him and his main concern was that it should contain as many
vituperative answers to the critics of *Lavengro* and as many
scurrilous attacks upon those he imagined to be his enemies
as he could possibly pack into its pages. It was not surprising
therefore that *The Romany Rye* became less a continuation of
his autobiography than what Dr. Knapp rightly described as
a "sort of ante-room to Hades". He was, however, in no hurry
to send the completed manuscript to Mr. Murray, and it must
be confessed that, disappointed as he had been over the
Lavengro failure, Mr. Murray was in no hurry to receive it.

The one lasting good effect of the Cornish visit was that it
turned Borrow's thoughts to the planning of other tours in
different parts of the country, and when he rose from his
desk after a day spent in writing pages of abuse of Mr. Peto,
or Dr. Bowring, or the Lord-Lieutenant of Suffolk, he occupied

his evening in discussing with his wife and Henrietta where he should go that summer.

But Mrs. Borrow had had quite enough of her dear George's lonely wanderings. She did not like what she had heard about Cornwall or his curious kinsmen and thought the trip had improved neither his habits nor his manners. Besides, she and Henrietta had "a hankering after what is fashionable", so she said decidedly that they would *all* go to Harrogate or Leamington where there would be plenty of congenial company and she and dear George could take the waters. Borrow retorted that he hated fashionable life more than anything in the world and that he had quite made up his mind to go on a walking tour in Wales. Whether Mrs. Borrow was so shaken by this sudden self-assertion on her husband's part that she gave way out of sheer surprise, or whether she felt that dear George would get through too many five-pound notes if allowed to meander off alone again is not known; but on 27 July, 1854, the three left Yarmouth, spending one night at Peterborough and three at Chester before reaching Llangollen on 1 August.

II

One is glad to record that for Borrow at least the sixteen weeks he spent in Wales were entirely successful ones. "There never was such a place for poets," he wrote, "you meet a poet, or the birthplace of a poet, everywhere."[1] And the people!— why the poorest peasant knew all about those heroes of his own youth, Ab Gwilym and Gronwy Owen, and could repeat Huw Morris off by heart. Enthusiasm was "never scoffed at by the noble simple-minded genuine Welsh, whatever treatment it may receive from the coarse-hearted, sensual, selfish Anglo-Saxon".[2] "Oh, what a blessing it is," he cried, "to be able to speak Welsh!"[3] although he did admit that he read the language much better than he spoke it, and William Thomas the mason—he "who stood for a moment or two, as if transfixed, a trowel motionless in one of his hands, and a brick in the other" when Borrow asked him the way to somewhere

1, 2, 3 *Wild Wales.*

before answering in "tolerable Spanish"[1]—laughed until his sides were sore at the stranger's queer pronunciation.

Little Ellen Jones too, whom Borrow encountered at Llanfair when he was looking for Ty Gronwy, the birthplace of Gronwy Owen, said long afterwards that he "had bright eyes and shabby dress, more like a merchant than a gentleman, or like a man come to buy cattle. But dear me! he did speak *funny* Welsh. He could not pronounce the 'll', and his voice was very high; but perhaps that was because my grandmother was deaf."[2]

All her life Ellen treasured the pocket-book Borrow gave her when he discovered she was a descendant of the poet:

" 'Can you write?' said I to the eldest child, a little stubby girl of about eight, with a broad flat red face and grey eyes, dressed in a chintz gown, a little bonnet on her head, and looking the image of notableness.

"The little maiden, who had never taken her eyes off me for a moment during the whole time I had been in the room, at first made no answer; being, however, bid by her grandmother to speak, she at length answered in a soft voice, 'Medraf, I can.'

" 'Then write your name in this book,' said I, taking out a pocket-book and a pencil, 'and write likewise that you are related to Gronwy Owen—and be sure you write in Welsh.'

"The little maiden very demurely took the book and pencil, and placing the former on the table wrote as follows:

" 'Ellen Jones yn perthyn o bell i gronow owen.'[3]

"That is, 'Ellen Jones belonging from afar off to Gronwy Owen.' "[4]

Borrow was enraptured by everyone he met; but we cannot say the same of Mrs. Borrow, who found the Welsh people uncouth and spent her days in the rooms they had taken at Llangollen, where she wrote to her mother-in-law:

[1] *Wild Wales*.
[2] From Mr. George Porter of Denbigh.
[3] Ellen really wrote—"Ellen Jones yn pithyn pell . . ."
[4] *Wild Wales*.

T

"He (George) is very regular in his morning and evening devotions so that we all have abundant cause to be thankful." This sinister sentence gives the impression that there were times when dear George refused to attend family prayers, perhaps when his melancholy moods were upon him. But the remainder of Mrs. Borrow's letter strikes a more cheerful note: "As regards your dear son and his peace and comfort, you have reason to praise and bless God on his account . . . He is fully occupied. He keeps a *daily* Journal of all that goes on, so that he can make a most amusing book in a month,[1] whenever he wishes to do so."

On 27 August Borrow decided to walk from Llangollen to Bangor, leaving his women-folk to travel by train. It was on the road between Cerrig y Druidon and Cernioge Mawr that he met the Irish fiddler—

"a man with a game leg, that is, a leg which, either by nature or accident, not being so long as its brother leg, had a patten attached to it, about five inches high, to enable it to do duty with the other. He was a fellow with red shock hair and very red features, and was dressed in ragged coat and breeches, and a hat which had lost part of its crown and all of its rim; so that, even without a game leg, he would have looked rather a queer figure. . . ."[2]

Borrow asked him if he could play the Orangemen's song *Croppies Lie Down*, to which the man indignantly replied:

" 'I cannot, your hanner; my fingers never learnt to play such a blackguard tune; but if ye wish to hear *Croppies Get Up* I can oblige ye?'

" 'No,' said I, 'it's a tune that doesn't please my ears. If, however, you choose to play *Croppies Lie Down*, I'll give you a shilling."

" 'Your hanner will give me a shilling?'

" 'Yes,' said I, 'if you play *Croppies Lie Down*; but you know you cannot play it; your fingers never learned the tune.'

[1] Borrow actually took several years to write *Wild Wales*; it was published in 1862.
[2] *Wild Wales*.

Snowdon from Llyn Llydaw

By courtesy of British Railways

Cader Idris, near Dolgelly

" 'They never did, your hanner; but they have heard it
played of old by the blackguard Orange fiddlers of Dublin
on the First of July, when the Protestant boys used to walk
round Willie's statue on College Green[1]—so if your hanner
gives me the shilling, they may, perhaps, bring out something
like it.'

" 'Very good,' said I; 'begin . . .' "[2]

The following verses to the tune played by the fiddler were
cut out from the published edition of *Wild Wales*, and when
one remembers the trouble Borrow had already got into because
of his attacks on the Holy Catholic Church the reason is not
far to seek:

> O! Croppies, ye'd better be quiet and still,
> Ye shan't have your liberty, do what ye will;
> As long as salt water is found in the deep,
> Our foot on the neck of the Croppy we'll keep.
> Remember the steel
> Of Sir Phelim O'Neill
> Who slaughtered our fathers in Catholic zeal;
> And down, down, Croppies lie down!
>
> The day of the Boyne was a brave gallant day,
> The Croppies had then all the worst of the fray;
> Then pale and aghast from our presence they fled,
> With Shamus the runagate king at their head,
> When crossing the ford
> In the name of the Lord
> The Protestant brandished his protestant sword;
> And down, down, Croppies went down!
>
> Yes, down ye went then, and ye down shall remain
> As long as the sun and the moon we retain;
> Whilst we the brave lads of the Orange cockade
> Shall laugh at our foemen confused and dismayed.
> Whoop! Protestants, Whoop!
> And drink full of hope,
> Bad luck to the Devil, Pretender, and Pope!
> And down, down, Croppies lie down!

[1] Statue of William III, hero of the Battle of the Boyne, fought 1 July,
1690, against James II.
[2] *Wild Wales*.

Borrow sang the words while the fiddler played, but when he had finished the man protested: "More blackguard Orange words I never heard! Divil a bit farther will I play—at any rate till I get the shilling."

But when he received this he asked curiously why his companion had asked for such a "blackguard song" which was quite out of date. Borrow answered him: "I used to hear the tune in my boyish days, and wished to hear it again; for though you call it a blackguard tune, it is the sweetest and most noble air that Ireland, the land of music, has ever produced. As for the words, never mind where I got them; they are violent enough, but not half so violent as the words of some of the songs made against the Irish Protestants by the priests."

"Well, your hanner," said the man, "the Orange is now in the kennel and the Croppies have it all their own way."

"And perhaps," said Borrow, "before I die, the Orange will be out of the kennel and the Croppies in, even as they were in my young days—Farewell!"

"Farewell, your hanner," whined the fiddler, "and here's another scratch of the illigant tune your hanner is so fond of, to cheer up your hanner's ears upon your way."

"And long after I had left him," wrote Borrow, "I could hear him playing on his fiddle in first-rate style the beautiful tune of *Down, Croppies Lie Down!*"

At Bangor Mrs. Borrow and Henrietta were waiting for him, and nothing would satisfy him but that he and Henrietta should climb Snowdon, which they did arm-in-arm accompanied by a boy guide. On the summit Borrow declaimed some poetry in Welsh, much to the amusement of some English tourists and the amazement of a Welshman who demanded to know if he were—of all things—a *Breton*. Borrow often took his stepdaughter with him on his long walks, for the two got on remarkably well as a rule, and he wrote of her:

"I generally call her daughter, and with good reason, seeing that she has always shown herself a daughter to me —that she has all kinds of good qualities, and several accomplishments, knowing something of conchology, more of botany, drawing capitally in the Dutch style, and playing remarkably well on the guitar—not the trumpery German thing so-called—but the real Spanish guitar."

On the same page in *Wild Wales* he also paid a handsome tribute to Mrs. Borrow:

"Of my wife I will merely say that she is a perfect paragon of wives—can make puddings and sweets and treacle posset, and is the best woman of business in East Anglia."

But by the time the party had returned to Llangollen for another three weeks and the September mists clouded the valley while dear George roamed to Carnarvon, Bala, and Festiniog, Mrs. Borrow was sighing for the comfort of Yarmouth. Accordingly she and Henrietta went home, and Borrow bought a little leather satchel, popped into it "a white linen shirt, a pair of worsted stockings, a razor and a prayer-book" and set out on foot for South Wales, a journey which took him three weeks. He returned to Yarmouth about the middle of November with four fat note-books on his travels and a host of stories about his adventures. Yet despite his love for Wales and his impassioned interest in her literature and history he had not been wholly happy. For an hour or two at a time while he spoke to people in the tap-room or on the open road he was eager, jovial, laughing. As he strode alone over the dead bracken and felt the chill autumn wind in his face he ached for the orange trees of Seville, the broad lands of the Alemtejo, the granite-faced quays of the Nevski Prospect; and melancholy swept him.

III

Borrow's first task on his return was to put the finishing touches to the Appendix to *The Romany Rye*, and the tears sprang to his eyes as he wrote:

"It is true he went to Spain with the colours of that

society on his hat—oh! the blood glows in his veins! oh! the marrow awakes in his old bones when he thinks of what he accomplished in Spain in the cause of religion and civilisation with the colours of that society in his hat, and its weapon in his hand, even the sword of the word of God; how with that weapon he hewed left and right, making the priests fly before him, and run away squeaking: '*Vaya! qué demonio es este!*' Ay, and when he thinks of the plenty of Bible swords which he left behind him, destined to prove, and which have already proved, pretty calthrops in the heels of Popery. . . .''

Suddenly his interest in the book revived and he knew an intense desire to have it published, so packed it off to Mr. Murray. It never entered his head that the folk at Albemarle Street might raise their eyebrows at some of his more vindictive passages or that they might be a shade disappointed that he still persisted in shrouding the years 1826 to 1833 in mystery and placed all the action of his book in the year 1825. Once he had dispatched the package and received a brief acknowledgment he took for granted that it had gone to press and began to work on his Cornish notes with a view to making a volume out of them. He also took up again the correspondence he had begun with the gentle Edward Fitzgerald a year earlier and seemed, for him, to be in a tolerably calm and cheerful frame of mind. It was therefore a tremendous shock to receive the following letter from Mr. Murray[1]:

"MY DEAR BORROW,—I have read with care the MS. of THE ROMANY RYE and have pondered anxiously over it; and in what I am about to write I think I may fairly claim the privilege of a friend deeply interested in you personally, as well as in your reputation as an author, and by no means insensible to the abilities displayed in your various works. It is my firm conviction then, that you will incur the certainty of failure and run the risk of injuring your literary fame by publishing the MS. as it stands. Very large omissions seem to me—and in this Elwin,[2] no mean

[1] Dated 27 January, 1855, but Mr. Murray wrote in 23 December, 1854.
[2] The Rev. Whitwell Elwin, editor of the *Quarterly Review* from 1853.

judge, concurs—absolutely indispensable. That *Lavengro* would have profited by curtailment, I stated before its publication. The result has verified my anticipations, and in the present instance I feel compelled to make it the condition of publication. You can well imagine that it is not in my *interest* to shorten a book from two volumes to one unless there were really good cause.

"*Lavengro* clearly has not been successful. Let us not then risk the chance of another failure, but try to avoid the rock on which we then split. You have so great store of interesting matter in your mind and in your notes, that I cannot but feel it to be a pity that you should harp always upon one string, as it were. It seems to me that you have dwelt too long on English ground in this new work, and have resuscitated some characters of the former book (such as F. Ardry) whom your readers would have been better pleased to have left behind. Why should you not introduce us rather to those novel scenes of Muscovite and Hungarian life respecting which I have heard you drop so many stimulating allusions. Do not, I pray, take offence at what I have written. It is difficult and even painful for me to assume the office of critic, and this is one of the reasons why this note has lingered so long in my desk. Fortunately, in the advice I am tendering I am supported by others of better literary judgment than myself, and who have also deep regard for you. I will specify below some of the passages which I would point out for omission.—With best remembrances, I remain, my dear Borrow, Your faithful publisher and sincere friend,

JOHN MURRAY."

The Borrow of 1845 would have flown into a wild rage, swooped upon Albemarle Street, thumped Mr. Murray's desk, and, by sheer force of personality, bludgeoned the publisher into accepting *The Romany Rye* with precious little, if any, alteration. The Borrow of 1855 was filled with a different sort of anger, a cold emotion which was born of fear. As he read Mr. Murray's letter one phrase, and one only, thrummed through his head—"*Have you ever been to Kiakhta?*" From that phrase, however he chose to deny the fact, fear had sprung, and the damning arguments among the critics of *Lavengro* as to what was truth and what was fiction had merely suckled an already lusty child. Now that child was a stripling of eight years old, standing alert and eager in the background of Borrow's mind, and as he scanned Mr. Murray's letter the child moved forward with an earnestness that would not be denied and said: "The mountains separating the years between 1826 and 1833 are as the mountains of the moon, which no man can scale."

It must be remembered that Mr. Murray was rightly not concerned with what posterity might, or might not, think of *The Romany Rye*. He was a publisher who, so far as was compatible with his undoubted literary taste, very naturally published books which had some hope of sale. It must also be remembered that any hint at criticism was immediately translated by Borrow as a reference to the "veiled period" he had created in a fit of grandeur when sure of himself and his evangelical mission, and that within him he was fumbling for just such a definition of autobiography as he was to give Watts-Dunton some ten years later—"Is it a mere record of the incidents of a man's life? Or is it a picture of the man himself—his character, his soul?"

The child in his mind—and that child was omnipresent throughout his life—shrank back from Murray's reasonable letter; shrank yet farther back from his "suggestions for omission":

"The Hungarian. In No. 6.
The Jockey Story, terribly spun out, No. 7.
    Visit to the Church, too long.
Interview with the Irishman, Do.
Learning Chinese, too much repetition in this part of a very
    interesting chapter.
The Postilion and Highwayman.
Throughout the MS. condensation is indispensable. Many of
    the narratives are carried to a tedious length by details
    and repetition.
The dialogue with Ursula, the song, etc., border on the

indelicate. I like much Horncastle Fair, the Chinese scholar, except objection noted above.

Grooming of the horse.

"January 27th, 1855."

Now how on earth, without scaling the mountains of the moon, was he going to introduce enough *fact* to satisfy Murray. The public—as he was too well aware—liked their autobiography pedestrian and starred with footnotes, and he was totally incapable of giving them what they wanted. They would not be satisfied, as he well knew, by the adventures of a man who raced through life for twenty-two years, went abruptly into eclipse for seven, and emerged a limping supplicant at the feet of Mr. Brandram of Earl Street at the age of twenty-nine. Yet he would not, could not, court disaster— after all, Dr. Bowring was presumably still alive and kicking in Canton?

In his fear—in the eyes of posterity ridiculous, but in the eyes of 1855—and dear Carreta—indubitably right—Borrow took refuge in the penning of the most impossible letter surely sent by any well-known author to any publisher. Worse still, he wrote it under his wife's name, a subterfuge detected by Dr. Knapp's magnifying-glass when he was so assiduously buying all data for his Borrovian shrine at New Haven, U.S.A.[1]:

"Jan: 29, 1855.

"DEAR MR. MURRAY,—We have received your letters.[2] In the first place I beg leave to say something on a very principal point. You talk about *conditions* of publishing. Mr. Borrow has not the slightest wish to publish the book. The MS. was left with you because you wished to see it, and when left, you were particularly requested not to let it pass out of your own hands. But it seems you have shown it to various individuals whose opinions you repeat. What these opinions are worth may be gathered from the following fact.

[1] The writer has been debarred, owing to her country's need for dollars, from examination of Dr. Knapp's "shrine".

[2] There seems to have been a second letter from Mr. Murray. We can only imagine that it was short and to the point.

"The book is one of the most learned works ever written; yet in the summary of the opinions which you give, not one single allusion is made to the learning which pervades the book, no more than if it contained none at all. It is treated just as if all the philological and historical facts were mere inventions, and the book a common novel . . .

"With regard to *Lavengro* it is necessary to observe that if ever a book experienced infamous and undeserved treatment it was that book. It was attacked in every form that envy and malice could suggest, on account of Mr. Borrow's acquirements and the success of the *Bible in Spain*, and it was deserted by those whose duty it was, in some degree, to have protected it. No attempt was ever made to refute the vile calumny that it was a book got up against the Popish agitation of '51. It was written years previous to that period—a fact of which none is better aware than the Publisher. Is that calumny to be still permitted to go unanswered?

"If these suggestions are attended to, well and good; if not, Mr. Borrow can bide his time. He is independent of the public and of everybody. Say no more on the Russian subject. Mr. Borrow has had quite enough of the press. If he wrote a book on Russia, it would be said to be like the *Bible in Spain*, or it would be said to be *un*like the *Bible in Spain*, and would be blamed in either case. He has written a book in connection with England such as no other body could have written, and he now rests from his labours. He has found England an ungrateful country. It owes much to him, and he owes nothing to it. If he had been a low ignorant impostor, like a person he could name, he would have been employed and honoured.—I remain—Yours sincerely,
                                        "MARY BORROW."

Doubtless the "low ignorant impostor" was Bowring, and one wonders that the business-like Mrs. Borrow allowed the letter to be sent at all. It did, in fact, partially destroy the very pleasant relationship which had endured for fourteen years between the house of Murray and George Borrow, while the rebuke about the MS. having been criticized by "various

individuals" was calculated to hurt Elwin, who had already
been snubbed by Borrow when he had asked him to write an
article for the *Quarterly* and received the scornful answer,
"Never! I have made a resolution never to have anything to
do with such a blackguard trade."[1]

IV

For the next year Borrow ignored the fate of *The Romany
Rye*. In the summer of 1855 he, his wife and Henrietta visited
the Isle of Man, the ladies staying in Douglas for September
and most of October while Borrow tramped all over the island
collecting information about the Manxmen and their language.

"He was not slow in discovering that they possessed a
literature of their own, entirely manuscript. This literature
consists of ballads on sacred subjects which are called *carvals*,
a corruption of the English word carol. It was formerly the
custom in the Isle of Man for young people, who thought
themselves endowed with the poetic gift, to compose carols
some time before Christmas, and to recite them in the
Parish Churches. Those pieces which were approved of by
the clergy were subsequently chanted by their authors
through their immediate neighbourhoods both before and
after the holy festival. Many of these songs have been handed
down in writing to the present time. Some of them possess
considerable merit, and a printed collection of them would
be a curious addition to the literature of Europe . . . The
Carvals are preserved in uncouth-looking, smoke-stained
volumes in lone farmhouses and cottages in gills and
glens . . ."[2]

In all likelihood it was Borrow's delving into Manx literature that was responsible for the formation, three years later,
of the Manx Society, a body which set about the deciphering
and publication of the Runic inscriptions found on so many
tombs in the island. He also translated several old Manx

[1] *Some 19th Century Men of Letters*, Ed. Warwick Elwin, 1902.
[2] From Borrow's Notes on the Isle of Man.

Ballads, including the *Ballad of Illiam Dhone* ("Brown William"), which told the story of William Christian, Receiver-General of the Isle of man who was executed on Hangoe Hill in 1662 or 1663 because he had surrendered to Cromwell:

> Let no one in greatness too confident be,
> Nor trust in his kindred, though high their degree;
> For envy and rage will lay any man low:
> Thy murder, Brown William, fills Mona with woe . . .[1]

"In the whole world," wrote Borrow, "there is not a more honest, kindly race than the genuine Manx." For a time, indeed, his enthusiastic admiration for the island people threatened to supersede his love for the Welsh. He was out of love with England and the English—as he had made all too plain in his letter to Mr. Murray—and his interest in the supernatural had of late years become almost an obsession, so the legends he drew from the country folk concerning piskies, hobgoblins, mermaids and satyrs delighted him, while he was tremendously excited at coming across further legends of that "mighty man of valour and swift runner", Finn McCoyle—or Ma Coul.

On 10 October, when he was in Douglas, he received news of the death of a cousin, William Borrow, who had gone to America to seek his fortune. This event led to one of those explosions which were growing rapidly more frequent:

"My wife brought me intelligence of the death of William Borrow in America. He had accomplished great things there; won a prize for a new and wonderful application of steam, but had shortly afterwards died from excess of mental fatigue—a sacrifice, like my brother, to the greediness of the wretched English aristocracy. Were talent properly patronized in England, he might have stayed at home and have become an ornament to his country. But there are no employments or honours in England for any but the connexions and lick-spittles of the aristocracy. Read in the newspapers that Leicester Curzon, the son of Lord Howe, had been made a Lieutenant-Colonel for bringing despatches

[1] From Borrow's Notes on the Isle of Man.

(from the Crimea). William Borrow, the wonderful inventor, dead, and Leicester Curzon . . . a Colonel! Pretty justice!"

This entry in Borrow's *Diary* proves how ill-balanced his mind was in the mid-fifties. Not by the widest stretch of imagination could John Borrow's early death in Mexico be attributed to the "wretched aristocracy"—although his brother had long deluded himself that if Lord Orford had granted John a regular commission, or at least allowed him to continue drawing half-pay, the boy would miraculously have survived the perils and diseases of Central America. William Borrow, so far as can be found out, went to America entirely on his own initiative and nobody in England, high or low, could be blamed for the venture. As for the Hon. Leicester Curzon, he most assuredly deserved his promotion and was only dragged in because Borrow had hated every bearer of that name since the episode of the *Codex Sinaïticus*.

Back at Yarmouth Borrow amused himself setting his Isle of Man notes in order, did some desultory work on his proposed Cornish book, and greatly annoyed the tenants of Oulton Hall by bathing in the mere in full view of their windows and in a remarkably skimpy costume suitable neither to decorum nor the English winter climate. *The Romany Rye* was not mentioned until April 1856, when he asked Mrs. Borrow to send this terse note to Mr. Murray:

"Will you have the kindness to send the MS. which my husband left with you. (November 1854!) Please to *book* it and direct it to 'George Borrow, No. 37, Camperdown Place, Great Yarmouth,'—which is our present residence, and should we remove, you shall know our address."

But during the short three days which elapsed before the arrival of the manuscript by rail, Borrow had again lost interest in it and pushed it into a tin box without so much as a glance. One is, however, forced to the conclusion that the essential child in his character was indulging in a game of "let's pretend", and that in reality his every action during 1855 and 1856—the ecstatic tour of the Isle of Man, the long lonely tramps through Norfolk and Cambridgeshire, the vituperative outbursts in his *Diary*—was only a cover behind which he hid his continuous anxiety about *The Romany Rye*. He believed it to be a great book—and posterity has shown that belief to be a right one. He also believed—and therein lay the rub—that his Appendix was the complete and perfect answer to the critics of *Lavengro*. Here, of course, he was entirely wrong. The Appendix detracted from, rather than added to, the book's value. It was, indeed, the most colossal piece of stupidity ever perpetrated by any great author—and Borrow most definitely *was* a great author.

During that spring of 1856 Borrow's secret brooding over *The Romany Rye* drove him out and across the wide spaces of East Anglia. He walked from Yarmouth to Ely, returning home by way of Cromer, Holt, Lynn and Wisbech. It was during this tour that he called upon Miss Anna Gurney[1] at her home in North Repps, but fled the house when she put an Arabic grammar into his hand and asked his advice on some particular point, talking rapidly as she waited for his answer. "I could not," said Borrow passionately, "study the Arabic grammar and listen to her at the same time, so I threw down the book and ran out of the room." Whether he simply could not stand the searching questions of Miss Gurney and the stuffy atmosphere of her room, or whether he had forgotten the Arabic he most certainly knew at an earlier period we do not know; but soon afterwards he met the Rev. Arthur W. Upcher of Sheringham Hall, Cromer, who wrote a letter to *The Athenæum* in 1893—twelve years after Borrow's death—about their conversation:

"He told us there were three personages in the world whom he had always had a desire to see; two of these had slipped through his fingers, so he was determined to see the third. 'Pray, Mr. Borrow, who were they?' He held up three fingers of his left hand and pointed them off with the forefinger of the right: the first Daniel O'Connor, the second Lamplighter (the sire of Phosphorus, Lord Berner's winner of the Derby), the third, Anna Gurney. The first two

[1] Anglo-Saxon scholar and first woman member of the British Association (1795–1857).

were dead and he had not seen them; now he had come to see Anna Gurney, and this was the end of his visit."[1]

Borrow carried his usual note-book during this and a second walking-tour through much the same country, but made few entries of interest. On leaving Miss Gurney he went to "Tucker's" in Cromer and ordered an immensely fine dinner with which he drank brandy and water—presumably to recover from the shock of the Arabic grammar. Outside the Globe Inn at Lynn he remonstrated with a driver for beating a fallen horse, and cried, "Give him a pint of ale, and I will pay for it!" The astonished ostlers gave the horse *two* pints, which revived it so quickly that it scrambled to its feet and was seen a quarter of an hour later "pulling merrily past the Globe with the other horses".

Ale was Borrow's panacea for all ills—but it had to be good ale "with plenty of malt in it, and as little hop as well may be—ale at least two years old", and he asserted he would like to see an Act of Parliament passed which would force brewers to brew none but the best beer. Old Burton was his favourite, and he was also a connoisseur of good port, although on his tramps round the countryside he would deliberately drink the thin, wishy-washy liquid known as "swipes", partly because that was the tipple of his gypsy friends and partly through some strange desire to mortify his stomach. When Elizabeth Harvey told him about some "lady who was attached to a gentleman", he said sharply, "Well, did he make her an offer?" and upon learning that he had not, said emphatically, "Ah, if she had given him some good ale he would!"

One cannot say, alas, that Borrow made a good impression upon the country folk he met with in his East Anglian wanderings. Some thought he was "a missionary out of work"; others that he "kep' hisself to hisself" and was a bit queer in the head. Many a fisherman in lake or river, many an eel-catcher, was scared out of his wits by sudden sight of a leonine white head and massive shoulders rearing out of the water with roars and splutters and went home to tell his awe-struck family he had seen "one of they monsters".

[1] 22 July, 1893.

Old Mrs. Borrow had a little land and a thatched cottage at Mattishall Burgh, a mile and a half from Dumpling Green, and her tenant was a "proper character", a small holder called Henry Hill, who seems to have been the only real friend Borrow had in the district. Henry was a mine of information about herbs and their uses, had taught himself to play the 'cello—he played it each Sunday in the Congregational Chapel —and had also taught himself how to repair watches. He became the star Sunday attraction for the neighbourhood through his bees, for he was supposedly the first man ever to keep bees under glass and he affirmed that they actually talked to him and regarded him as a friend. People came from far and wide on Sabbath afternoons to see Henry's bees and listen to his lectures on their habits. Such a man was naturally one after Borrow's own heart, and for hours together he would march beside Henry as he ploughed his fields, asking eternal questions and listening raptly to the old man's answers.

But Henry Hill was an exception, and when he was succeeded by his son John, Borrow was not altogether welcome at Church Farm, Mattishall, partly because he once told John he should be responsible for his half-brother's debt (apparently owed to Borrow); and partly because the family sensed the "queerness" complained of by so many other yokels. Norfolk men were always conservative folk and the sharp social divisions which existed all over England in the eighteen-fifties were even sharper in that county than elsewhere. To their minds it simply was not right for a "gentleman" collecting his rents to sit down by the fire with hunks of bread and cheese, quizz Mrs. Hill about London—where she originally hailed from—sing foreign songs, make long quotations from the Scriptures, and recite outlandish poems. Since they possessed a deeply ingrained sense of hospitality they treated him courteously and gave civil answers to questions they privately regarded as interfering; but when bedtime came they packed him off to one of the seven poor inns in Mattishall although they had room and to spare.

The reasons behind Borrow's local unpopularity were obvious ones. People in those parts had long memories and busy tongues. There wasn't a man, woman, or child from

29 Along the pathway as I trod
    A beggar met my eye,
    And at her cries the Almighty God
    Descended from on high.

30 O counsel, precious counsel, yield
    Sweet Jorm, in my need,
    How I may get my jars refill'd
    Myself and bairns to feed.

31 The priest of Villa Franca bold
    Proclaimeth far and wide,
    That he the law which Gypsies hold
    Is bent to set aside.

32 And see, adown the road doth prance
    The priest in full array,
    In fear before his countenance
    Facundo runs away.

Facsimile of four stanzas from an unpublished Gypsy poem by
George Borrow

Oulton Broad to King's Lynn who did not know of the fuss over Mr. Peto's railway, the dog-fight correspondence with Mr. Denniss, the noisy evenings spent round gypsy camp-fires. To them, indeed, Borrow appeared much as the piskies appeared to Cornishmen, and when he strode into the bar of an inn, gulped a pint of "swipes" with ostentation, and began to talk in a loud, overbearing voice, they slid their mugs stealthily along the counter and huddled in a corner, mute and suspicious.

Most strangely Borrow, that hypersensitive being, seemed unaware of the hostility which charged the atmosphere each time he entered a public-house or visited a farm. His egoism wrapped him about as securely as the Spanish cloak he still affected and until the day of his death he fondly imagined that the people of Suffolk and Norfolk thought of him as a god. The truth was, of course, that Borrow, from the publication of *Lavengro* onwards, was so obsessed by his hatred of the outside world that he tended to live more and more in a world of the mind into which time did not enter. Everything he said, everything he did, belonged to those glorious moments he had once shared with Hasfeld in St. Petersburg, with the gypsies of Badajoz and Granada, with Antonio Buchini and Benedict Mol, with the old apple-woman of London Bridge and the host of queer characters he had met on his vagabond rovings through England—the moments he had shared with Jasper Petulengro and that tall woman with the braided hair, Isopel Berners. . . .

People said she was a figment of his imagination—ah, but they had not crouched with her over the fire in Mumper's Dingle,[1] known her every mood, realized what it meant to a man with good red blood in his veins to win—and lose—the love of that Amazonian woman who frightened the Flying Tinker and so nearly became Jasper Petulengro's second living wife:

Jasper. "My mind at present rather inclines towards two wives. I have heard that king Pharaoh had two, if not more. Now, I think myself as good a man as he; and if he

[1] Near Willenhall, Staffordshire; now a most unromantic place of slag-heaps.

had more wives than one, why should not I, whose name is Petulengro?"

Borrow. "But what would Mrs. Petulengro say?"

Jasper. "Why, to tell you the truth, brother, it was she who first put the thought into my mind. She has always, you know, had strange notions in her head, *gorgiko* notions, I suppose we may call them, about gentility and the like, and reading and writing. Now, though she can neither read nor write herself, she thinks that she is lost among our people and that they are no society for her. So says she to me one day, 'Pharaoh,' says she, 'I wish you would take another wife, that I might have a little pleasant company. As for these here, I am their betters.'—'I have no objection,' said I; who shall it be? Shall it be a Cooper or a Stanley?'— 'A Cooper or a Stanley!' said she, with a toss of her head, 'I might as well keep my present company as theirs; none of your rubbish; let it be a *gorgie*, one that I can speak an idea with'—that was her word, I think. Now I am thinking that this here Bess of yours (Isopel) would be just the kind of person both for my wife and myself. My wife wants something *gorgiko*, something genteel. Now Bess is of blood gorgious; if you doubt it, look in her face, all full of *pawno ratter*, white blood, brother; and as for gentility, nobody can make exceptions to Bess's gentility, seeing she was born in the workhouse of Melford the Short,[1] where she learnt to read and write. She is no Irishwoman, brother, but English pure, and her father was a farmer.

"So much as far as my wife is concerned. As for myself, I tell you what, brother, I want a strapper; one who can give and take. The Flying Tinker is abroad, vowing vengeance against us all. I know what the Flying Tinker is, so does Tawno. The Flying Tinker came to our camp. 'Damn you all,' says he, 'I'll fight the best of you for nothing.'— 'Done!' says Tawno, 'I'll be ready for you in a minute.' So Tawno went into his tent and came out naked. 'Here's at you,' says Tawno. Brother, Tawno fought for two hours

---

[1] A girl child born at Long Melford, Suffolk, workhouse in the early years of the nineteenth century, eventually ran away with the gypsies and became the woman Borrow called Isopel Berners.

with the Flying Tinker, for two whole hours, and it's hard to say which had the best of it or the worst. I tell you what, brother, I think Tawno had the worst of it. Night came on. Tawno went into his tent to dress himself and the Flying Tinker went his way.

"Now suppose, brother, the Flying Tinker comes upon us when Tawno is away. Who is to fight the Flying Tinker when he says: 'D . . . n you, I will fight the best of you?' Brother, I wouldn't fight the Flying Tinker for five pounds; but I couldn't for less. The Flying Tinker is a big man, and though he hasn't my science, he weighs five stone heavier. It wouldn't do for me to fight a man like that for nothing. But there's Bess who can afford to fight the Flying Tinker at any time for what he's got, and that's three ha'pence. She can beat him, brother; I bet five pounds that Bess can beat the Flying Tinker. Now, if I marry Bess, I'm quite easy on his score. He comes to our camp and says his say. 'I won't dirty my hands with you,' says I, 'at least not under five pounds; but here's Bess who'll fight you for nothing. I tell you what, brother, when he knows that Bess is Mrs. Pharaoh, he'll fight shy of our camp; he won't come near it, brother. He knows Bess don't like him, and what's more, that she can lick him. He'll let us alone; at least I think so. If he does come, I'll smoke my pipe whilst Bess is beating the Flying Tinker. Brother, I'm dry, and will now take a cup of ale."[1]

But after all Isopel Berners had refused the Pharaoh's offer and had stayed on in the dingle with the *gorgio* who had a lock of white hair flaring above his forehead. He had hoped that she might remain with him for always, that together they might walk, lawless and unafraid, all the way to Finisterre— but then there was no telling with Isopel Berners, and when he came home one day, limping tiredly beside his creaking tinker's cart, to find the dead ash of a gypsy fire, he knew she had gone as she was perhaps bound to go, away down the winds of time with her hair unbraided and streaming behind her. Only a

[1] A fragment of manuscript in Borrow's handwriting discovered by Dr. Knapp.

letter she had left him, yet for his life long he would keep that scrap of paper close to his heart:

"Fear God, and take your own part.

"There's Bible in that, young man; see how Moses feared God, and how he took his own part against everybody who meddled with him. And see how David feared God, and took his own part against all the bloody enemies which surrounded him—so fear God, young man, and never give in! The world can bully, and is fond, provided it sees a man in a kind of difficulty, of getting about him, calling him coarse names, and even going so far as to hustle him: but the world, like all bullies, carries a white feather in its tail, and no sooner sees the man taking off his coat, and offering to fight its best, than it scatters here and there, and is always civil to him afterwards. So when folks are disposed to ill-treat you, young man, say, 'Lord have mercy upon me!' and then tip them Long Melford, to which, as the saying goes, there is nothing comparable for shortness all the world over; and these last words, young man, are the last you will ever have from her who is nevertheless,

"Your affectionate female servant,
"ISOPEL BERNERS."[1]

Borrow, not Isopel Berners, wrote that letter; yet the real Isopel, the tall, striding companion of his wandering youth, inspired the writing.

There certainly had been an Isopel Berners in Borrow's life; but whether he had really loved and lived with her in the dingle, or whether he had built up the whole affair out of a handful of chance meetings nobody will ever know. In all his writings about her he was peculiarly careful to emphasize the fact that their relationship was platonic—but that might have been done for his wife's sake. One can only hope that he did once know happiness with Isopel Berners, and that their romance was complete.

---

[1] *The Romany Rye.*

V

The winter of 1856-1857 passed slowly in the Yarmouth lodgings. Borrow saw Edward Fitzgerald occasionally and had much pleasant correspondence with him, principally about Turkish Dictionaries and the translation of *Omar Khayyam*:

> "How I enjoyed my evening with you a month ago" (Fitzgerald wrote in October 1856). "I wanted to ask you to read some of the *Northern Ballads* too; but you shut the book . . . I must tell you. I am come up here (London) on my way to Chichester to be—married! to Miss Barton (of Quaker memory) and our united ages amount to 96!—a dangerous experiment on both sides. She at least brings a fine head and heart to the bargain—worthy of a better market. But it is to be, and I dare say you will honestly wish we may do well."

The gentle Fitzgerald had an excellent effect on Borrow, his sweetness being proof against his friend's touchiness and suspicion. Others, alas, were so offended by his rudeness, his sudden fits of rage, or his failure to answer their letters that they soon drifted away. At some time in the 'fifties Charles Darwin sent an inquiry through a mutual acquaintance: "Is there any Dog in Spain closely like our English Pointer, in *shape* and size, and *habits*—namely in pointing, backing, and not giving tongue. Might I be permitted to quote Mr. Borrow's answer to the query? Has the improved English Pointer been introduced into Spain?" In all probability Borrow simply ignored this query from the man of science, for there is no record of any reply.

It was in February 1857 that Borrow took the manuscript of *The Romany Rye* from its tin box, solemnly read it through, and wrote to Mr. Murray:

> "DEAR SIR,—I write this to say that the work must go to press, and that unless the work is forthwith commenced, I must come up to London and make arrangements myself.

Time is passing away. It ought to have appeared many years ago. I can submit to no more delays.—Yours truly,

"GEORGE BORROW."

It was to Mr. Murray's eternal credit that he swallowed this piece of sheer impertinence and agreed to publish *The Romany Rye* "just to oblige Mr. Borrow". He saw squalls ahead, however, and these were not long in blowing up. Both he and Elwin were absolutely determined on certain alterations and Elwin, who had magnanimously forgiven Borrow for earlier insults and was genuinely aware of the essential greatness of the book, wrote begging him to "give his sequel to *Lavengro* more of an historical, and less of a romancing air". To his surprise Borrow agreed, and in March Elwin was able to write to Mr. Murray:

" 'It is not the statements themselves which provoke incredulity, but the melodramatic effect which he tries to impart to all his adventures.' Instead of 'roaring like a lion', in reply, as Elwin had expected, he returned quite a 'lamb-like' note, which gave promise of a greater success for his new work than its precursor."[1]

In truth Borrow was a very weary lion and one sadly aware that his fighting days were done. The amended manuscript was sent to the printer, but when Elwin was writing a review from the proof-sheets for the *Quarterly* he was horrified to find that Borrow had slipped in—presumably while correcting his proofs—an unforgivable paragraph:

"When the review was almost finished, it was on the point of being altogether withdrawn, owing to a passage in *The Romany Rye* which Elwin said was clearly meant to be a reflection on his friend Ford, 'to avenge the presumed refusal of the latter to praise *Lavengro* in the *Quarterly*. I am very anxious,' he said, 'to get Borrow justice for rare merits which have been entirely overlooked, but if he persists in publishing an attack of this kind I shall, I fear,

[1] *Some XVIII Century Men of Letters*, Ed. Warwick Elwin, 1902.

not be able to serve him.' The objectionable paragraphs had been written by Borrow under a misapprehension, and he cancelled them as soon as he was convinced of his error."[1]

Not quite so soon, unfortunately, as Mr. Warwick Elwin inferred. The cancellation only followed a stern rebuke from Mr. Murray:

"MY DEAR BORROW,—When I have done anything towards you deserving of apology I will not hesitate to offer one. As it is, I have acted loyally towards you, and with a view to maintaining your interests.

"I agreed to publish your present work solely with the object of obliging you, and in a great degree at the strong recommendation of Cooke. I meant (as was my duty) to do my very best to promote its success. You on your side promised to listen to me in regard to any necessary omissions; and on the faith of this, I pointed out one omission, which I make the indispensable condition of my proceeding further with the book. I have asked nothing unfair nor unreasonable —nay, a compliance with the request is essential for your own character as an author and a man.

"You are the last man that I should ever expect to 'frighten or bully'; and if a mild but firm remonstrance against an offensive passage in your book is interpreted by you into such an application, I submit that the grounds for the notion must exist nowhere but in your own imagination. The alternative offered to you is to omit or publish elsewhere. Nothing shall compel me to *publish* what you have written. Think calmly and dispassionately over this, and when you have decided let me know.—Yours very faithfully,

"JOHN MURRAY."

Borrow's answer was typical—not for the world would he admit that he had deliberately inserted the passage about Richard Ford, that gay, generous friend who had helped him so much. As always, when his sins found him out, he was at his most autocratic. He demanded that Mr. Cooke should come all the way to Yarmouth to see him—"*after* Monday, when I

[1] Ibid.

shall be disengaged". He went on with a fervour worthy of the Rev. Mr. Andrew Brandram:

"You call a chapter heavy, and I, not wishing to appear unaccommodating, remove or alter two or three passages for which I do not particularly care, whereupon you make the most unnecessary comments, obtruding your private judgment upon matters with which you have no business, and of which it is impossible that you should have a competent knowledge. If you disliked the passages you might have said so, but you had no right to say anything more. I believe that you not only meant no harm, but that your intentions were good; unfortunately, however, people with the best of intentions occasionally do a great deal of harm. In your language you are frequently in the highest degree injudicious; for example, in your last letter you talk of obliging me by publishing my work. Now is not that speaking very injudiciously? Surely you forget that I could return a most cutting answer were I disposed to do so . . . I believe, however, that your intentions are good, and that you are disposed to be friendly."

The Romany Rye appeared in two volumes on 30 April, 1857,[1] and at the end of the book Borrow gave a grandiloquent and detailed list of no fewer than *nine* "works by the Author of the *Bible in Spain*, ready for the Press",[2] which included his old friend the *Kiempe Viser* translation and books on Cornwall and the Isle of Man.

The book had even less success than had *Lavengro*, and the critics were almost unanimous in their condemnation. "No author," said *The Athenæum* nastily, "has, to use a gypsy phrase, *drabbed* so much *drao* into literary dough as the author whose dullest gypsy preparation we have now read . . . Yes, *kosko divvus, Romany Rye*, say we; and so, we fancy, will our readers."

The Saturday Review struggled nobly, in a long and detailed article, to give genius its due; while Elwin wrote an excellent criticism in the *Quarterly* drawing attention to the fact that *Lavengro* had not obtained the fame which it deserved. "It

[1] First edition, 1,000 copies; Second edition (1858), 750 copies.
[2] Only two books in the list, *Wild Wales* and *The Sleeping Bard*, were published in Borrow's lifetime.

contains passages which in their way are not surpassed by anything in English literature. The truth and vividness of the descriptions, both of scenes and persons, coupled with the purity, force, and simplicity of the language, should confer immortality upon many of its pages . . ."

But neither the *Saturday* nor the *Quarterly* could stomach the Appendix, that masterly piece of invective wherein Borrow lashed savagely at his enemies, giving them the pseudonyms of Priestcraft—Foreign Nonsense—Gentility Nonsense—Canting Nonsense—Pseudo-Critics—Pseudo-Radicals, before gathering the hatred of years for his wild attack on Bowring, so thinly disguised as "The Old Radical".

Assuredly the Appendix damned *The Romany Rye's* chance of even limited success; but the thing went deeper than that. This man, George Borrow, was writing in advance of his time, using a post-impressionist method of conveying autobiographical adventures to his reader which utterly confused a public accustomed to life stories and memoirs which were nothing more nor less than clear—and, in some cases, remarkable unprepossessing—photographs. They retreated uncomfortably from the riot of colour straggling across the pages of *The Romany Rye* and could not understand the "air of mystery" in which Borrow wrapped his own character. That he was attempting the picture of a man's soul never occurred to them; indeed, such an idea would have shocked them, for they felt most strongly that souls should not be mentioned in any except strictly "religious" works. They said flatly that Mr. Borrow was a liar—and a vagabond to boot—and struck his name from their list of readable authors.

Even Fitzgerald was sadly worried, and wrote to Professor Cowell in June 1857:

"Within hail almost lives George Borrow who has lately published, and given me, two new Volumes of *Lavengro* called *Romany Rye*, with some excellent things, and some very bad (as I have made bold to write him—how shall I face him!) You would not like the Book at all, I think."[1]

[1] *Letters and Literary Remains of Edward Fitzgerald*, 1889.

The failure of *The Romany Rye* cast a sombre melancholy over the little company at Yarmouth. Only twice did the old lion raise his tired head and growl forth protest; once when a friend told him the book was the greatest piece of literary invective since Swift, and he answered bitterly, "Yes, I meant it to be; and what do you think the effect was? No one took the least notice of it!"[1] And again when he wrote to Mr. Murray in the September:

> "It is of course unpalatable to many; for it scorns to foster delusion, to cry 'peace where there is no peace', and denounces boldly the evils which are hurrying the country to destruction, and which have kindled God's anger against it, namely, the pride, insolence, cruelty, covetousness, and hypocrisy of its people, and above all the rage for gentility, which must be indulged in at the expense of every good and honourable feeling."

Sick and sulky, Borrow again took to roving the countryside. Mrs. Borrow and Henrietta, significantly enough, no longer accompanied him. Alone with his memories and his hatred he tramped through South Wales from Carmarthen to Pembroke, from Haverfordwest to Cardigan Bay, from Builth to Mortimer Cross in Herefordshire and Shrewsbury in Shropshire, trying vainly to recapture the old enthusiasm he had felt for the Welsh race. On his return from this sadly unprofitable journey he sent Mr. Murray his translations of the *Visions of the Sleeping Bard* on which he had once pinned his youthful faith almost thirty years earlier. Murray refused it, gently but firmly, after spending several months wading through a manuscript which was practically indecipherable owing to a mass of corrections. But Borrow's allegiance to Ab Gwilym had not waned with the passing of time, and he wrote that he proposed to have the book printed locally and at his own expense. "I think it would sell, more especially with three engravings by Cruikshank. One might be the Dance of the Fairies in the first part; another the old Poet in Hades flinging a skull at the head of Ellis Wynne in the second, and the last the personification of Sin in the third

[1] A. Egmont Hake in *The Athenæum*, 13 August, 1881.

part, at the very conclusion." There was a poignant postscript: "I really want something to do; and seeing the work pass through the press might amuse me."

But for the moment nothing could amuse him or still his restless thoughts. He flung the manuscript into a drawer, turned the key on it, and spent his time striding impatiently about Yarmouth and asking his inevitable questions of every passer-by. Mrs. Borrow, whose decision to share her husband's hypochondriacal tendencies had not faltered, lay on her sofa or took airings in a Bath chair, and bemoaned to her "inseparable", as she called her daughter, the lack of success which seemed to haunt all dear George's literary undertakings. Twenty years of marriage to George Borrow had seen the death of all her great ambitions for him, but she could not altogether forgive him for their passing.

In August 1858 old Mrs. Borrow died suddenly at Oulton of "pulmonary congestion" in her eighty-seventh year, and was buried in Oulton Churchyard. To her son the shock was overwhelming. He remembered the days of childhood when she protected him unswervingly from his father's wrath and the uncomplimentary opinions of relatives, friends and school-masters; her loyalty throughout those terrible years when he had come home again and again with the miserable confession that the world would have none of him or his works; her delight in his St. Petersburg appointment; her glory in his work for the Society in Spain and the subsequent fame of his book about those "happiest years". . . .

"No more earthly cares and affections now, my mother? Yes, one. Why dost thou suddenly raise thy dark and still brilliant eye from the volume with a somewhat startled glance? What noise is that in the distant street? Merely the noise of a hoof—a sound common enough. But it draws nearer and nearer; it stops before the gate. Singular! And now there is a pause, a long pause. Ha! thou hearest something—a footstep, a swift but heavy footstep! thou risest, thou tremblest; there is a hand on the pin of the outer door; there is someone in the vestibule; and now the door of thy apartment opens; there is a reflection on the mirror behind

thee—a travelling hat, a grey beard, a sunburnt face. 'My
dearest Son!'—'My darling Mother!' ''[1]

Her death—and Mr. Murray's uncompromising verdict on
The Sleeping Bard, "there is no money in it"—sent Borrow
nearly distracted. In an effort to regain his mental balance he
set off on a long and exceedingly rough tour of Scotland in the
autumn. Edinburgh "was wonderfully altered since I was
there, and I don't think for the better", and as he made his
way northwards he gained black looks from the inhabitants
because of his deplorable faculty of saying the wrong thing at
the wrong moment. One could not imagine, for example, any
member of the Catholic Macdonnel clan appreciating the advice,
"Trust in Christ, not in the Virgin Mary and graven images";
nor any Highlander relishing the reproof, "You should not say
a *soft* day, but a wet day".

At Inverness Borrow was "swindled out of a shilling by
rascally ferrymen" while crossing the firth to Beauly where he
"saw the gate of the pit where old Fraser used to put the
people whom he owed money to", and found the "present
family rather uneasy . . . for though they are flaming Papists
they are very free of their money", owing to the claims of a
descendant of Simon Fraser's brother to the Lovat title and
lands. "Old Fraser's brother (who had fled to Wales after
committing murder in 1690) was called Black John of the
Tasser. The man whom he killed was a piper who sang an
insulting song to him at a wedding . . . He was dressed very
finely, and the piper sang:

> 'You're dressed in Highland robes, O John,
> But robes of straw would become ye better;
> You've silver buckles your shoes upon
> But leather thongs for them were fitter.'

Whereupon John drew his dagger and ran it into the piper's
belly."

After this extraordinary bowdlerization of Scottish history
Borrow proceeded to Fort Augustus by the Loch Ness steamer,
meeting a "strange man—tall gentleman—half doctor" in a
"dreadful hurricane of wind and rain", and enjoying a

[1] Lavengro.

gargantuan repast of "herrings, first-rate—black ale, Highland mutton—pudding and cream", after which he talked with "a kind, intelligent woman from Dornoch—no Gaelic"—who spoke of "Alexander Cumming, a fat blacksmith and great singer of Gaelic songs.

"I was never in such a place in my life for cheating and imposition," he wrote mournfully to his dear Carreta, but apparently his view was coloured by the atrocious weather and the refusal of a Macdonell to give him shelter—"A savage, brutish Papist and a hater of the English", who lived by the Spean river.

At Invergarry on Loch Oich Borrow had a "vision" of his mother, which we cannot but attribute to his over-indulgence in a noted Scottish dish. "Dinner of haggis; met a conceited schoolmaster," runs his *Diary*. "This night, or rather in the early morning, I saw in the dream of my sleep my dear departed mother—she appeared to be coming out of her little sleeping-room at Oulton Hall—overjoyed I gave a cry and fell down at her knee, but my agitation was so great that it burst the bonds of sleep, and I awoke."

His Scottish journeyings took him to Tobermory on the Island of Mull, to Helmsdale, Wick and Thurso, and across to the Orkneys and Shetlands—he preserved a bill for "shawls, veils and hosiery" from Lerwick—but he was heartily glad to travel southwards to Yarmouth, his wife, and the rows of medicine bottles decorating the shelves in his bedroom.

The following year, Borrow, his wife, and Henrietta went to Dublin, whence he "walked to Connemara, and from there to the Giant's Causeway. My expedition upon the whole afforded me much pleasure, though I was frequently wet to the skin and indifferently lodged." Yet even Ireland, that land of faery so loved by Borrow in his childhood, failed to soothe the restless, embittered man of 1859, for on 4 November, we find his wife writing to Mr. Murray: "We intend (D.V.) to return for the present to our old winter quarters at Yarmouth, near which most of our property lies. If all be well, in the Spring I shall wish to look around and select a pleasant healthy residence within three to ten miles of London . . ."

VI

It was a very subdued George Borrow who called at Albemarle Street in April 1860 to tell Mr. Murray that he had arranged with a Yarmouth printer to print 250 copies of *The Sleeping Bard*,[1] and to ask permission to use Mr. Murray's name above that of J. M. Dewey, the printer. This was gladly given and the book came out in the early summer; but Borrow soon found how difficult it was to dispose of without the backing and advertisement of the House of Murray. The only review it received, indeed, was one written by Borrow himself and published anonymously in the *Quarterly* of January 1861. This had the effect of finding buyers for those copies which he had not given away, and produced in his mind a momentary elation which led him to ask Mr. Murray to print a second edition, a demand which was politely refused.

Meanwhile the Borrows had moved into 22 Hereford Square, Brompton, where they had the misfortune, as it turned out, to have as neighbour that well-known writer, Miss Frances Power Cobbe, who afterwards trounced him so thoroughly in her *Autobiography*.[2] An alert, inquisitive woman with a caustic tongue, Miss Cobbe could not abide Borrow.

". . . If he were not a gypsy by blood" (she wrote) "he *ought* to have been one . . . My friend (Miss Lloyd, who lived with her) was amused by his quaint stories and his real or sham enthusiasm for Wales, and cultivated his acquaintance. I never liked him, thinking him more or less of a hypocrite. His missions, recorded in the *Bible in Spain*, and his translations of the Scriptures into the out-of-the-way tongues for which he had a gift, were by no means consonant with his real opinions concerning the veracity of the said Bible."

Perhaps it would have been better if Miss Lloyd, who was a cheerful Welshwoman, had not struck up a friendship with the Borrows and continually invited them to "share a dish of tea"; for these visits almost always ended in disaster. Miss Cobbe liked to lead the conversation in her own house: Borrow

---

1 The total cost to Borrow was £15 16s. 8d.
2 *The Life of Frances Power Cobbe, by Herself*, 1894.

relapsed into gloom unless *he* was allowed to do so. Miss Cobbe delighted in laying traps for him and into these he fell with remarkable alacrity. If she deplored the lack of educational facilities for women he flashed back that it was *right* they should be ignorant, and that no man could endure a clever wife. Miss Cobbe laughed and asked what he thought of the Brownings, whereat he was stung into saying foolishly that he had heard the name but did not know anything about them, as he read no modern writer later than Scott, while when Miss Cobbe egged him on to discussion of Norse and Irish poetry he usually jumped from his chair and hurried from the house.

There is no doubt that Borrow was capable of Johnsonian rudeness on occasion. An emissary from the Russian Embassy called upon him with much pomp to crave a copy of his *Targum* for the Tsar, and was told his Imperial master could come and fetch it himself. In argument with a man of great erudition he suddenly roared, "Sir, you're a fool!" On the other hand he could be immensely courteous, and his native kindness of heart was infinitely greater than that of his acidulated neighbour at No. 26.

Literary folk he shunned whenever possible, spending his days wandering about London, poking into old bookshops, visiting the gypsy encampments at Wandsworth, watching prize-fights and races, notably one between Seerfoot, the Seneca Indian, and Jackson, known as the American Deer, at Brompton. The publication of *Wild Wales* in 1862 meant little to him, and despite the fact that only *The Spectator* praised the book he remained strangely quiet in face of criticism. At intervals he had a sudden spurt of energy and wrote notes for his *Romano Lavo-Lil*, and he arranged with the magazine *Once a Week* to publish some of the translations over which he had slaved so long ago in his Millman Street attic; otherwise his only connection with writing was when he gave rare but lavish dinners at the Star and Garter, Richmond, to Mr. Murray and a few other friends.

It might have been thought that a countryman such as Borrow would feel sadly confined in London, but he had an outlet of which he took full advantage. His old friend Dr. Hake had returned from America and gone to live at Roehampton,

and Borrow often walked there from Brompton. It was through
Dr. Hake that he met the man who perhaps understood his
strange character better than anybody else—Theodore Watts-
Dunton. Together these two strode across Wimbledon Common
or Richmond Park, Watts-Dunton listening eagerly to stories
of the gypsies. Together they drank beer in The Bald-Faced
Stag and toasted the sword of the highwayman Jerry Abershaw,
which hung there, and Watts-Dunton had many stories of
Borrow breaking the ice on the Fen Pond in order to bathe in
mid-winter, and of his intensely superstitious nature which led
him to "touch" the trees for luck as he passed them.

In 1865 Henrietta Clarke decided to marry a Dr. William
McOubrey of Belfast, who was curiously described in the
marriage register as "a physician of Sloane Street", but on his
tombstone as a "barrister". The following year Mr. and Mrs.
Borrow crossed to Ulster to stay with the McOubreys, and
after a few days Borrow left his wife, crossed to Stranraer
and walked through the Stewartry and the Border country of
Scotland, collecting as he went more notes for his *Lavo-Lil*.
When he reached Carlisle he found a letter from Mrs. Borrow,
saying she was far from well but telling him not to worry.
By the time he got back to Ulster, however, she seemed
recovered, though on their return to London she became very
nervous and hysterical, a condition which grew gradually
worse until the year 1868, when she forced herself to make the
journey to Oulton since she had many business matters there
to attend to. For an account of Borrow at this period we are
indebted to the acid Miss Cobbe:

"Mr. Borrow says his wife is very ill and anxious to keep
the peace with C. (a litigious neighbour). Poor old B. was
very sad at first, but I cheered him up and sent him off
quite brisk last night. He talked all about the Fathers
again, arguing that their quotations went to prove that it
was *not* our gospels they had in their hands. I knew most of
it before, but it was admirably done. I talked a little theology
to him in a serious way (finding him talk of his 'horrors')
and he abounded in my sense of the non-existence of Hell,
and of the presence and action on the soul of *a* Spirit,

v

rewarding and punishing. He would not say 'God'; but repeated over and over again that he spoke not from books but from his own personal experience."[1]

But on 24 January, 1869, Mrs. Borrow was taken suddenly ill. Agitated beyond measure at finding their own doctor was away, Borrow sent for a Dr. W. S. Playfair of Curzon Street, who later confided to his fellow-physician that he had "found great difficulty in making the case out exactly. . . . I could detect no marked organic affection about the heart or lungs, of which she chiefly complained. It seemed to me to be either a very aggravated form of hysteria, or, what appears more likely, some more serious mental affection. In any case, the chief requisite seemed very careful and intelligent nursing or management, and I doubt very much, from what I saw, whether she gets that with her present surroundings . . ."

Both doctors were clearly of the opinion that Borrow, who had succumbed to an attack of the "horrors" the day his wife became so much worse, was the last possible person to be with her. Perhaps fortunately, the poor lady died of "valvular disease of the heart and dropsy" on 30 January. On 4 February she was buried in Brompton Cemetery—where her gravestone bears the strange inscription: "To the Beloved Memory of My Mother, Mary Borrow, who fell asleep in Jesus", and has no mention of her husband's existence.

Now George Borrow was truly, desperately alone. For the past thirty years, through all his wild moods, his dear Carreta had been beside him to soothe and distract, to read him little lectures, to nurse his ailments and to manage all business affairs. Mary Borrow had turned her dear George into a hypochondriac no doubt; but she had been a very gallant partner to one of the most difficult husbands a woman ever had. From behind her Nottingham lace curtains kind Miss Lloyd watched the tall figure in black, with square shoulders suddenly stooped and with white leonine head bowed, and her eyes filled with tears. Never had she seen anybody look so utterly lost and dejected.

[1] *The Life of Frances Power Cobbe, by Herself,* 1894.

CHAPTER EIGHT

"THERE IS NO PEACE IN THE WORLD"

(From a letter from George Borrow to Mr. Murray).

(1869–1881)

I

BORROW wandered aimlessly through the days following his wife's death. Miss Lloyd did her best, sending him innumerable little notes about tea-parties, but her efforts were nullified by Miss Cobbe's antagonistic attitude—which found its culmination in a scurrilous letter to James Hooper of Norwich more than twenty years after Borrow's death:

". . . I do not think that what is contained in my book is 'bitter' at all. But if I were to have told of my last interview with him—when I was driven practically to drive him out of our house, more or less drunk, or mad with some opiate— the charge might have had some colour. He was not a good man, and not a true or honourable one, by any manner of means."

Until he left Hereford Square for Oulton in 1874, the lady contented herself with nasty hints about Borrow's "drinking" and "drugging"—in her view any *gentleman* who went into low public-houses, frequented the Gypsyries at Wandsworth, and was seen ushering most common people up the steps of No. 22, was a brand which could not be snatched from any burning. Miss Cobbe was entirely wrong. In the whole record of his life there is not one single jot of evidence that he was a "bad" man in any sense of the word. His integrity was beyond dispute, his business dealings were strictly honourable, and nobody who really knew him ever so much as suggested that he either took too much to drink or was a drug addict.

A very different description was given by Mr. A. T. Story,[1]

---

[1] *London Daily Chronicle,* 9 July, 1913.

who met Borrow about 1872 in Mr. James Burns's publishing office in Southampton Row, and went to a spiritualistic seance with him in Mr. Burns's drawing-room, of which he said, "it would not take me long to sum up that little man (the medium) as a humbug, but a very clever humbug". Later Story came across Borrow standing on Westminster Bridge, gazing down into the river:

> "When I approached him he said: 'I have been standing here for twenty minutes looking round and meditating. There is not another city like this in the world, nor another bridge like this, nor a river, nor a Parliament House like that—with its little men making laws—which the Lawgiver that made yonder stars—look at them!—is continually confounding—and will confound. O, we little men! How long before we are dust? And the stars there, how they smile at our puny lives and tricks—here today, gone tomorrow. And yet tonight how glorious it is to be here!' "[1]

With a tremendous effort Borrow roused himself sufficiently to set his *Romano Lavo-Lil*, that Word-Book of the Romany over which he had laboured so long and so lovingly, into some semblance of order: and in the autumn of 1870 he received a letter from the American Charles G. Leland, who had published a collection of satirical German Ballads under the name of *Hans Brietmann* and was even then at work on his book, *The English Gypsies and Their Language*.[2] Leland wrote enthusiastically of Borrow's own books, told him he was entirely responsible for developing his interest in Romany matters, and said that "though I have had the impudence to write a Romany *gili*, I am far from being proficient in the language". The two met in 1871, when Leland honestly confessed that he was writing a book on the English Gypsies, and this was a little more than Borrow could stand. Living apart from the world, he had no idea that he had long since been outstripped in knowledge of the Romany folk and their language by such men as F. Hindes Groome and Leland

[1] *London Daily Chronicle*, 9 July, 1913.
[2] Published, London and New York, 1873.

himself. There was only one *El Gitano*—and that was George Borrow.

Unfortunately, Borrow had already contracted with Murray to edit new editions of *Lavengro* and *The Romany Rye* in one volume each, and was also busy with a complete reconstruction of the Gospel of St. Luke in *Calo*-Gypsy, which he had published in Madrid in 1830. Try as he would, he could not finish his *Romany Lavo-Lil* before Leland's book was published, and when Mr. Murray eventually brought it out in 1874 the scornful comments from Romany students regarding its "out-datedness" came as a blow from which he never recovered. To think—just to think—that he, the only man of his day in England who knew the "people out of Egypt" should be told he was outdated!

II

But this time there were no violent outbursts, no thumping of Mr. Murray's desk, no Appendices to *The Romany Rye*. Old and broken, Borrow crawled back to Oulton Cottage, where he lived a morose and lonely existence with a shaggy grey sheep-dog as his sole companion. His only recreation was quarrelling with his tenants—for Mrs. Borrow had left him all her property —and this he seems to have done with something of his old vigour, for people shook in their shoes when they saw him striding up the path with his "great dog". Maidservants whispered in fright, "It's Mr. Borrow and we dassent go!" Children fled at his approach. Rumours of his supernatural powers ran round the neighbourhood. In his *George Borrow in East Anglia* Mr. W. A. Dutt wrote:

"During his latter years his tall, erect, somewhat mysterious figure was often seen in the early hours of summer
mornings or late at night on the lonely pathways that wind
in and out from the banks of Oulton Broad . . . the village
children used to hush their voices and draw aside at his
approach. They looked upon him with fear and awe . . .
In his heart, Borrow was fond of the little ones, though it

amused him to watch the impression his strange personality made upon them. Older people he seldom spoke to when out on his solitary rambles; but sometimes he would flash out such a glance from beneath his broad-brimmed hat and shaggy eyebrows as would make timid country folk hasten on their way filled with vague thoughts and fears of the evil eye."

Borrow lived, during this period, in a state of appalling discomfort. He himself had no ideas of tidiness, and the local women were so afraid of him that it was only with the utmost difficulty he found one to "do" for him—and she did as little as possible before snatching her money and flying down the lawn as though the piskies were after her. He did not really mind; he was too occupied in reliving the glorious, fantastic days of youth. Yet when he read, in 1878, that Her Majesty Queen Victoria had been graciously pleased to visit Ambrose Smith, the gypsy, and his wife Sanspirella, at Knockenhair Park, near Dunbar, the old yearning for his friend returned. Jasper Petulengro, the blood-brother, the man whose sturdy championship had never faltered! He remembered the fights, the talks, the fires on Mousehold Heath, as he strode through the Suffolk darkness with his dog at his side. And when he learned that same autumn that Ambrose Smith had died he knew such loneliness that he asked Henrietta and her husband to come to live with him at the Cottage.

They came, but the joint *ménage* was scarcely successful. Henrietta, with her twin passions for conchology and guitar-playing, had left all domestic management to her capable mother. Dr. McOubrey was very much of an age with Borrow and about as untidy. They puttered along somehow, but the Cottage and its garden grew steadily more dilapidated and their owner steadily more intractable. Borrow did not, one feels, really like Dr. McOubrey, because he sent for his solicitor in 1880 and made a will leaving everything he possessed in trust for his stepdaughter, and from time to time he let the Ulsterman know that his tongue could still lash. More and more he kept to a hermit-like retreat in one room, taking his walks abroad only at dead of night; and when a new Vicar from Lowestoft arrived to pay a duty call and was ill-advised enough to inquire his host's age, Borrow flashed, "Sir, I tell my age to no man!" and stumped indoors to write an article on "People's Ages":

"Never talk to people about their age. Call a boy a boy, and he will fly into a passion and say, 'Not quite so much of a boy either; I'm a young man.' Tell an elderly person that he's not so young as he was, and you will make him hate you for life. Compliment a man of eighty-five on the venerableness of his appearance, and he will shriek out, 'No more venerable than yourself,' and will perhaps hit you with his crutch."

On a fine summer morning in July 1881 Dr. and Mrs. McOubrey announced their intention of driving into Lowestoft for the day. Borrow protested, saying he felt exceedingly ill and knew his last hour was at hand. Now it must be remembered that probably he had made just the same passionate statement many times before; yet after all he was seventy-eight years old and Dr. McOubrey, as a medical man, should surely have examined him at least. One can only surmise that the cantankerous Borrow had in some way antagonized his—almost equally cantankerous—relatives, for they drove off early and returned, many hours later, to find him dead.

What did he think of, that grand old lion, that *El Gitano* of Spain, in the few brief minutes before death claimed him? One hopes, despite recent querulous disparagement of "the wind on the heath nonsense", that he thought of the conversation with Jasper Petulengro which proved him, when all is said and done, a man of far greater achievement than any of his critics past or present. One likes to think that, despite all the hatreds which marred his later years, he remembered at the last the days spent with Jasper on windy Mousehold Heath, the evenings spent with that strange, shining figure Isopel Berners, in Mumper's dingle. He was a rebel, maybe the most significant one that the nineteenth century produced; and he never knew that posterity was to realize the genius behind the rebellion. There were few to mourn his passing; perhaps only one who understood the tragic history of the man put decorously to rest in Brompton Cemetery under a stone carved with the lettering:

IN LOVING REMEMBRANCE OF

GEORGE HENRY BORROW, Esq.,

Who died July 26th, 1881 (at his Residence "Oulton Cottage, Suffolk")
in his 79th Year.

(Author of The Bible in Spain, Lavengro—and other Works)

"IN HOPE OF A GLORIOUS RESURRECTION."

All very right and very proper—but so unlike the tempestuous George Borrow. Yet out of the obscurity which shrouded his old age—most people believed he had died even before the publication of *Romano Lavo-Lil*—stepped Theodore Watts-Dunton with Borrow's true epitaph:

". . . Of Borrow it may be said, as it was said of a greater man still, that 'after Nature made *him* she forthwith broke the mould'. The last time I ever saw him was shortly before he left London to live in the country. It was, I remember well, on Waterloo Bridge, where I had stopped to gaze at a sunset of singular and striking splendour, whose gorgeous clouds and ruddy mists were reeling and boiling over the West-End. Borrow came up and stood leaning over the parapet, entranced by the sight, as well he might be. Like most people born in flat districts, he had a passion for sunsets. Turner could not have painted that one, I think, and certainly my pen could not describe it; for the London smoke was flushed by the sinking sun, and had lost its dunness, and, reddening every moment as it rose above the roofs, steeples, and towers, it went curling round the sinking sun in a rosy vapour, leaving, however, just a segment of a golden rim, which gleamed as dazzlingly as in the thinnest and clearest air—a peculiar effect which struck Borrow deeply. I never saw such a sunset before or since, not even on Waterloo Bridge; and from its association with 'the last of Borrow' I shall never forget it. . . ."[1]

> We talked of "Children of the Open Air"
> Who once in Orient valleys lived aloof,
> Loving the sun, the wind, the sweet reproof
> Of storms, and all that makes the fair earth fair,
> Till on a day, across the mystic bar
> Of moonrise, came the "Children of the Roof",
> Who find no balm 'neath Evening's rosiest woof,
> Nor dews of peace beneath the Morning Star.
> We looked o'er London where men wither and choke,
> Roofed in, poor souls, renouncing stars and skies,
> And lore of woods and wild wind-prophecies—
> Yea, every voice that to their fathers spoke:
> And sweet it seemed to die ere bricks and smoke
> Leave never a meadow outside Paradise.

Seville, June 1949—Claverton Lodge, Bath, July 1950.

---

[1] *The Athenæum*, 10 September, 1881.

v*

BIBLIOGRAPHY

of Principal Works Consulted

LIFE, WRITINGS AND CORRESPONDENCE OF GEORGE BORROW, by William I. Knapp, Ph.D., LL.D., 2 vols.: London, John Murray; New York, G. P. Putnam's Sons, 1899.

GEORGE BORROW, THE MAN AND HIS WORK, by R. A. J. Walling. Cassell, 1908.

GEORGE BORROW, THE MAN AND HIS BOOKS, by Edward Thomas. Chapman & Hall, 1912.

GEORGE BORROW AND HIS CIRCLE, by Clement King Shorter. Hodder & Stoughton, 1913.

LETTERS OF GEORGE BORROW TO THE BRITISH AND FOREIGN BIBLE SOCIETY, edited by T. H. Darlow. Hodder & Stoughton, 1911.

LIST OF GEORGE BORROW'S WORKS

1825

Celebrated Trials, and Remarkable Cases of Criminal Jurisprudence, from the Earliest Records to the Year 1825. Six volumes, with plates. London.

Faustus: His Life, Death, and Descent into Hell. Translated from the German of F. M. von Klinger. W. Simpkin and R. Marshall, London.

1826

Romantic Ballads. Translated from the Danish: and Miscellaneous Pieces. S. Wilkin, Norwich.

1835

Targum: or, Metrical Translations from Thirty Languages and Dialects. St. Petersburg. Later reprinted by Jarrold & Son, Norwich.

The Talisman. From the Russian of Alexander Pushkin. With Other Pieces. St. Petersburg. Later reprinted in same volume as *Targum* by Jarrold & Son, Norwich.

1841

The "Zincali; Or, An Account of the Gypsies of Spain. With an Original Collection of their Songs and Poetry, and a Copious Dictionary of their Language. Two volumes. John Murray, London.

1842

The Bible in Spain; or the Journeys, Adventures, and Imprisonments of an Englishman in an Attempt to Circulate the Scriptures in the Peninsula. Three volumes. John Murray, London.

1851

Lavengro; The Scholar—The Gypsy—The Priest. Three volumes. John Murray, London.

1857

The Romany Rye: a Sequel to *Lavengro.* Two volumes. John Murray, London.

1860

The Sleeping Bard; or, Visions of the World, Death and Hell. Translated from the Cambrian British of Elis Wyn. Printed by Dewey, Yarmouth, with imprint of John Murray, London.

1862

Wild Wales: Its People, Language, and Scenery. Three volumes. John Murray, London.

1874

Romano Lavo-Lil: Word-Book of the Romany; or, English Gypsy Language. With Many Pieces of Gypsy, Illustrative of the Way of Speaking and Thinking of the English Gypsies; with Specimens of their Poetry, and an Account of Certain Gypsies or Places Inhabited by Them, and of Various Things Relating to Gypsy Life in England. John Murray, London.

1884

The Turkish Jester; or the Pleasantries of Cogia Nasr Eddin Effendi Translated from the Turkish. W. Webber, Ipswich.

1892

The Death of Balder. Translated from the Danish of Evald. Jarrold & Sons, Norwich.

Itinerary of

GEORGE BORROW'S JOURNEY
from MADRID to FINISTERRE in 1837

May 15.—Madrid, Guadarrama, San Chidrian, Peneranda, Salamanca.

June 10.—Salamanca, Pitiegua, Pedroso, Medina del Campo, Tordesillas, Simancas, Valladolid.
June 19.—Valladolid, Dueñas, Palencia, Sahagun, Leon.
June 30.—Leon to Astorga.
July 4.—Astorga, Puerto de Manzanal, Bembibre, Cacabelos, Villafranca, Puerto de Fuencebadon, Nogales, Lugo.
July 13.—Lugo, Betanzos, Coruña.
Aug. 1.—Coruña, Santiago.
Aug. 14.—Santiago. Padron, Pontevedra, Vigo.
Aug. 20.—Vigo, Pontevedra, Padron, Noya, Corcuvion, Finisterra, Corcuvion, Santiago, Coruña.
Sept. 15.—Coruña, Ferrol.
Sept. 21.—Ferrol, Novales, Santa Maria, Coisa d'Ouro, Viviero.
Sept. 22.—Viviero, Foz.
Sept. 23.—Foz, Rivadeo.
Sept. 24.—Rivadeo, Castropol, Navia, Luarca.
Sept. 25.—Luarca, the Caneiro, Las Bellotas, Soto Luino, Muros.
Sept. 26.—Muros, Aviles, Gijon.
Sept. 27.—Oviedo.
Oct. 5.—Oviedo, Villaviciosa.
Oct. 6.—Villaviciosa, Colunga, Ribadesella.
Oct. 7.—Ribadesella, Llanes, Colombres.
Oct. 8.—Colombres, San Vicente, Santillana.
Oct. 9.—Santillana, Santander.
Oct. 20.—Santander, Renedo, Puente Viesco, Ontaneda, Oña, Bribiesca, Burgos, Valladolid, Guadarrama, Madrid (Oct. 30).

INDEX

NOTE.—Since a full bibliography of Borrow's own works and of books consulted is given none of these are included in the index.